Reg. 49296

Grammar, Structure, and Style

A Practical Guide to A-Level English

Shirley Russell

WITHDRAWN

D1340085

Oxford University Press

* 000103773 *

Oxford University Press, Great Clarendon Street, Oxford OX2 6DP

Oxford New York
Athens Auckland Bangkok Bogota Bombay
Buenos Aires Calcutta Cape Town Dar es Salaam
Delhi Florence Hong Kong Istanbul Karachi
Kuala Lumpur Madras Madrid Melbourne
Mexico City Nairobi Paris Singapore
Taipei Tokyo Toronto

and associated companies in
Berlin Ibadan

Oxford is a trade mark of Oxford University Press

© Shirley Russell 1993

Published by Oxford University Press 1993

Reprinted 1993, 1994, 1995, 1996, 1997

All rights reserved. No part of this publication may be reproduced,
stored in a retrieval system, or transmitted, in any form or by any
means, without the prior permission in writing of Oxford University
Press. Within the U.K., exceptions are allowed in respect of any fair
dealing for the purpose of research or private study, or criticism or
review, as permitted under the Copyright, Designs and Patents Act,
1988, or in the case of reprographic reproduction in accordance with
the terms of licences issued by the Copyright Licensing Agency.
Enquiries concerning reproduction outside those terms and in other
countries should be sent to the Rights Department, Oxford University
Press, at the address above.

A CIP catalogue record for this book is available from the British
Library

ISBN 0 19 831179 6 School edition
ISBN 0 19 831198 2 Bookshop edition

For Alice Russell

Orders and Enquiries to Customer Services:
Tel. 01536 741519 Fax. 01536 454519

Printed in Great Britain

Contents

The language of society

The role of language in literature

Practical writing skills

The origins of English vocabulary

· ·

The family background of English

English belongs to the Germanic branch of the great Indo-European family of languages.

One theory suggests that all these languages evolved from one earlier one, spoken by a people who (according to Colin Renfrew) farmed Anatolia in eastern Turkey at some time before 6500 BC. The influence of this early ancestor can be seen in the table below, showing obvious similarities in the conjugation of verbs within the Indo-European family:

English	Sanskrit	Greek (Doric)	Latin	Old High German	Old Slavonic
I bear	bharami	phero	fero	biru	bera
(thou bearest)	bharasi	phereis	fers	biris	beresi
he bears	bharati	pherei	fert	birit	beretu
we bear	bharamas	pheromes	ferimus	berames	beremu
you bear	bharata	pherete	feris	beret	berete
they bear	bharanti	pheronti	ferunt	berant	beratu

F. Bodmer, *The Loom of Language*

The evolution of one language into many

The theory also suggests that the Indo-European language was spread, not by war and conquest, but by a peaceful process of expansion known as 'the wave of advance'. The process worked like this:

1 The farmers moved outwards from Anatolia, field by field, carrying their language first into Greece and Crete, then west across Europe to the British Isles and south-east into India.
2 As new areas of land were colonized, dialect forms of the original Indo-European language began to evolve.
3 These dialect forms began to harden into distinct sub-families of language, such as Old High German and Latin.
4 These sub-families evolved in turn into the separate languages spoken in various parts of Europe, India, and the Middle East. The 'Romance' languages, for example – French, Italian, Spanish, Portuguese, Catalan, and Romanian – all began life as 'dog-Latin', the form of the language spoken in the streets and bars, as opposed to the elite written form studied in schools and colleges: *horse*, for instance, is *equus* in classical Latin, *caballus* in the common form (Fr. *cheval*, Sp. *caballo*, It. *cavalto*). Dog-Latin would have been spoken with a different accent in the different

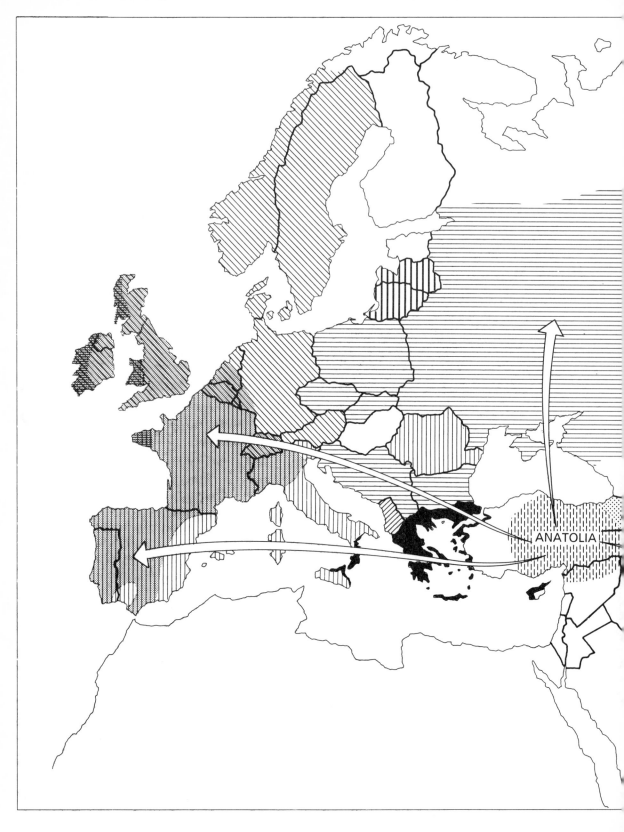

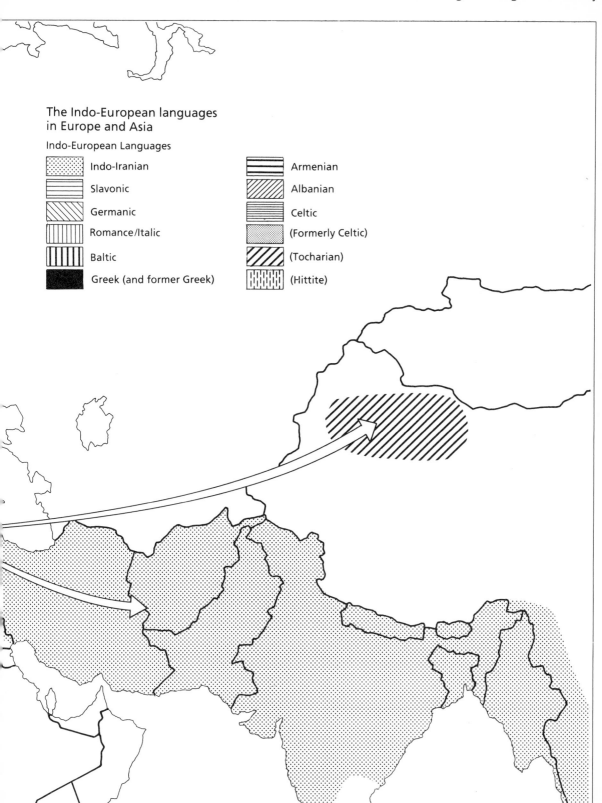

The Indo-European languages
in Europe and Asia

Indo-European Languages

Indo-Iranian	Armenian
Slavonic	Albanian
Germanic	Celtic
Romance/Italic	(Formerly Celtic)
Baltic	(Tocharian)
Greek (and former Greek)	(Hittite)

regions of the Roman Empire, but it was recognizably the same language. In the same way, German, English, Dutch, Danish, Swedish, and Icelandic all began as the same form of Old German before evolving their own identities and going their separate ways. The unmistakable signs of this common ancestry are shown below:

Da nobis hodie panem nostrum quotidianum	(Latin)
Donne-nous aujourd'hui notre pain quotidien	(French)
Danos hoy nuestro pan cotidiano	(Spanish)
Dacci oggi il nostro pane cotidiano	(Italian)
O pão nosso de cada dia dai-nos hoje	(Portuguese)
Gib uns heute unser täglich Brot	(German)
Geef ons heden ons dagelijksch brood	(Dutch)
Giv os i Dag vort daglige Brød	(Danish)
Giv oss i dag vårt dagliga bröd	(Swedish)
Gef oss i dag vort daglegt brauð	(Icelandic)

F. Bodmer, *The Loom of Language*

The arrival of English in Britain

Because of its situation on the western fringes of Europe, Britain has always been a last resort for peoples escaping from wars and famines on the Continent itself. Wave after wave of Celtic tribes colonized the country in prehistoric times, known only by vague labels such as the *Beaker People* (from archaeological finds). When the Germanic Angles, Saxons, and Jutes arrived in about 450 AD, they soon came to dominate the Celts, many of whom were driven into the mountains, islands, and coastal fringes. (The Romans, who had ruled them for five hundred years – a period equal to that between the early days of Elizabeth I and 1937 – had just gone, leaving them unprotected.)

The Celtic stock survived – not only among the Irish, the Welsh, and the Scots, but also among the people we now think of as 'English' – but the old Celtic language was overwhelmed by Anglo-Saxon and has left few traces: the element *coombe* (a deep valley) in place names like *Ilfracombe*; a few river names such as *Dart* and *Nene*; and a small number of nouns such as *ass*, *bannock*, *brock*, and *binn*.

An indication of the language that evolved out of the dialects of the Angles, Saxons, and Jutes – Anglo-Saxon or Old English – will be given in the section, *The grammar English has lost*, page 51.

The nature of English

Modern English is made up of three layers of vocabulary:

1 Anglo-Saxon (with additions from the Viking language, Old Norse)
2 French
3 Latin (with additions from Greek, often through Latin).

The Anglo-Saxon basis of English

Look at the passage below and you will see how much of the oldest part of our language has survived into the present day (words of Anglo-Saxon origin are in italic):

> *English was not* merely *the* product *of the* dialects *brought to England by the Jutes, Angles, and Saxons. These* formed *its* basis, *the* sole basis *of its* grammar, *and the* source *of by far the* largest part *of its* vocabulary. *But there were other* elements *which* entered *into it.*

Look at what is left when these are removed –

> merely . . . product . . . dialects . . . formed . . . basis . . . sole basis . . . grammar . . . source . . . largest part . . . vocabulary . . . elements . . . entered

– and you will see that it would be impossible for us to speak or write intelligibly without the help of Old English, simply because all the little *structure words* that hold sentences together – like *a, the, in,* and *that* – are Anglo-Saxon.

Other indispensable English structure words are:

- the personal pronouns *I, you, he, she, we, us*;
- the demonstrative pronouns *this, that, these, those*;
- the auxiliary verbs *can, shall*;
- the conjunctions *as, and, but, so, then*;
- the prepositions *on, in, under, over, down, up, to, by*;
- the adverbs *when, while, where.*

Many of our most familiar *content words* (the words that carry ideas) are also Anglo-Saxon in origin. For example:

Nouns

house (hūs)	love (lufu)	heart (heorte)	wife (wīf)
husband (hūsbonda)	father (fæder)	son (sunu)	friend (frēond)
ship (scip)	food (fōda)	grass (græs)	leaf (lēaf)
fowl or bird (fugol)	saddle (sadol)	water (wæter)	moon (mōna)
sun (sunne)	winter (winter)	spring (spryng)	fall (feall)
day (dæg)	night (niht)	king (cyning)	

Adjectives

right (riht)	evil (yfel)	cold (cald)	busy (bisig)
bloody (blōdig)	bitter (biter)	broad (brād)	black (blæc)

Verbs

eat (etan)	drink (drincan)	sleep (slǣpan)	live (libban)
fight (feohtan)			

Most names for parts of the body, most numbers, and most strong verbs also come from Anglo-Saxon. (Strong verbs are those that form their past tense by changing the vowel, e.g. *speak/spoke*: for instance *ride, sing, think, fight, find, sit, stand, drink, have, hold, do, be.*)

Finally, most rude names for parts of the body and its functions – *arse* and *fart*, for example (these two are found across the whole range of Indo-European languages) -- are Anglo-Saxon in origin. So are most of the 'four-letter words' that used to be written with initial and final letters and a row of asterisks in between: *sh*t*, *c**t*, and *f**k*, for example, although there are no written records of the last two before the twelfth century. Once perhaps terms acceptable in ordinary conversation, they have acquired obscene connotations over the centuries and cannot now be used in ordinary social contexts, nor on the television at peak viewing times.

Old Norse additions to Anglo-Saxon vocabulary

No sooner had Angles, Saxons, and Jutes begun to unite into one nation under Alfred the Great than they began to be invaded by Scandinavian Vikings. After harrassing the English continuously from 787 to 1014, the Danes finally conquered them, and ruled the country for twenty-eight years.

The effect on the English language was relatively slight. The Germanic language spoken by the invaders – Old Norse – was so like Old English that Danes and Anglo-Saxons could understand one another as readily as Danes and Swedes do today, and the two languages eventually blended into one.

The following words, remarkably similar in sound and style to Old English vocabulary, all derive from Old Norse:

bank   birth   brink   bull   leg   loan   dirt   dregs   race   root
steak   thrift   trust   window   fellow   freckle   gap   guess   seat
skill   skin   skirt   sky   awkward   flat   ill   loose   low   meek
rotten   tight   weak   muggy   crawl   die   droop   gasp   get   give
glitter   raise   rake   scare   scowl   snub   sprint   take   thrive   thrust

The stylistic qualities of Old Norse words

As the above lists show, Old English and Old Norse words generally have a direct, forceful, no-nonsense quality. Many are monosyllabic; many, such as *sky*, *skin*, *skill*, *scrupe*, *scrub*, *screech*, *bask*, *whisk*, contain consonants that sound harsh to the ear. (The Romans remarked, rather rudely, that listening to the speech of Germanic tribes was like listening to the cawing of crows.) Many of the harsher sounds of English derive from Old Norse. While Old English modified sharp Germanic 'sk' to a softer 'sh' sound, Scandinavian kept 'sk': hence, for example, OE *shirt*, ON *skirt*. The same is true of 'k' and 'g': when these are pronounced hard, as in *kid*, *dyke* (cf *ditch*), *get*, *give*, *egg*, etc., the words in which they occur are generally Old Norse in origin.

The sounds of Old Norse have made their contribution to English poetry. The English county of Yorkshire was once part of the Danelaw – the kingdom ceded to the Danes by King Alfred – and many Scandinavian words linger on in its dialects – *gill* for stream, for instance. The most famous poet born in that region, Ted Hughes, ignores actual dialect words but exploits the harsh sounds of Anglo-Saxon and Old Norse in poems like the following:

Thistles

Against the rubber tongues of cows and the hoeing hands of men
Thistles spike the summer air
Or crackle open under a blue-black pressure.

Every one a revengeful burst
Of resurrection, a grasped fistful
Of splintered weapons and Icelandic frost thrust up

From the underground stain of a decayed Viking.
They are like pale hair and the gutterals of dialects.
Every one manages a plume of blood.

Then they grow grey, like men.
Mown down, it is a feud. Their sons appear,
Stiff with weapons, fighting back over the same ground.

Ted Hughes

Only ten words of this poem – *hoeing*, *blue*, *revengeful*, *resurrection*, *pressure*, *pale*, *gutterals*, *dialects*, *plume*, and *appear* – are from Latin or French; with the exception of *rubber* (origin unknown), the remaining eighty-one are either Old English, Old Nors᠎, Old Swedish, or Old German in origin.

Activity

Explain the similarities Hughes sees between thistles, Viking warriors, and the old Germanic dialects.

▨rench additions to English vocabulary

Although the Norman French who ruled England from 1066 onwards were from the same stock as the Danes who had invaded England three centuries earlier, they were by now a very different people: thoroughly civilized and thoroughly French. (*Norman* means Northman or Viking.)

For three hundred years the Normans lorded it over the English in every way, controlling the government, the legal system, the army, and the church, and laying the foundations of the class divisions that have plagued English society ever since.

Activity

1 a Look up the entry under *punishment* in Roget's or any other thesaurus.
  b Check the derivation of the word and its given synonyms (words that have similar meanings).
  c Write a paragraph on what this indicates about the Conquest.
2 Read the first two pages of *Ivanhoe* by Sir Walter Scott.
3 Look up the word *marshal* in an encyclopaedia such as Longman's *English Larousse* and write a paragraph on what it reveals about French control of English society.

The English language suffered, too. For two hundred years after the Conquest, the kings of England spoke French, governed part of France, and took French women for their wives. Since French was the language of the Court, the upper and middle classes spoke French also, leaving only the unambitious and the peasants to speak English.

Nevertheless, although it took them a lot longer than it did their earlier Scandinavian kin, the Norman French did eventually settle down to become English and speak the Anglo-Saxon tongue. In the process, hundreds of French words passed into English, covering a wide range of contexts from cookery to religion to heraldry and the law. The resulting language, known as Middle English, is far closer to the language we speak today than was its Old English predecessor.

■ *The stylistic qualities of French loan words*

Although many humble words such as *bucket* come originally from French, most French borrowings are elegant words, with connotations of chivalry, courtliness, refinement, and romance. The French brought new and softer sounds into English, and, because they stressed their words differently, more varied rhythms also.

The rhythms of Middle English poetry and prose could be rather monotonous, thanks to the Anglo-Saxon habit of forward stress – the habit of placing the strongest stress on the first syllable of most words (or on the second if the first was a prefix; e.g. *bóard*, but *abóard*). Early borrowings from French were Anglicized by being stressed in this way: *góvernment, míracle, próperty*. Later ones, however, retained both a little of their original French pronunciation and the French system of giving equal stress to all the syllables of a word, as in *chócólát* (English *CHOClate*): *prémiére, clíché, néglígée, élíte, débútánte*, and so on.

Activity	Here is a list of English words and phrases which mean the same as words we have borrowed from the French. (The first letter of each word is given in brackets as a guide):

an illicit sexual affair (l)
a secret meeting (r)
remission given to a convict (p)
face fungus (m)
girl with dark hair (b)
public eating place (r)
an engaged person (f)
what success brings (p . . . . . . e)

1 Write down the appropriate word against its definition.
2 Check that you
   a pronounce it with something of a French accent,
   b distribute the stress over its several syllables.

The process reversed

> ### Sound Bites
> ·····································
> Un scoop, un one-man-show, une duty-free
> shop, un escalator, le fast-food, un jumbo-jet,
> un ferry, hot money, le Walkman, le bulldozer.
> **'Barbarous Anglo-Saxon terms' proscribed**
> **by the fifth edition of the Official Dictionary**
> **of Neologism, published by French**
> **Government this week**
>
> The Guardian, 31 December 1988

The result of borrowing from French is a variation in sound and rhythm that softens the brusqueness of plain Anglo-Saxon English writing, as the examples below will show. The first extract, from Langland's *Piers Plowman*, is an example of native English alliterative poetry, which had four stresses to a line, two on either side of a mid-line pause. (*Alliterative* refers to the fact that the stressed words in each half of the line usually begin with the same consonant, the technique of repeating consonants in close proximity to one another being known as alliteration.)

a

I was wéry forwándred	and wént me to réste
Vnder a bróde bánke	bi a bórnes síde,
And as I láy and léned	and lóked in the wáteres,
I slómbbred in a slépyng	it swéyued so mérye.

Langland, *Piers Plowman*, 1367 onwards

Each line here echoes the one before in rhythm and movement, rising very slightly towards the pause and falling equally gently away from it – a somewhat monotonous effect created largely by blunt English mono-syllables and forward stress.

The same insistent native beat can be heard at times behind Chaucer's five-stress line, the *iambic pentameter* borrowed from French and Italian poets. In lines like the ones below, four strong stresses fall on the key words, overwhelming the normal iambic pattern of alternating light and heavy stresses.

And tíl that týme he léyd was on his béere,

He knéw that Gód was ful of mýght and gráce . . .

Compare the stiff regularity of these lines with the freer movement and more varied intonation of extract (b), full of French borrowings, taken from the opening sentence of the *General Prologue to the Canterbury Tales*:

b
> Whan Zephirus eek with his sweete breeth
> Inspired hath in every holt and heeth
> The tendre croppes, and the yonge sonne
> Hath in the Ram his halve cours yronne,
> And smale foweles maken melodye,
> That slepen al the nyght with open ye
> (So priketh hem nature in hir corages);
> Thanne longen folk to goon on pilgrimages . . .
>
> Chaucer, *The Canterbury Tales*, 1387

c
> *To Mistress Margaret Hussey*
>
> Merry Margaret
> As midsummer flower,
> Gentle* as falcon   *noble
> Or hawk of the tower:
> With solace and gladness,
> Much mirth and no madness,
> All good and no badness;
> So joyously,
> So maidenly,
> So womanly
> Her demeaning
> In every thing,
> Far, far passing
> That I can indite,
> Or suffice to write
> Of Merry Margaret
> As midsummer flower
> Gentle as falcon
> Or hawk of the tower.
>
> Anonymous, sixteenth century

Activity
> Compare the diction of these last two extracts with that in 'Jolly Good Ale and Old' (number 57 in *The Oxford Book of English Verse*), discussing the different qualities of sound and rhythm that French words introduced into English.

Latin and Greek additions to English vocabulary

Greek has been included with Latin here rather than treated separately in its own right. This is because Latin words are

a more numerous than Greek,
b more relevant to most people's experience.

It is true that twentieth-century scientists have drawn on Greek rather than Latin for words to name their inventions and discoveries. Medicine, for instance, has adapted the Greek suffixes *-itis* and *-osis* to signify disease, creating words like *arthritis*, *appendicitis*, *bronchitis*, *halitosis*, *neurosis*, *tuberculosis*, and *psychosis*. But the fact remains that Latin has made a far deeper and wider impact on the English language. Greek borrowings have to do with more specialized and esoteric concerns, as the following sample will show:

grammar logic rhetoric arithmetic geometry astronomy
music academy atom acrobat Bible diphthong harmony
ecstasy nymph tyrant drama theatre comedy tragedy
climax catastrophe episode scene dialogue chorus prologue
epilogue irony alphabet elegy dilemma caustic basis pathos
epic theory orchestra pandemonium museum hyphen
dogma clinic bathos philander phase pylon therm agnostic

Activity	Look up the derivation of *homo* in words like *homosexual* and *homogeneous*, and of *hetero* in words such as *heterosexual*, *heterogeneous*. You will need to know the latter for the next section.

Although English was once a largely homogeneous Germanic or Teutonic language, well over half its vocabulary today is derived from Latin. We began to borrow wholesale from Latin during the Middle Ages, when scholars throughout Europe wrote and spoke to one another in that language. As a result, we lost our habit of coining new words out of existing English elements (*hand-book* for L. *manual*, for instance, and *Threeness* for *Trinity*) and started taking words directly from Latin texts instead. Interestingly, Modern German, although sprung from the same Teutonic roots as Anglo-Saxon, has kept this ability. Where we borrowed from Latin, they formed new words out of existing German elements:

English	**German**
contradict	widersprechan
(from L. *contra* = against,	(from G. *wider* = against
dicere, dictum = to speak)	*sprechan* = to speak)
solidarity	Zusammengehorigkeitsgefuhl
(from L. *solidus* = of dense	(from G. *zusammen* = together
consistency, firm,	*gehorigkeit* = belonging
substantial)	*gefuhl* = feeling)

Just how widely we've borrowed from Latin is shown in the following list. (Those of you who are studying German or French or Spanish might like to check the equivalent words in those languages.)

pauper proviso equivalent legitimate index scribe simile
memento requiem collect (noun) diocese mediator tolerance
abject adjacent allegory conspiracy contempt custody
distract frustrate genius gesture history homicide immune
incarnate include incredible incubus incumbent index

individual infancy interior infinite innate innumerable
intellect interrupt juniper lapidary legal limbo

Note: not all of these words came directly from Latin. Some, like
equivalent, collect, diocese, mediator, tolerance, conspiracy, and
homicide, are Latin words which found their way into Old French before
they were borrowed by English. In the same way, *allegory* and *history*
originally came into Latin from Greek. Words borrowed from the Romance
languages have a mixed parentage: the Romans borrowed from the Greeks,
the French borrowed from the Romans, and we in turn have borrowed
their borrowings. Loan words may therefore have been taken straight from
the original language or have entered indirectly via another language, in a
slightly modified form.

Activity

> 1 Look up any words in the above list that you do not know.
> 2 Write clear definitions of the first six words on the list.
> 3 What is the most striking difference between the Latin words and
>   your definitions of them?
> 4 Argue the case for and against getting rid of Latin loan words by
>   'translating' them into native English elements – *ungettatable* for
>   *inaccessible,* say; *unseethroughable* for *opaque.* (Don't forget to take
>   spelling as well as comprehensibility into account.)

Today we would find it hard to manage without such Latin prefixes as
anti, re, pro, trans, post, pre, sub, and *de*; and suffixes such as *-ate, -ic,* and
-al (as in *educate, elastic, normal, abysmal*). And to appreciate the
importance of Greek and Latin roots, we have only to look at Greek *logos*
(a speaking or discourse on, i.e. the science or study of), and *-nomia*
(arrangement, management, regulation, i.e. classification of, science of),
found in the form of *-ology* and *-onomy* in words like *biology, astronomy,*
and countless other scientific terms. The academic world would collapse
without them.

▓ *The stylistic qualities of Latin loan words*

Generally speaking, the words we have borrowed from Latin are lengthy,
impressive, and polysyllabic. They carry prestige and authority.

▓ *The advantage of a heterogeneous language: precision*

Thanks to the mingling of Latin, French, and native Anglo-Saxon
elements, English is rich in synonyms. The French have a word for
everything, we are told. We have at least three, with different qualities that
fit them for different purposes in different contexts. We have:

* Anglo-Saxon words that are familiar, immediate, and therefore warm
  in tone;
* French borrowings that are more formal and polite;

⁕ more esoteric and learned Latin loan words, that seem weightier, solemn, and more remote.

In theory, therefore, English speakers can always find the exact word they need for a particular context: the Saxon word for ordinary situations; the sophisticated French word for more fashionable contexts; the more recondite Latin word for more abstract, metaphysical concerns. The distinctive qualities of these different kinds of word can be seen in the following sets, where the first word is always native English, the second French, and the third Latin in origin:

ask–question–interrogate	thin–spare–emaciated	folk–people–nation
help–aid–assistance	goodness–virtue–probity	fast–firm–secure
fire–flame–conflagration	holy–sacred–consecrated	time–age–epoch

Baugh, *A History of the English Language*

Activity

> 1 Put the following groups of three into the same English–French–Latin sequence as above, judging which word belongs to which language purely on sound and 'feel'.
>   a impecunious, needy, financially distressed
>   b inept, incompetent, gauche
>   c residence, domicile, house
>   d reserved, close-mouthed, uncommunicative
>   e harden, solidify, coagulate
> 2 Check that you are correct by consulting *The Concise Oxford Dictionary*.
> 3 Write sentences using all the words of each set.
> 4 Discuss the different tone and atmosphere of the sentences you have created out of each set of synonyms. What impression do they make on you? How do they sound?

▧ *The use of Latinate words in English literary writing*

Writers who use a predominantly Latinate style do so for one or more of the following reasons:

1 They find a sensuous appeal in the quality of Latin words. They love the fullness and richness of their vowels, the strength (without harshness) of their consonants. (Examples: Sir Thomas Browne, John Milton, Thomas Babington Macaulay, Henry James, Joseph Conrad.)

2 They feel that nothing less than elevated Latinate diction can match the dignity and importance of their subject-matter. (Johnson criticized Shakespeare for using the humble word 'blanket' in the context of a tragedy.) (Examples: Jonathan Swift, Samuel Johnson.)

3 They have no choice but to use Latinate diction since the metaphysical nature of their themes – the nature of love, the conflict in the heart between good and evil, the concept of individual responsibility, the problem of guilt, for instance – can be fully discussed only in such terms. (Examples: Milton, Swift, Johnson, James, Conrad.)

4 The education of their time being based upon the study of Greek and Latin, they believe a Latinate style to be the mark of an educated man. (Examples: Alexander Pope, John Dryden, Joseph Addison, Richard Steele.)

To describe the styles that result, however different, critics use adjectives of an appropriately Latinate kind: when critics are in favour, *sonorous, resonant, magnificent, dignified,* and *eloquent* are used; when they are not, *over-elaborate, unnatural, inflated, pretentious, pompous* and *excessively formal.*

Below are brief extracts from the work of three of the main exponents of the Latinate style in English: Milton, Conrad, and Henry James. (Latinate words in all three extracts are printed in italics.)

A
> Him the Almighty Power
> Hurl'd headlong flaming from th'*Ethereal* Sky
> With *hideous* ruin and *combustion* down
> To bottomless *perdition,* there to dwell
> In *Adamantine* Chains and *penal* Fire,
> Who durst defy th'*Omnipotent* to Arms . . .
>
> Milton, *Paradise Lost*

B
> She was *savage* and *superb,* wild-eyed and *magnificent;* there was something *ominous* and *stately* in her *deliberate progress.* And in the hush that had fallen *suddenly* upon the whole sorrowful land, the *immense* wilderness, the *colossal* body of the *fecund* earth and *mysterious* life seemed to look at her, *pensive,* as though it had been looking at the image of its own *tenebrous* and *passionate* soul.
>
> Conrad, *Heart of Darkness*

C
> Felix had *observed* on the day before his *characteristic pallor,* and now he *perceived* that there was something almost *cadaverous* in his uncle's high-featured white face. But so clever were this young man's quick *sympathies* and *perceptions* that he had already learned that in these *semi-mortuary manifestations* there was no cause for alarm. His light *imagination* had gained a glimpse of Mr Wentworth's *spiritual mechanism,* and taught him that, the old man being *infinitely conscientious,* the *special operation* of *conscience* within him *announced* itself by several of the *indications* of *physical faintness.*
>
> Henry James, *The Europeans*

Each is a great writer in his own particular way; none of the three should be judged on little snippets taken out of context.

▨ *The rise and fall of Latinate vocabulary*

Latin words began to flood into English at the beginning of the Renaissance, from the 1430s onwards. During the seventeenth and eighteenth centuries English writers and scholars modelled their work on classical literature and borrowed still more. Philosophers such as Francis Bacon and scientists like Sir Isaac Newton wrote their treatises in Latin, and attempts were even made to teach grammar school students in that language. (Shakespeare learned his 'little Latin and less Greek' at Stratford Grammar and got his revenge later by mocking pedants who talked in Latin, in plays like *Love's Labours Lost*.)

Nevertheless, up to 1650, English writers could take or leave Latin borrowings. If a Latin word was useful in making a point it would find a place in a sentence, but the surrounding vocabulary would be predominantly English.

The situation changed dramatically in the second half of the seventeenth century, when the roles of the two languages were almost reversed. A glance at the table below will show the percentage of native English and Latin loan words in the work of the 'best' English writers:

		English	Latin
The Authorized Version of the Bible	1611	94%	6%
Shakespeare	1564–1616	90%	10%
Spenser	1552–1599	86%	14%
Milton	1608–1674	81%	19%
Addison	1672–1719	82%	18%
Swift	1667–1745	75%	25%
Pope	1688–1744	80%	20%
Johnson	1709–1784	72%	28%
Hume	1711–1776	73%	27%
Gibbon	1737–1794	70%	30%
Macaulay	1800–1859	75%	25%
Tennyson	1809–1892	88%	12%

Baugh, *A History of the English Language*

The larger the number of Latinate words in a piece of writing therefore, the greater the likelihood that it was written between 1650 and 1800. The main exceptions to this rule of thumb are Sir Thomas Browne, 1605-1682, who took to Latinisms rather earlier than most other writers, and Thomas Babington Macaulay, who took to them much later. (The five-year-old Macaulay, asked how he was feeling after being scalded by a cup of hot tea, replied, 'Thank you, ma'am, the agony is much abated'.) Not until Wordsworth's stand for 'language such as men do use' did things begin slowly to change, and he was soundly criticized for his efforts. Here is an example of Wordsworth's 'common' language, 'such as men do use':

> In the sweet shire of Cardigan,
> Not far from pleasant Ivor-hall,
> An old man dwells, a little man,
> I've heard he once was tall.

> Of years he has upon his back,
> No doubt, a burthen weighty;
> He says he is three score and ten,
> But others say he's eighty.
>
> William Wordsworth, *Simon Lee, The Old Huntsman*, 1798

And here is a contemporary critic's opinion of it, full of the kind of Latinate vocabulary he would have preferred Wordsworth to use for the dignity of English poetry:

> Long habits of seclusion, and an excessive ambition of originality can alone account for the disproportion which seems to exist between this author's taste and his genius . . . Solitary musings [among his lakes and mountains] might no doubt be expected to nurse up the mind to the majesty of poetical conception, – (though it is remarkable, that all the greater poets lived, or had lived, in the full current of society): – But the collision of equal minds – the admonition of prevailing impressions – seems necessary to reduce its redundancies, and repress that tendency to extravagance or puerility, into which the self-indulgence and self-admiration of genius is so apt to be betrayed, when it is allowed to wanton, without awe or restraint, in the triumph and delight of its own intoxication.

Activity

The great Greek writer Aristotle ruled that plays should obey the three dramatic unities of time, place, and action:

* the unity of action: there should be only one main plot, and any sub-plots there might be should be related to this;
* the unity of place: the main plot should be seen to unfold in one and the same location;
* the unity of time: the action of the plot should occupy the space of twenty-four hours only.

Below are two extracts on the last two unities, one from a sixteenth, one from an eighteenth century writer. Read them and answer the questions that follow.

a 'Gorboduc' is very defectious in the circumstauces, which greeueth mee, because it might not remaine as an exact model of all Tragedies. For it is faulty both in place and time, the two necessary companions of all corporall actions. For where the stage should alwaies represent but one place, and the vttermost time presupposed in it should be, both by Aristotles precept and common reason, but one day, there is both many dayes, and many places, inartificially imagined. But if it be so in 'Gorboduc', how much more in all the rest, where you shal haue Asia of the one side, and Affrick of the other, and so many vnder-kingdoms, that the Player, when he commeth in, must euer begin with telling where he is, or els the tale will not be conceiued? Now ye shal haue three Ladies walke to gather flowers, and then we must beleeue the stage to be a Garden. By and by, we heare newes of shipwracke in the same place, and then we are to blame if we accept it not for a Rock. Vpon the backe of that, comes out a hideous Monster, with fire and smoke, and then the miserable beholders are bounde to take it for a Caue. While in the mean-time two Armies flye in, represented with foure swords and bucklers, and then what hearde heart will not receiue it for a pitched fielde? Now, of time they are much more liberall, for ordinary it is that two young Princes fall in loue. After many trauerses, she is got with childe, deliuered of a faire boy; he is lost, groweth a man, falls in loue, and is ready to get another child; and all this in two hours space: which, how absurd it is in sence, euen sence may imagine, and Arte hath taught, and all auncient examples iustified . . .

Sir Philip Sidney

b The necessity of observing the Unities of time and place arises from the supposed necessity of making the drama credible. The criticks hold it impossible, that an action of months or years can be possibly believed to pass in three hours; or that the spectator can suppose himself to sit in the theatre, while ambassadors go and return between distant kings, while armies are levied and towns beseiged . . . The mind revolts from evident falsehood, and fiction loses its force when it departs from the resemblance of reality.

From the narrow limitation of time necessarily arises the contraction of place. The spectator, who knows that he saw the first act at Alexandria, cannot suppose that he sees the next at Rome . . . he knows with certainty that he has not changed his place; and he knows that place cannot change itself . . . Such is the triumphant language with which a critick exults over the misery of an irregular poet . . .

The objection arising from the impossibility of passing the first hour at Alexandria, and the next at Rome, supposes that when the play opens the spectator really imagines himself at Alexandria, and believes that his walk to the theatre has been a voyage to Egypt, and that he lives in the days of Antony and Cleopatra. Surely he that imagines this, may imagine more . . . Delusion, if delusion be admitted, has no certain limit; if the spectator can be persuaded, that his old acquaintance are Alexander and Caesar, that a room illuminated with candles is the plain of Pharsalia, or the bank of Granicus, he is in a state of elevation above the reach of reason, or of truth, and from the heights of empyrean poetry, may despise the circumscriptions of terrestrial nature.

The truth is, that the spectators are always in their senses and know, from the first act to the last, that the stage is only a stage, and that the players are only players . . .

By supposition, as place is introduced, time may be extended. The drama exhibits successive imitations of successive actions, and why may not the second imitation represent an action that happened years after the first, if it be so connected with it, that nothing can be supposed to intervene? Time is, of all modes of existence, most obsequious to the imagination; a lapse of years is as easily conceived as a passage of hours. In contemplation we easily contract the time of real actions, and therefore willingly permit it to be contracted when we only see their imitation.

Samuel Johnson

1 Allowing for the difference in length of the two passages, which writer do you think uses:
    a a largely native vocabulary with a number of Latinisms;
    b shorter and simpler sentence-constructions;
    c an inconsistent and idiosyncratic system of orthography (spelling);
    d a more intimate and personal way of addressing the reader;
    e punctuation stops that indicate where the writer might pause if he were addressing his audience orally, rather than in writing;
    f a livelier, more good-humoured, more humorous tone?

2 Which writer uses:
    a a great number of Latinate words and phrases;
    b a greater number of abstract nouns;
    c longer sentence constructions with several dependent clauses;
    d no direct address to the reader;
    e a formally correct, predominantly *written* style, with nothing about it of the 'speaking voice';
    f punctuation stops that divide sentences into units of sense by marking where one clause or phrase ends and another begins;
    g a more modern system of paragraphing;
    h a consistent and almost modern system of orthography;
    i a vehement and slightly angry tone?

3 Which of the following adjectives would you choose to describe the style and tone of passage (a), which of passage (b)?:
    lively, informal, humorous, ironical, personal, varied, persuasive, formal, correct, authoritative, consistent, didactic, serious.

4 A writer's tone of voice and mode of address to his readers are influenced by his individual cast of mind as well as by the age in which he lives. With this reservation in mind, write notes for yourself on the five major differences between sixteenth and eighteenth century prose. Set out your notes logically, using headings and sub-headings, for example:

Differences between sixteenth and eighteenth century prose
   i vocabulary
       a C16th   b C18th

English as a world language

Whether they are learning English in their own countries or as emigrants to an English-speaking country, speakers of Germanic and Romance languages find English readily accessible and easy to pick up because they find echoes of their own languages in its mixed vocabulary.

As a result, English, rather than German, French, Spanish, or Italian, is fast becoming the *lingua franca* of a common European civilization, and the major language of the world.

Latin and Greek elements

Since so many of our most important words are drawn from Latin and Greek, knowledge of the elements that make them up improves writing and reading skills enormously. Teachers in New York ghetto schools recently tried teaching low-achieving black children the most important Latin and Greek elements and roots; their vocabulary, reading ability, and behaviour all improved dramatically. They had been given a key to understanding language, and it helped.

Browse through the following list of Latin and Greek elements and then carry out the activities suggested below.

Prefixes

a, an (Gk) *a-, an-* not, un-, -less, without: *agnostic, amoral, amorphous*

ab, abs, a (L) *a, ab, abs* away, from, away from: *abduct, aberration, abstinence*

ad, a (L) *ad* towards, against, at: *adhere, adjacent, admire, advent*

amb(i) (L) *ambo, amb(i)* both, around, about: *ambidextrous, ambiguous, ambivalent*

ant(e) (L) *ante* before: *antecedent, antediluvian, antenatal, anteroom*

ant(i) (Gk) *anti* against, opposite: *Antarctic, antibiotic, antidote*

aut(o) (Gk) *autos* self, by oneself: *autistic, autobiography, autograph*

bene (L) *bene* well: *benediction, benefactor, benefit, benevolent*

bi, bin, bis (L) *bi* two, twice: *biceps, biennial, bilateral, bilingual*

circa, circum (L) *circum* around: *circuit, circumcision, circumlocution*

com, con, co (L) *co* with, together: *coeducation, cohabit, compatriot*

de (L) *de* down from, away from, off: *decelerate, declivity, decrease*

dis, di (L) *dis-, di-* apart; *different, digress, discordant, dislocate, disrupt*

dys (Gk) *dys* badly, ill-: *dysentery, dysfunction, dyslexic, dyspepsia*

en, em (Gk) *en* in: *emblem, empathy, energy, enthusiast*

equ(i), iniqui (L) *aequus* equal: *equanimity, equidistant, equilibrium*

eu (Gk) *eu-* well-: *eulogy, euphonious, euphuistic*

ex, e (L) *e, ex* from, out of, away from: *effluent, effulgent, effusion*

hyper (Gk) *hyper* over: *hyperactive, hyperbole, hypercritical*

in, im, i (L) *in-* in, into, upon, un-: *illicit, immure, impose, incarnate*

orth(o) (Gk) *orthos* straight, right: *orthodox, orthography, orthopaedics*

par(a) (Gk) *para* beside, beyond: *paramedic, paramilitary, paranormal*

poly (Gk) *poly-* much, many: *polygamy, polyglot, polygon, polymath*

post, poster (L) *post* after: *postdate, posterity, posthumus, postprandial*

pre (L) *prae* before, in front: *precede, preclude, precursor, predict*

re (L) *re-* back, again: *recline, recurrent, regress, reject, rejuvenate*

retro (L) *retro* backwards: *retroactive, retrograde, retrogress, retrospective*

sub (L) *sub* under: *subaqua, subhuman, subplot, suburb, suffix, suppress*

Roots

acer(b), acid, acri(d), acu (L) *acer, acr-* sharp, bitter: *acerbic, acrimony, exacerbate*

amic, am(or), imic (L) *amor* love, *amicus* friend: *amateur, amicable, inimical*

anim (L) *animus* mind, *anima* mind, spirit, soul: *animated, animosity, magnanimous*

ann, enn (L) *annus* year: *annuity, biennial, centennial, millennium*

arch (Gk) *-arches/os* ruler, ruling: *anarchy, hierarchy, oligarchy, patriarch*

arch(i) (Gk) *archi-* first, chief: *archbishop, archduke, archetypal, architect*

ast(e)r(o) (Gk) *aster* star: *asterisk, astrology, astronaut, disastrous*

aud(io) (L) *audire, audit-* to hear: *audible, audience, audition, auditorium*

bio (Gk) *bios* life: *amphibious, antibiotic, biochemistry, biography*

capit (L) *caput, capit-* head: *capital, capitation, capitulate, decapitate*

chron(o) (Gk) *chronos* time: *anachronistic, chronic, chronological, synchronize*

cosm(o) (Gk) *kosmos* world, universe: *cosmic, macrocosm, microcosm*

cred (L) *credere, credit-* to trust, believe: *credible, creditable, credulous*

cur(r), curs (L) *currere, curs-* to run: *concur, concurrent, precursor*

dem(o) (Gk) *demos* the people: *demagogue, endemic, epidemic, pandemic*

dic(t) (L) *dicere, dict-* to say, speak: *contradict, dictator, diction*

duc(t) (L) *ducere, duct-* to lead: *aqueduct, deduce, educate, seduce*

exter(n), extr(a), extrem (L) *exterus* outside, outward: *exterior, extracurricular*

fac(t), fect, fic, fiat (L) *facere, fact-* to make, do: *affect, benefactor, fact*

fin (L) *finis* boundary, end: *affinity, confine, define, finite*

hetero (Gk) *heteros* other: *heterodox, heterogeneous, heterosexual*

(h)om(o) (Gk) *homos* same, *homalos* even, level: *anomaly, homogeneous*

hydr(o) (Gk) *hydor* water: *dehydrate, hydrant, hydraulic, hydrophobia*

labor (L) *labor* work: *collaborate, elaborate, laboratory, laborious*

loc (L) *locus* place: *allocate, dislocate, local, location, locum*

magn(i) (L) *magnus* big: *magnanimous, magnate, magnificent, magnum opus*

mal(e) (L) *male* badly, ill, *malus* bad, evil: *malaria, malediction, malfunction*

mar(in) (L) *mare* the sea: *marinade, marine, maritime, submarine*

medi (L) *medius* middle: *intermediary, medi(a)eval, mediate, mediocre*

mon(o) (Gk) *mono-* alone, single: *monarch, monastery, monograph, monolith*

nom(ic) (Gk) *-nomia* arrangement, management: *astronomy, economy*

nom(in) (L) *nomen, nomin-* name: *denomination, ignominy, misnomer, nomenclature*

omni (L) *omnis* all: *omnibus, omnipotent, omniscient, omnivorous*

oper, opus (L) *opus, oper-* a work: *cooperate, magnum opus, modus operandi*

pass, pat (L) *pati, pass-* to suffer: *compassion, impassive, patience*

phot(o), phos (Gk) *phos, phot-* light: *phosphorus, photograph, photosynthesis*

sci (L) *scire* to know: *conscience, conscious, nescient, prescience*

scrib, script (L) *scribere, script-* to write: *describe, inscription, scribe*

spir (L) *spirare, spirat-* to breathe: *aspire, conspire, expire, inspire, spirit*

super, suprem (L) *super* above: *insuperable, superfluous, supernatural*

syn (syl, sym, sys, sy) (Gk) *syn* with: *synchronize, synonym, synthesis*

tel(e) (Gk) *tele* far: *telegram, telepathy, telephone, telescope*

ter(r)(estr) (L) *terra* the earth: *terrestrial, extraterrestrial, Mediterranean*

the(o), thus (Gk) *theos* God: *apotheosis, atheist, enthusiasm, pantheist*

tract (L) *trahere, tract-* to draw, drag: *abstract, attract, contract*

tra(ns) (L) *trans* across: *trajectory, transact, transatlantic, transcend*

urb (L) *urbs* city: *conurbation, suburb, urban, urbane*

Mary Byrne, *Eureka*

Activity

1 Using *The Concise Oxford Dictionary*, look up the meaning of any unknown words in the above list.

2 The element *jur* from L *jurare*, to swear, occurs in several important English words. Find words containing this element with the following meanings:
   * to swear away or renounce
   * to perform magical tricks
   * a body of people sworn to deliver a verdict
   * the swearing of a falsehood.

3 Use the element *liber* (L for *free*) to form words with the following meanings:
   * generous
   * to set free
   * free thinker or person of loose morals.

4 Using the elements *man(i)* and *manu* (from L *manus*, hand) create words with the following meanings:
  * to control things (by hand)
  * hand care
  * to influence someone's behaviour for one's own ends
  * an instruction booklet
  * to produce something commercially
  * (thing) written by hand.

5 *Inter* derives from the Latin word for *among, between*. Find words containing this element with the following meanings:
  * among other things (two Latin words are used for this)
  * a go-between
  * between nations
  * mutually communicating
  * (cause a) break between
  * between continents
  * scatter between
  * mutual dependence
  * period between two events
  * to throw in, interpose (remark, etc.)
  * to come between.

6 Use the elements *jug, junct*, and *jung* from Latin *jungere*, to join, to form words that mean the following:
  * relating to a married pair
  * a word that joins other words or clauses
  * a joining
  * a crucial moment or point in time
  * to bring under control, conquer.

7 Bigamy means the state of being married to two people at the same time. What is meant by *monogamy, polygamy*, and *hypergamy*?

8 *Dogma* and *dox* come from Greek *dokeein*, to think, and *doxa*, opinion. What do the following words mean: *dogma, dogmatic, heterodox, orthodox, paradox*?

9 Look up the meaning of *panacea, pandemonium, panorama, pantheism*, and *pantheon*. What is the derivation of the element they all have in common?

10 *Path(o)* from Gk *pathos* signifies *suffering, experience, feeling*. What kinds of feeling are indicated by the following words with this element: *antipathy, sympathy, empathy, apathy, telepathy*?

11 a Look up the derivations of *citizen, civil, civilization; savage*, and *primitive*.
   b Define as clearly as you can the difference between a primitive and a civilized society.

c What other meaning can you find for *civilized*? Can the natives of certain primitive societies be called civilized in this sense of the word? Can the industrialized societies of the West?

12 The following elements are particularly useful to students of English language and literature. Look them up and make notes on them for your own use:

bath(y) (Gk) *bathos* depth
cris, crit (Gk) *krisis* judgment
gram (Gk) *gramma, grammat-* thing written, writing, letter, line
graph (Gk) *graphein* to write
loc, loq (L) *loqui, locut-* to speak
log (Gk) *logos* a speaking, speech, saying, word, discourse, thought, reasoning, reckoning, ratio
morph (Gk) *morphe* form, shape, figure
onym, onomast, onomato (Gk) *onoma, onomat-* name
or(at) (L) *orare, orat-* to speak, make a speech, plead, pray
phras (Gk) *phrasis* a speaking, speech
romanc, romant (L) *Roma* (Rome) romance
thes(is), thet (Gk) *thesis* a placing, setting
verb (L) *verbum* word

The prescriptivist attitude towards vocabulary

Like pronunciation and grammar, vocabulary undergoes a constant process of change. We make up new words to express new ideas or to dress up old ones (*interface*; *state of the art*); we extend the meaning of existing words by using them metaphorically (*the bottom line*); we alter the meaning of existing words by using them in mistake for others. *Prevaricate*, for example, is presently being confused with *procrastinate* by speakers as diverse as Mrs Thatcher (she accused General Galtieri of prevaricating when he was playing for time – enough to start a war in itself had his English been good enough) and a Radio 2 sports commentator – a fair indication that a shift of meaning is underway.

This last practice rouses the anger of prescriptivists – people who would like words to be used only with their 'original' meanings.

Activity

Read the passage that follows and carry out the suggested tasks.

It is certainly a rather sterile pursuit to attack what we know (or what dictionaries could tell us) are thoroughly established words. Despite strong opinion to the contrary, it is futile to try to stop words from being used in a sense different from that in which they were used at
5 some earlier period. Such an 'etymological fallacy' betrays, in any case, a lamentable ignorance of the nature of language. We are still occasionally told that it is incorrect to use *tremendous* in the sense of huge because the word 'really' means 'that which causes trembling', the 'really' deriving its force from the fact that *tremendous* comes from the

10   gerundive of the Latin verb *tremere*, to tremble. If such pedantic considerations are taken as the basis of 'correctness', then the 'correct' meaning of style is a pointed instrument and the 'correct' meaning of like, a body. One could not speak of arriving at King's Cross, because King's Cross has no shore, and the word's derivation shows that at one

15   time it meant to come to the shore . . .

Change of meaning is commonplace, and indeed it would appear to be fundamental in living language. One reason for the futility of objecting to a modern meaning lies in the fact that almost every word we use today has a slightly different meaning from the one it had a

20   century ago: and a century ago it had a slightly different meaning from the one it had a century before that. Or rather meanings. For it is natural for a word to have more than one, and we can even say that, the commoner the word, the more meanings it has: and this is a further reason for seeing the search for a 'correct' or 'basic' meaning as futile.

25   In his fascinating, recent book, *Studies in Words*, Professor C.S. Lewis explains the steps by which even an apparently simple word like 'sad' has radically changed its meaning over the years. It once meant 'full to the brim', 'well-fed'; one could be thoroughly 'sad' with food and drink (sated, satiated, satisfied, and saturated are etymologically related to

30   it). From this it came to mean 'solid' as well; a good spear could be sad, and one could sleep sadly. This idea of solidness was then metaphorically applied to human character, and a person who was reliable and firm could be called sad. It is now easy to see how the chief modern sense could come into existence; a well-fed person may feel

35   solid, heavy, and dull, and thus be sober-faced on that account: we must not forget the slang use of the expression 'fed-up' which offers something of a semantic parallel. Alternatively, a person who is reliable and firm is a serious person, and serious is the opposite of light-hearted and gay.

40   In the face of so universal a natural process, one may as well sit on the shore and order back the advancing tide as attempt to turn back the tide of semantic change. The conclusion is obvious (and has been accepted by dictionary makers for generations): the only practical and reasonable standard of a word's acceptability at all or in a particular

45   sense is usage. If lay-by is in use among lorry-drivers, Ministry of Transport and local Government officials, that is enough: the word can be recorded in our dictionaries with the meaning that is current among those who use the word. If guts is used for courage, but with some contextual restriction, the lexicographer will still record this sense, but

50   will add a note on the particular restriction he has noticed ('informal' or 'colloquial' perhaps). In either case, he will be accurately and objectively representing the usage as he observes it: he will not be sitting as a magistrate, frowning upon the 'ugly', 'atrocious', or vile.

Randolph Quirk, *The Use of English*

1 In paragraph 1 the writer castigates prescriptivists for ignorance and pedantry.

   a What etymological fallacy are prescriptivists working on if they suppose that words can always be used in their original meaning?

   b Why could their 'pedantic considerations' never be taken as the basis of 'correctness'?

2 With particular reference to the second half of the last sentence, 'he will not be sitting . . .' discuss what the writer thinks of prescriptivist *attitudes* towards the use of words.

3 What do you understand by a 'contextual restriction' (line 45)?

4 Look up the following words in the micro-print edition of *The Oxford English Dictionary*, tracing their change of meaning through the centuries:

horrible   awful   enormous   extravagant   disgusting   nice modern   admiration   sophisticated   gay

5 Use the following words in sentences of your own devising: aggravate, chronic, disinterested.

Look up the dictionary definition of these words and make notes for your own use.

If your use of the above three words agrees with one of the formal definitions given, does that make it correct? If so, in what way is it correct?

If your use of the words corresponds to the entries followed by the note, '(coll.)', does that mean it is wrong? If not, in what sense can it be said to be right?

If these three words eventually survive only in their colloquial meaning, will anything be lost?

Do you agree with the writer when he says that the sole criterion of a word's acceptability is usage?

If not, what methods could you suggest for preserving important meanings?

The concept of register

The different layers of English vocabulary outlined in the previous section allow us to speak or write differently to different people in different situations or contexts.

Key word

> *Register*: a form of language considered to be appropriate to a particular social situation or a particular kind of subject-matter. Based on the classical concept of decorum, it can be further defined as 'a particular usage required by politeness or decency'.

Look at the chart below, and you will see the full range of registers available to us. In the centre we have the common register – the great common pool of language on which we draw for our conventional speech and writing; basically Anglo-Saxon but with a large sprinkling of Latin roots. Latin disappears as we move down-market into the informal language registers – colloquial English and slang – but really comes into its own in the scientific and technical registers on the left of the diagram. It doesn't exist in the literary register for the simple reason that there is no recognizable literary register. As Crystal remarks in his *Cambridge Encyclopaedia of Language*, 'Literature reflects the whole of human experience, and authors thus find themselves drawing on all varieties of language (or even on different languages) as part of their expression.' A single work of Eliot or Joyce may draw on the registers of commerce, nursery rhyme, religion, philosophy, psychology, demotic speech, and popular song.

Formal and informal registers

The main division in registers is between *informal* (used to speak to family and friends) and *formal* (used to speak to people in the wider world of society). The informal includes the *colloquial*, *slang*, and *dialectal* registers at the bottom of the chart; the formal embraces all the rest.

We learn to use registers as we learn to talk – by listening to other people. Nobody actually tells us to say 'Hello' or 'Hi' to friends but 'Good morning' to people we know less well. We pick it up from listening to our parents, probably before we're even out of our prams. And our knowledge of registers increases as our world expands. We learn not to use words like 'poo' and 'willy' in front of parents; not to greet teachers with 'Hi man, how's tricks?'; not to call employers by their first names without being asked. We learn, in other words:

1 to use the formal register.
2 to adapt the way we speak to:
   ⊛ the person we're addressing,
   ⊛ the situation (or 'context') we find ourselves in.

Activity

> Discuss the appropriateness of the following registers, taken from Randolph Quirk's *The Use of English*:
>
> 1 Bye-bye, Your Holiness. See you!
> 2 Hi, John: I'm just phoning to say your sister has croaked.
> 3 Professor Crowell, I think I understand your first two points, but could you explain that last fucker?

At the same time we learn not to equate formality with politeness. Say, 'Thank you so much for a lovely meal; it was very kind of you to get it for me', to your mother instead of 'Thanks, Mum', and she will probably burst into tears. Politeness in this context means talking to her in the intimate register of family relationships; address her in the formally polite language you would use to an acquaintance and she will be hurt. In the same way, reply in extremely formal terms to somebody who has been talking to you in dialect and you will seem rude and aloof. *Appropriateness* to both the person and the context is what you should remember when discussing register. Choose what is appropriate and politeness will take care of itself.

Activity

> 1 a Something happens to you (anything you like, real or imaginary). Write out how you would describe this same event to
>   ⊛ your friends,
>   ⊛ your parents,
>   ⊛ your personal tutor or other authority figure.
>   b Analyse the differences you note in your use of language.
>
> 2 a How would you react to an unfamiliar doctor or solicitor who received you in his office wearing jeans and sweat-shirt and gold chains and who greeted you with the words, 'OK man, what's going down?'
>   b Basing your remarks on your reactions to the situation outlined above, write a paragraph on the purpose and function of
>   ⊛ formal dress,
>   ⊛ formal registers.

But the range of registers doesn't stop at formal and informal. Just as the informal register has many different sub-registers, so there are formal sub-registers for every social context you can think of, from buying something in a department store to taking part in a church service to greeting a member of the Royal Family ('Your Royal Highness', or 'Your Majesty' in the case of the Queen, followed by 'Ma'am').

Activity

1 Test the range of the informal register by both listening carefully and taking notes of the way in which you find yourself speaking or writing in the following contexts:

   a at home with your family (do you have any special words that outsiders wouldn't understand? Do you always talk in complete sentences?);

   b trying to get something out of your (reluctant) mother or father;

   c with friends of the same sex;

   d with friends of the opposite sex;

   e with friends of both sexes;

   f alone with the person you love;

   g playing a game or taking part in sport of some kind.

   (You need not give the exact words used if you find it embarrassing: just explain the general nature of the language used; i.e. made-up words, baby-talk, swear-words, and so on.)

2 Now do the same for the formal register in one of the following contexts (if you have never attended a committee meeting, or been interviewed for a job, your tutor will help you to set one up in class first):

   a an interview with a Head Teacher, Head of Department, or Principal;

   b a committee meeting;

   c a letter applying for a job or a place at college/university;

   d an interview with a prospective employer;

   e an orchestra rehearsal or music lesson;

   f any other social context in which you find yourself and/or others employing some kind of specialized terminology.

3 Discuss any noticeable differences you found between

   a the formal and informal registers;

   b the sub-registers of each of these major registers.

It would be interesting to consider your general body language and the tone and loudness of your voice in the different registers, as well as the actual vocabulary used.

The scope of individual register use

'No man's English is *all* English', remarks the Preface to the *Oxford English Dictionary*. To put it another way, no one uses *all* the registers that are available. The common register, as its name implies, is used by all; the colloquial and slang by most, and dialect forms by many. After that, it's a question of where our occupations and interests take us. The wider an individual's interests, the wider their command of register and the scope of their knowledge.

The common register

No one has used the common register for writing better than George Orwell. Good writing, he believed, should resemble a pane of clear glass: it should allow readers to see straight through to the meaning without distracting them with decorations or flaws of its own – foreign words and phrases, clichés, and stale imagery, for example. His writing has the clarity that comes from words exactly used. When writing is as forceful and immediate as this, we feel the writer must be telling the truth:

> Here I am sitting writing in front of my comfortable coal fire. It is April but I still need a fire. Once a fortnight the coal cart drives up to the door and men in leather jerkins carry the coal indoors in stout sacks smelling of tar and shoot it clanking into the coal-hole under the stairs. It is only very rarely, when I make a definite mental effort, that I connect this coal with the far-off labour in the mines. It is just 'coal' – something that I have got to have; black stuff that arrives mysteriously from nowhere in particular . . . You could quite easily drive a car right across England and never once remember that hundreds of feet below the road you are on the miners are hacking at the coal. Yet in a sense it is the miners down there who are driving your car forward. Their lamp-lit world down there is as necessary to the daylight world above as the root is to the flower.
>
> George Orwell, 'Down the Mine', from *Inside the Whale and Other Essays*

Talking point

> Discuss the appropriateness of
> **a** the diction,
> **b** the concluding image,
> to the subject Orwell is discussing.

Colloquial language and slang

The colloquial register uses words like *chap* and *bloke* for the common register's neutral *man* (see line 3 of the extract above) and more formal *gentleman*. It talks of rows rather than arguments, requests people to chuck things rather than to throw, calls odd behaviour dodgy rather than suspicious. It is relaxed, matey, and largely unrefined. But how does it differ from slang?

Heavy is current slang for *serious*, *difficult*, or *tragic*, but is *to make heavy weather of* slang? Or colloquial language? Is *I've got the message* or *the penny's dropped* colloquial language, or slang? Or are all these examples of dead slang that has become fossilized as colloquial language?

Recent dictionaries such as Birmingham University's *Cobuild* refuse to attempt a clear distinction between colloquial language and slang, preferring to classify words instead by their degree of informality – 'informal' and 'very informal'. But how do we tell the informal from the very informal? Is *guy* more informal than *bloke*? *Iffy* than *dodgy*? Who is to say? Other dictionaries drop 'colloquial' in favour of 'informal', but still retain slang as a separate category. It is all very confusing.

A more useful distinction between the two might be made on the criteria of freshness and originality. 'Colloquial' might be used for words and phrases that have been around for a long time and have lost their freshness. 'Slang' could be used to describe language that is new and fresh and inventive – like 'he's strictly read-from' to describe somebody too 'thick' (colloquial or slang?) to take anything in. (This metaphor is taken from computing, where you insert information into a file by 'writing to' a disk as opposed to extracting information by 'reading from' one.)

▓ *Differences between colloquial language and slang*

1 Colloquial language is conventional: it is what we expect people to use when they are at ease in informal situations. Colloquial words are old, much-used, 'matey', sanctioned by custom and habit. They give the impression of being used not from choice but because they are the first words that come into the head.

Slang on the other hand is the language of non-conformity. It is created by those who dislike or are bored by the conventions of society expressed in conventional language. American informality creates some great slang: witness for example the American colonel interviewed on BBC Radio 4 after the U.S. invasion of Grenada. Where British top brass in their stiff-upper-lipped way would have described the situation as uncertain, fluid, or unresolved, he said that what they had there was a 'floating crap-game'. It is paradoxical that the very slang that sets out to destroy convention quickly becomes conventional itself (rather like its sartorial equivalent, blue jeans), but that does not invalidate the point.

2 The origins of many colloquial words – like *row* or *chuck* or *gink* – are unknown. Occasionally one is thought to be the result of a creative use of language – *geezer* for example may come from *guise* (dress or pretended appearance) plus *-er* – but many seem to have arrived ready-made. *Bloke*, for instance, was adopted from Celtic Shelta, the private language of itinerant Irish tinkers. If we class phrases like 'the penny's dropped' as colloquial, however, they may simply be dead slang that stuck fast in this register.

Slang is largely created out of existing language or objects by giving them a metaphorical twist and extending them to other contexts (as with the dropping penny above). Examples:

the bottom line (from book-keeping): the governing factor, the thing that controls the situation;
you can't put the toothpaste back in the tube: to signal that if you do a certain thing you will have committed yourself, performed an irrevocable action.

The best slang, as this last phrase and the similarly vivid *open a can of worms* shows, often has a pictorial quality.

3 Many colloquial words are class-bound, which is why, outside of literature, they exist almost exclusively in the spoken register. *Fag*, for example, is working class; *cigarette* is much more widely used.

Slang is classless. Helped by the media it spreads almost overnight throughout the country. Words like *bread* and *bonking* turn up everywhere on the social scale. Today, even Earls have been heard to talk of 'flogging their Canalettos'. Then, too, we find sub-registers of slang in every social or work group. Public schoolboys and Sloanes have their exclusive argots, as do state schoolchildren, criminals, athletes, climbers, and the police, and the term 'psychobabble' has been coined to describe the slang of affluent Americans obsessed with their mental and emotional health. This last includes *to come on to*, *hit on* (me, etc.) (behave offensively or threateningly); *into the pits* (depression); *lay on* (inflict); *trip* (experience); *hang loose* (relax); *hang in there* (hold on); *get centered* (find yourself); *get off on* (find satisfaction in); *get it/your head/your act together* (organize your behaviour/ideas/lifestyle); *get to* (hurt, annoy, disturb). Used in U.S. television imports like *Thirtysomething* and *L.A. Law*, it either irritates or delights according to the individual viewer's attitude to language.

4 Slang reveals its user's age; colloquial language does not. Nothing dates more quickly than slang. No one under the age of forty today would use the word *snazzy*, just as no one over the age of thirty would say 'What's the scam?'

5 Good slang expresses an idea so vividly and succinctly that it fills a need and often passes very quickly into the common register. Colloquial language does so far more rarely. *Blurb*, for example, was adopted by publishers, critics, and the quality Press almost as soon as it was coined. *Yuppy*, like *blurb*, is now completely assimilated into the common pool, and *window* (from computer programming) is following the same path, making itself valuable in contexts as different as social planning (finding a window in one's diary) to horticulture (finding a window in bad weather to sow crops), to A.A. reports (looking for a window in traffic congestion). Slang that does not make it into the common register either sinks without a trace or grows stale on the lips of those who are out of touch and out of date.

6 Colloquial language is used to show belonging, conformity; the user is 'one of the boys'; matey; unpretentious; not given to fancy talk.

Slang is used to show non-conformity and originality; the user is his own 'man' (of either sex). (Some slang, however, is used to show conformity to a particular social group; it is deliberately esoteric to repel outsiders. Cockney rhyming slang is of this kind.)

There is, however, one point of contact between colloquial language and slang: both can be used to make friendly overtures to people, or to break down social barriers.

In short, colloquial language can be thought of as familiar, easy, and slightly coarse; the kind of words and phrases we would expect to hear in a setting like the pub.

Slang can be thought of as newly invented expressions, or existing words and phrases given a new meaning by metaphorical extension.

Activity

1 Look up the entry under 'bird' in *The Concise Oxford Dictionary* and write notes on its different meanings in the informal register.

2 Below is a passage written in Cockney rhyming slang.

'Nice little battle this, ain't it?'
'Yer. Have a butcher's at the ice-cream on the 'aystack.'
'Filth?'
'Dunno. 'E's been eyeballing us ever since 'e came through the Rory.'
'Nah, 'e's sweet. I know 'is boat. 'E's an iron I was in the shovel with.'
''Ere, you're wanted on the odie. It's that bloke 'oo 'ad 'is collar felt for a bit of Bob Hope.'
'The gevalt that bloke gets into.'

Glossary

Rhyming slang
battle – battle cruiser
butcher's – butcher's hook
ice-cream – ice-cream freezer
hay-stack – hay-stack
Rory – Rory O'Moore
boat – boat-race
iron – iron-hoof
shovel – shovel and pick
odie – eau de cologne
Bob Hope – Bob Hope [American comedian]

Other slang
filth – police
sweet – fine, in order
'ad 'is collar felt – was arrested
gevalt – trouble (Jewish)

a Translate the dialogue above, which contains Cockney rhyming and other slang, into a formal register, using Latinisms where you can (*beverage* rather than *drink*, for example).
b Discuss the difference in the tone of the two pieces.
c Analyse the character that has emerged through your translation. What kind of person is he? What makes you think this?
d What insight has this given you into how playwrights create their characters?

3 a List as many colloquial/slang terms as you can for
  ◦ dying,
  ◦ sexual intercourse.

b Write a note on what this tells you about another function of the informal register.

4 Below is a piece of writing that deliberately contrasts the formal and informal registers to make a point. It is a review by British novelist Nigel Dennis of Theodore Sorensen's life of John F. Kennedy. Read the review, then answer the questions that follow.

America is vast – and so, by God, are her biographies. As for the Americans who write the biographies, they are giants with a thousand spectacles. Where humans have brains, these Titans have something like a Mississippi paddle-boat, churned interminably along by some force of
5   perpetual motion.

And how they struggle, these Magogs of the Tome, to assemble their continental masterpieces! Read this acknowledgement (one of many) at the end of Theodore C. Sorensen's 'Kennedy':

'The task of deciphering my illegible pen fell principally, as it has for
10   more than ten years, to Gloria Sitrin; and she was joined in this effort by Rebecca Cooley, Christine Petrone, Rose Franco, Sue Vogel Singer, David Sitrin, Toi Bachelder, Valerie Cooley, Christine Camp, Mary Connolly and Stella Thompson.'

Think of a bloke needing eleven disciples just to type his book! Why,
15   it only took four to write the Gospels. Or was Mr Sorensen's message more urgent?

No: the evidence shows that as Special Counsel to the late President Mr Sorensen resolved to do anything rather than get a move on. First of all, he seems to have murmured to himself, a slow music must mark the
20   opening of my prodigious labour:

'Across the muddy Potomac from the Lincoln Memorial a green and gentle slope rises gradually to what was once the home of Robert E. Lee . . .'

Obviously a steep trudge ahead, but never mind. Go on!
25   'From halfway up that hill one can see on a clear day most of the majesty that is Washington . . . In the distance the dome of the Capitol covers a milieu of wisdom and folly, Presidential ambitions and antagonisms, political ideals and ideologies. To the right is the stark and labyrinthian Pentagon . . .'
30   My dear Mr Sorensen! Your book turns my bathroom scales at more than two pounds and contains 3,000,000 words. Hanging on every last one of them are Gloria, Rebecca, Sue, David, Toi, Valerie, Christine, Mary and Stella. Could we not bat on a little faster?

'It was on just such a clear autumn afternoon, on October 20, 1962,
35   that President John Fitzgerald Kennedy stood on the second-storey back porch . . .'

No, no; clearly, Mr Sorensen's kingdom is not of this world. Books like his are not written for the living at all; they are just heavy industry's answer to death. Nor should they be reviewed like books. All they ask
40   (and it's a hell of a lot) is for some paid trusty to turn their autumnal leaves and tip off the innocent bystander as to what's buried there. So, here are some suggestions:

Pages 1–248: Skip the whole labyrinthian caboodle – unless you happen to be inordinately interested in United States politics, elections, campaigns, etc., and feel a genuine need to read everything you needn't know about the days *before* Kennedy became President. Be sure to take brandy and a stout spade.

Page 249: A small oasis here in the form of a funny story about what President Eisenhower's golfing shoes did to the White House parquet.

Pages 250–290: A snail's paced description of Kennedy settling down to his job and choosing his staff. As lively as a man with lumbago lowering himself into a chair.

Pages 291–309: Here's treasure – eighteen really interesting pages! They describe the famous 'Bay of Pigs' episode, when the novice President was caught short. Representing 'the worst defeat of his career', the incident made him exclaim bitterly: 'How could I have been so far off base? All my life I've known better than to depend on the experts. How could I have been so stupid, to let them go ahead?'

Pages 310–326: On Kennedy's relations with the Press. For newspapermen, possibly: general public may safely skip.

Pages 327–365: Mostly about Kennedy's relations with Congress. Of vital interest to Kennedy, of course, but not in prose like Mr Sorensen's.

Pages 366–389: Purely personal stuff about Kennedy's working-hours, marriage, children, reading, views on culture, etc.: 'He still favoured dark-coloured, lightweight, two-button suits, with a monogrammed shirt and a PT-boat tie-clasp.' Will pass a wet hour.

Pages 390–666: Absolute desert of dullness with nary a date palm. Domestic and foreign battles of first importance seem trifling compared with the reader's fight against sleep.

Pages 667–722: Very good stuff indeed. All about the second Cuban crisis and the ultimatum to Khrushchev to pull out his missiles. The remarkable dramatics of the situation are felt even by the author, who also gives a very good account of how Kennedy 'worked' it. Very instructive, too, about Kennedy's characteristic approach to things and about his 'experts' and advisory bodies.

Pages 723–758: Just epilogia pro vita sua.

That is about the best that can be done for Mr Sorensen's book, though before sending this review to eleven typists one might add that such a book should never have been written.

People who have special knowledge about a great man should begin by asking themselves how briefly and clearly they can convey it. They should bear in mind that mere accumulated verbiage is bound to make even the greatest hero seem as commonplace as the author. A great American need not fear the hand of his assassin; his real demise begins only when a friend like Mr Sorensen closes the mouth of his tomb with a stone.

Nigel Dennis, *The Listener*

a Which three of the following adjectives would you choose to describe
   * Sorensen's,
   * the reviewer's choice of words and phrases in this passage: pompous, pedantic, florid, obscure, Latinate, formal, colloquial, slangy, figurative (containing much imagery), precise, concise, economical? Quote to illustrate your points.

b Explain why the reviewer has chosen to use the informal register for much of the time. Quote his use of colloquial and slang terms in your answer.

c Do you detect a change in the reviewer's vocabulary, sentence structure, and tone in the final paragraph? If so, describe that change and suggest why it has been made.

d There are several biblical references in the review (ll.14–15, 37, 87). Why has the reviewer used them? What do they reveal about his attitude towards
   1 Sorensen,
   2 Kennedy?

e Find two examples of antithesis and explain how they help Dennis to make his points.

f Explain the difference between an ideal and an ideology.

g Referring particularly to what Dennis says about pages 1-248, say whether in your opinion this is a fair and useful book review.

C lichés

Cliché: a word or expression that has lost its force through over-use.

Clichés have been in use for so long that even the words commonly used to describe them – 'hackneyed', 'fly-blown', 'stale', 'outworn', for example – have themselves become clichés. They spring ready made to our lips (cliché), saving us the trouble of thinking for ourselves, and fall into three main categories: coarsely colloquial clichés, facetious clichés, and metaphorical clichés.

Coarsely colloquial clichés

suit yourself	you heard	fair enough
a bit dodgy	know what I mean?	bend over backwards
on the trot	I haven't a clue	be my guest
just the job	you're telling me	do you mind?
let's face it	that's your lot	just one of those things
big deal	you must be joking	when it comes to the crunch
watch it, mate	back to square one	

▓ *Facetious clichés*

These are the expressions used (largely by hearty men) when the middle classes forgather in pubs and clubs and meetings. 'Golf-club phrases' Simon Hoggart christened them: 'those tedious moribund locutions most of us use occasionally and some of us use all the time'. He points out that they differ from ordinary clichés in having a 'special flavour of boringness, enhanced by repetition'.

> It's people who always say 'Home James!' whenever they get into a car, or say 'This is Liberty Hall old boy' every single time you ask if you can use their loo or their phone who are the worst offenders. Stand in any bar frequented by businessmen and it's possible to hear entire conversations in this form.
>
>   'Charles, how goes it? Still in the land of the living I see!'
>   'Well, where have you been hiding your face?'
>   'Well met by moonlight, say I. Care for a little noggin?'
>   'Since you twist my arm.'
>   'Let me do the honours. What's your poison?'
>   'Spot of the old vino, if you don't mind.'
>   'Prefer the grape to the grain, eh?'
>   'Got to watch the old ticker. Not getting any younger.'
>   (Drinks arrive.)
>   'What's the damage? Just see if I've got the where-withal.'
>   'Cheers! Down the hatch! How's the good lady wife?'
>   'The better half? Positively blooming. And how's business? Nose to the grindstone?'
>   They don't drink, but 'wet the whistle', don't say 'yes please' but 'I wouldn't say no'. Pubs are always hostelries, landlords always 'mine host'. They don't eat, but 'partake of a little sustenance', don't think, but 'exercise the little grey cells'.
>
> Simon Hoggart, *The Guardian*

Activity

> Find 'golf-club phrases' for the following:
> to switch on a lamp; to write; to go to the lavatory; to go to bed; to look something up in a reference book; a cup of tea; an aeroplane.

▓ *Metaphorical clichés*

Clichés of a metaphorical kind abound in English. They have an air of proverbial wisdom about them, which is probably why they have lasted so long.

Talking point

> **1** Pick out the metaphorical clichés in the following article, written in response to an attempt to discover which recorded clichés were still current in English:
>
>   . . . the custodians of the Archive of English Cliché, an organization

where every question is vexed and every problem knotty, will have
to look to their laurels. Over the weeks ahead they will need to put
their hands to the plough and their shoulders to the grindstone
to ensure that no stone is left unturned in purging outmoded
exhibits. For observation purposes, whatever the cries of the animal
welfare lobby, pigs will have to be thrust into pokes, bees into
bonnets, fish into pretty kettles, and dogs into mangers (or, should
they prove to be Cerberus, given sops). Trained staff will lead horses
to the water and try to make them drink: should any be found to be
dead, they will, of course, try to flog them. Gnats will be strained at
and geese said 'boo' to. In one particularly ambitious experiment, a
representative group of parrots will be tested against a control group
of other avian species to see which lot gets sicker when England lose
. . . But because of logistic difficulties, the Archive does not expect to
measure with very much accuracy the velocity of a bat out of hell . . .

2 In an unquoted sentence of the article, the writer claims that 'the
Guardian's style-book has long insisted that clichés must be avoided
like the plague'. Explain why this claim is ironical.

Clichés are not all bad, however. They can be the source of wit and of new
insights into human nature. They can be used ironically to attack, say,
corruption, in 'It's an ill wind that blows nobody any good', and, most
importantly, since they are known to everyone, they can express a sense of
shared human experience, as in 'Oh well, it'll all be the same in a hundred
years'. It is this quality of speaking for us all that makes clichés last.

They can, of course, also distract us from thinking for ourselves.

Journalese

Journalese – the language used by newspapermen – is a register full of
clichés and stereotyped expressions. As Fritz Spiegl has pointed out,

Nothing ever falls but 'plunges', 'plummets' or 'hurtles'; every attempt is
a 'bid', every mundane decision a 'vow', every journey a 'dash' – 'mercy
dash' if someone is helped. Things are never expected but 'set' to
happen; and police do not arrest but 'swoop' or 'pounce' (except in the
dear *Guardian*, where they have been known to 'ponce').

In the tabloids, opponents either 'clash', 'snub', or 'rebuff' each other,
doctors 'battle' to save lives, prices 'rocket', flames 'leap' or 'sweep',
temperatures 'soar', and unfortunates who do wrong are 'slammed',
'slated', or 'blasted' – all to inject drama into a story and sell copies. The
technique can be seen at its best in headlines, where the maximum
impact must be made with the minimum number of strong words: 'boost'
is used for increase, 'curb' for restrict or restriction, 'axe' for cut, 'hit' for
affect badly, 'key' for important or vital, 'link' for connection or contact,
'oust' for drive out or replace, 'probe' for investigate or investigation,
'riddle' for mystery, 'scare' for public alarm or alarming rumour, 'top' for
exceed.

The journalist Liz Gill admits that the tabloids also sensationalize their stories with the help of strongly emotive language:

> They tell of *agony, anguish, torture, ordeals, going through hell.* Events are *horrifying, historic, tragic, heart-warming, shattering, staggering, amazing, scandalous, astonishing, devastating, cataclysmic, outrageous, stunning, moving, disastrous.*

Over-use of such words is however counter-productive, and any power they once had to stir emotion is long gone. The same is true of the cliché'd nouns and adjectives used in the tabloids' treatment of sex – the verbal equivalent of the dirty seaside postcard: *tease, showgirl, dish, love-nest, romps, canoodling, dishy, saucy, sizzling, hot, cheeky, exotic, titillating.* Titillating is the last thing they are.

The people who appear in the stories are similarly stereotyped by a series of cliché'd adjectives, often hyphenated to compress as much as possible into a small space: any woman not actually ugly is described as *attractive, raven-, dark-,* or *blond-haired, blue-* or *brown-eyed*; similar clichés for men are *handsome, dashing, muscular.* Clichés can be used to hint, too. When dashing playboy and raven-haired beauty get together they are euphemistically described as *close personal friends* or *constant companions* (i.e. lovers). Those who don't go in for long-standing relationships are stereotyped as *fun-loving* or *party-going* (i.e. promiscuous), while those who are not interested in heterosexual relationships are described as *confirmed bachelors* or *active feminists.*

Utterly predictable and appalling puns are another kind of cliché dear to the tabloids, however serious the subject: 'Take-away thieves last night ransacked a Chinese restaurant . . .'; 'It was a black day for coalman Ted . . .'. Teachers are caned, butchers get a roasting, maritime projects are sunk, scuppered, or torpedoed (unless they succeed, when, improbably, they 'ride high'). Musicians always strike notes – high, low, or sour. 'Biscuit hopes crumbled last night . . .' was the jolly start to a story about the closure of a biscuit factory in Liverpool, while an article about hip replacement carried the headline 'HIP HOORAY!' Even the *Guardian* feels compelled to 'entertain' in this way, but it does it more wittily: 'THE BIGGEST ASP DISASTER IN THE WORLD' (of a bad review of *Antony and Cleopatra*), 'HOT UNDER THE CHOLERA' (of an epidemic). Liz Gill has a theory about the 'cliché-ridden, stereotyped style' so many reporters use:

> Almost all news is bad news. Death, violence, cruelty, mayhem, natural and manmade disasters, pain and sorrow are the daily diet of newspapers. And readers do not, I believe, want to experience them intensely or genuinely sympathize with the subjects of the stories day after day. We do not really want to peer into the bottomless pit of human misery every morning over breakfast. We take such small doses at our convenience from poetry and fiction, not newspapers.
>
> And that is why newspaper language though dealing daily in such

> matters does not bring them too close. The style serves to distance us from the real world, while at the same time bringing its horrors into our homes. Otherwise we would go mad.

The scientific and technical register

The two registers on the left of the diagram on page 33 – scientific and technical – can be grouped together for our purposes. They have three things in common:

1   Both have many sub-registers: the technical register embraces the terminology of thousands of occupations from the making of false teeth through the programming of computers to the building of ships; the scientific register includes the terminology of professions as diverse as nuclear physicist and professor of environmental science, astronomer, and forensic surgeon.
2   Both draw heavily on the Latin side of English for their terminology.
3   Both contain large amounts of something called 'jargon'.

More about jargon

Key word

> *Jargon*: the set of words and phrases (the terminology) peculiar to a trade, profession, or occupation.

Philip Howard offers the following definition of jargon:

> 'Jargon' comes from a delightful old French word which means 'the twittering of birds'. In English it now has three principal meanings. First it can mean a medley of more than one language. This meaning is otiose [no longer useful]. Second, it means the technical vocabulary of a science, trade, or other hermetic group [hermetic = closed to outsiders]. The third kind of jargon in English is the nastiest. This is pretentious language conspicuous for its abstractitis, circumlocution, and avoidance of plain English . . . Most of us are liable to fall into this kind of jargon occasionally, if we are not careful. It takes time to say things simply . . .
>
> Philip Howard, *The State of the Language*

The definitions that concern us here are 2 and 3.

▪ *Jargon as technical vocabulary*

The jargon of definition 2 can range from slangy expressions like the prison officer's *black aspirin* (a kick with a heavy boot) through the rock-climber's *deep-sixer* (a fall off a steep cliff resulting in death) to the dignified terminology of the Law and other learned professions. This latter kind – the specialized vocabulary used when expert talks to expert – is what is important for our purposes. It is used for two main reasons:

1 It is a kind of shorthand. Much quicker to refer to a *lien* than to 'a right to retain another person's property pending discharge of a debt'; to talk of *quarks* than of 'hypothetical elementary particles postulated together with their antiparticles to be fundamental units of baryons and mesons', and of *irony* rather than 'the sarcastic use of words to imply the opposite of what they normally mean'.

2 It is more exact than everyday language; being drawn largely from 'dead' Latin and Greek, it does not change as living English does, altering its connotations or acquiring new meanings.

However unintelligible to the layman, therefore, jargon is never obscure – as long as it is used in its proper context. Used by experts to laymen who do not understand it, however, it is both a form of bad manners and a barrier to communication.

▨ *Pseudo-jargon*

The kind of terminology discussed in Philip Howard's third definition – 'pretentious language conspicuous for its abstractitis, circumlocution, and avoidance of plain English' – might more properly be called 'pseudo-jargon', since it is used in imitation of jargon proper. It seeks to impress with learned-sounding abstractions, and the result is a terminology that nobody, not even its user, can clearly understand. 'Doublespeak' is the name William Lutz, following George Orwell, gives to such language:

> Farmers no longer have cows, pigs, chickens and other animals on their farms; according to the U.S. Department of Agriculture farmers have 'grain-consuming animal units' (which, according to the Tax Reform Act of 1986, are kept in 'single-purpose agricultural structures', not pig-pens and chicken coops). Attentive observers of the English language also learned recently that the multibillion dollar stock market crash of 1987 was simply a 'fourth quarter equity retreat'; that airplanes don't crash, they just have 'uncontrolled contact with the ground'; that janitors are really 'environmental technicians'; that it was a 'diagnostic misadventure of a high magnitude' which caused the death of a patient in a Philadelphia hospital, not medical malpractice (or even a doctor's mistake); and that President Reagan wasn't really unconscious while he underwent minor surgery, he was just in a 'non-decision-making form'.
>
> Doublespeak is a blanket term for language which pretends to communicate but doesn't, language which makes the bad seem good, the negative appear positive, the unpleasant attractive, or at least tolerable. It is language which avoids, shifts, denies responsibility, language which is at variance with its real or purported meaning. It is language which conceals or prevents thought . . .
>
> William Lutz, *The World of Doublespeak*

This ability of doublespeak to duck the consequences of its intentions by never fully spelling them out is all too clearly seen in times of war. During the American invasion of Vietnam, the destruction of villages was referred to as 'pacification'; the civilians killed as the result of bombing raids as 'collateral damage'.

Before the Gulf war, American senators advocated the carrying out of 'surgical strikes' against Iraq. The connotations of the word 'surgical' cluster round the concept of healing: a precise cut is made into diseased tissue in order to eliminate what is unhealthy and restore the body to wholeness. Is that what a surgical strike in military terms would do? Were these people blinding themselves with the use of such anodyne language?

Activity

> Explain the effect produced by changing abstract nouns like *inter-sibling rivalry* and *kill factor* into simple verbs like *hate* and *kill*.

Even in academic circles, where people might be expected to speak and write as clearly as possible, esoteric Latinate terms are used as a deliberate ploy to enhance prestige. And the ploy succeeds. Below, an American graduate testifies to the belief that the longer and more arcane a professor's vocabulary, the greater the gap between his intelligence and that of the rest of the world:

> Somewhere along the line, probably in college, I picked up on the fact that articulate people used big words, which impressed me. I remember taking two classes from a philosophy professor simply because I figured he must be really smart since I didn't know the meaning of the words he used in class . . . He sounded so smart to me simply because I didn't understand him . . . The way someone writes – the more difficult the writing style – the more intellectual they sound.

She openly admits the effect her attitude has had on her written style:

> Instead of choosing to write 'he lives at' I prefer 'he resides at'. Instead of saying 'Couples spend their extra money' . . . I'd choose 'surplus income'. It sounds more grown up. Here's a favourite of mine: 'predicated upon the availability of' is classier than saying 'exists because of' (or, for that matter, 'depends on'). Maybe it sounds more awesome . . . I think the point is that I am looking for a writing style that makes me look smart.

When motives are as false as this, judgement is impaired:

> When I read something and I don't know immediately what it means, I always give the author the benefit of the doubt. I assume this is a smart person and the problem with my not understanding the ideas is that I'm not as smart.

Activity

> 1 Give your considered opinion of
>   a the professor's use of language;
>   b the student's attitude towards it.

Generally speaking, in writing containing jargon the technical words themselves are the only source of obscurity to a layman. In passages of pseudo-jargon almost every word may be obscure, so that whole sentences may be impossible to pin down to a concrete meaning and translate.

Activity

Read the following extracts, then follow the instructions below:

a Comfort's catholicity of perception and image, strangely Whitmanesque in range, almost the exact opposite in aesthetic compulsion, continues to evoke that trembling atmospheric accumulative hinting at a cruel, an inexorably serene timelessness . . .

(Critical review)

b Nobody could fault Hakan Hardenberger's Haydn trumpet concerto, with flutter-tongue mordants, a bold cadenza and exquisitely musical phrasing. Nor could they fail to thrill to Ann Murray's Rossini fireworks from the last scene of *La Cenerentola*, with the Irish mezzo's amazing flexibility and beauty of tone, her cascades of fioritura and delicate coloratura.

(Critical review)

c Fallback is catered for on the Courier, though not to the extent that it is on the Hayes unit. In HST mode, the modem can fall from 14,400 cps through to 12,000, 9600, 7200 and 4800 cps, but in V32 mode this is reduced severely to just 9600 to 4800. However, HST modulations can also fall forward if the line speed improves in the middle of a transmission.

(Article on computers)

d '. . . He hails from a multi-delinquent family with a high incarceration index. Inter-sibling rivalry hindered his on-going relationships, making him an isolate in a stress-situation.'

(Letter from social worker to magistrate)

e The photographic image, however, does more than place the viewer; and these other functions, no less fraught with ideological implications, also need examination. A still image, for example, is a remarkably mute object testifying perhaps only to a 'having been there' of the image's referent at that single instant in time of its capture.

Meaning, though rich, may be profoundly imprecise, ambiguous, even deceiving. A large component of the work undertaken in the construction and reading of images becomes directed toward a distillation of that ambiguity of meaning into a more defined and limited concentrate.

(Article on photography for general readers)

1 In which extracts do the writers use
  a jargon proper,
  b pseudo-jargon?

2 In those extract(s) in which you feel language obscures meaning, does the source of the obscurity lie in the writer's wish to conceal or impress, or in an inability to think and write clearly?

3 Which extract would you find the greatest difficulty in translating into your own words? Why?

The grammatical structure of English

● ●

The grammar English has lost

Note: you are not asked to learn the grammar discussed in this section, but simply to be aware that it once existed.

Some people complain that English 'has very little grammar'. What do they mean?

They mean that the structure of individual words in modern English is less interesting than in certain other languages such as modern German and French because we have lost our habit of inflecting words: that is, showing their meaning by altering their form.

Inflections

Words can be inflected:

1 by changing the vowels inside a word, as we do with irregular plurals such as feet (singular 'foot');
2 by adding letters at the end, as we do when we add -s to regular nouns to make them plural, and -s and -ed endings to verbs to show number and tense:

> (I) walk, (he/she) walks, (you/we/they) walked.

Languages that inflect their words are called *synthetic* languages, as opposed to *analytical* ones, like English.

Take for example the Latin sentence, *Nero interfecit Agrippinam.* (Nero murdered Agrippina.) The fact that the word *Nero* has no inflection shows that he is the **subject** of the sentence – the agent or doer of the action. The -*m* inflection on *Agrippina* on the other hand shows her to be the **object** of the sentence, the receiver of the action. It would make no difference therefore if we altered the word order and wrote *Agrippinam interfecit Nero*, for the -*m* inflection on *Agrippina* gives it only one possible meaning: she was the victim of Nero's action – the murderee, as an American might say.

In modern English, on the other hand, we use word order to show meaning: subjects are always placed first and objects second. Change *Nero killed Agrippina* to *Agrippina killed Nero* and you change completely the meaning of the sentence.

Like Latin, Old English was a highly inflected language. Its words changed their forms to show
  a their function,
  b their agreement with other words in a sentence.

For example, Old English nouns had four inflections (or case-endings) to show their function in a sentence.

Inflections of noun and pronoun in Old English

* the **nominative** or **subject** case (showing that it was the subject)
* the **accusative** or **object** case (showing that it was the object. This case is sometimes also called the *direct object*.)
* the **genitive** or **possessive** case (showing that something belonged to it)
* the **dative** (showing that something was being done by, or to, or for it; it would also cover the meanings *in* and *on*, for which there was no separate *ablative* case, as there was in Latin. The dative case is sometimes also called the *indirect object*.)

For example:

N stān (*stone*)	cyning (*king*)
A stān	cyninge
G stānes	cyninges
D stāne	cyninge

Baugh, *A History of the English Language*

To see how the system worked, imagine having to inflect a common noun like *cat*. Instead of using the same form of the word whenever we mentioned the animal, we should have to vary it to suit its function in the sentence, like this:

The cat [*nominative case*] is hungry.
We have a nice cate [*accusative case*].
The cates [*genitive or possessive case*] food is in the cupboard.
Give some to the cate [*dative case*].

Any other nouns used in the sentence would also have to be inflected, of course: in the examples above involving the cat, *food* would take the accusative case-ending, *cupboard* the dative, for instance. And even then the complexities were not over: there was the **declension** to take into account.

Declension

Nouns that ended in a vowel took the case-endings of the weak declension; those that ended in a consonant took those of the strong. Thus, *stān* (see below) belongs to the strong declension, *gièfu* and *hunta* to the weak.

Singular				
	N	stān	gièf-u	hunt-a
	G	stān-es	gièf-e	hunt-an
	D	stān-e	gièf-e	hunt-an
	A	stān	gièf-e	hunt-an

Plural	N	stān-as	gièf-a	hunt-an
	G	stān-a	gièf-a	hunt-ena
	D	stān-um	gièf-um	hunt-um
	A	stān-as	gièf-a	hunt-an

Baugh, *A History of the English Language*

So, you had to remember

a to give each noun in a sentence the ending appropriate to its function;

b to make sure that that case-ending was in the correct declension.

And even then your work was not finished; there was still gender to cope with.

▨ *Gender*

Regardless of its natural sex (or lack of sex if inanimate), every noun was given a masculine, feminine, or neuter gender. Thus, *stone* and *hunter* (above) were masculine while *gift*, for no particular reason, was feminine. More absurdly still, *sunne* (sun) was feminine, *mōna* (moon) masculine, *wīf* (wife) neuter, and *wīf-mann* (woman) masculine (following the gender of the last element of the word).

The business of gender was made even more complicated by the fact that you didn't alter the nouns themselves, but the words that qualified those nouns. Demonstratives such as *this* and *that*, the definite and indefinite articles, *the* and *a* – all had to be given a masculine, feminine or neuter ending to suit the gender of their nouns:

the man	the woman	this man	this woman	(modern English)
se mann	þaet wif	þes mann	þis wif	(Old English)

Modern German and the languages derived from Latin still inflect to show gender in this way, which may be one reason why we find them so hard to learn.

l'homme	la femme	cet homme	cette femme	(French)
der Mann	die Frau	dieser Mann	diese Frau	(German)
l'hombre	la mujer	este hombre	esta mujer	(Spanish)
l'uomo	la donna	questo uomo	questa donna	(Italian)

All adjectives were inflected also, so if we wanted to expand our original sentence into 'We have a nice black cat', both *nice* and *black* would have to be made masculine, feminine or neuter to match the gender of *cat*, and inflected either strong or weak according to the word that preceded them – in this particular instance, the indefinite article *a*.

Finally, having got your nouns, articles, and adjectives into agreement you would have to cope with verbs, which were rather more heavily inflected than ours today.

▇nflections of the verb

▒ *Tense*

Like the nouns, Old English verbs were divided into two categories: strong and weak. Strong verbs formed their past tense and past participle by modifying (i.e. changing) their stem vowel, as some still do: for example *drink*, *drank*, *drunk*. Weak verbs on the other hand formed their past tense and past participle by tacking a suffix on to the end of their stem: for example, *burn*, *burned*, *burnt*.

▒ *Number*

Old English also had seven endings to show number (i.e. how many people were involved in the action of the verb): four singular endings in the present tense, and three in the past:

		present tense	**past tense**
Ist person sing.	(I)	ic luf-i(g)e	ic luf-ode
2nd person sing.	(you)	þu* luf-ast	þu luf-odest
3rd person sing.	(he/it/she)	he/hit/heo luf-aþ*	he/hit/heo luf-ode
Ist person plur.	(we)	we luf-iaþ	we luf-odon
2nd person plur.	(you)	ge luf-iaþ	ge luf-odon
3rd person plur.	(they)	hie luf-iaþ	hie luf-odon

Sweet, *A First Middle English Primer*

Can you see now what people mean when they say that Modern English has very little grammar?

Activity

> 1 Look at the text of any Shakespeare play and see how the old second and third person singular endings survived into the seventeenth century:
> *dost, hast, didst, beginst*, etc. (contracted from *doest, havest, didest, beginnest*);
> *doth* (contracted from *doeth*), *loveth, pleadeth*, etc.
>
> 2 Write out all the *persons* of the verb *to talk* in order to discover how many inflections to show number we use today (e.g. *I, you, she/he/it, we, you, they*).
>
> 3 Read the following passage and summarize its ideas in no more than seventy of your own words.
>
> I can't help feeling that the current TV series, *The Story of English*, is making rather heavy weather of the question of why English is so universally popular. The class of students I used to take in English as a foreign language had no doubts at all. English was incredibly easy; it had no grammar at all.
>   These foreign students – from Spain, Portugal, France and Germany – were used to a language that operated as a system. Each sentence in

---

* Anglo-Saxon had two letters to represent modern *th*: ð and þ. Either could be used to represent the two sounds of *th*, as in *thin* and *then*.

most European languages is a machine, like a gearbox, in which one moving part affects every other part. All the words are altered, or inflected, to agree with all the other words. English, on the other hand, is an almost entirely un-inflected language. Where German has three genders for nouns, English has one. Where German nouns have four cases to show their function in the sentence, English nouns rely entirely on pronouns to tell you what they are doing. If you take a regular English verb like *to jump* it only has three inflections, which are: *jumps, jumping, jumped*. Stick these together with a group of simple auxiliaries like *may, will* and *should,* and you can form every tense and person that you need with about thirty words. To do the same in French would take around three hundred. This makes English very easy to learn. It is more like learning a list than a system, which is why various forms of pidgin English, and the bastard English of computer languages and airline-speak are so popular. It also makes English very very corruptible, which is why we have more jargon, neologisms, and foreign importations than anybody else. A hideous neologism in a French sentence will make the gearbox grind, whereas an English sentence can swallow almost anything from a megadeath to a cul de sac. On the positive side, because English has no grammar it is highly compressible, which makes it the ideal language for advertising men, headline writers, and poets. 'Sex-tangle vicar slams street-crime link' is utterly untranslatable, as is a fine line from Yeats like 'A lonely impulse of delight, drove to this tumult in the clouds.'

The period of levelled inflections, 1150–1500

At the beginning of this period, English is so fully inflected that it looks like a foreign language. By the end of it, it has clear similarities with the language that we use today.

The different stages of this transition are illustrated in the three extracts that follow, taken from Roger Lass's book, *The Shape of English.* All are versions of the same biblical passage (St Luke 2:8-9), but (a) is in Anglo-Saxon or Old English, (b) in Middle English, and (c) in early modern English.

a   And hyrdas wæron on þam ylcan rice waciende, and nihtwæccan healdende ofer heora heorda. Þa stod Drihtnes engel wiþ hig, and Godes beorhtnes him ymbe scean; and hi him mycelum ege adredon.

b   And scheeperdis weren in the same cuntre, wakynge and kepynge the watchis of the nyȝt on her flok. And lo! the aungel of the Lord stood bisidis hem, and the cleernesse of God schinede aboute hem, and thei dredden with greet drede.

c   And there were in the same countrey shepheards abiding in ye field, keeping watch ouer their flocke by nyght. And loe, the Angel of the Lord came vpon them, and the glory of the Lord shone round about them, and they were sore afraid.

The only connection between (c) and (a), written four hundred years earlier, is the verb *were* (from Old English *wæron*). Both the vocabulary of (a) (*ylcan* for *same*, *Drihtnes* for *God's*, *ymbe* for *about*) and the order in which its words are arranged (notice the position of the verbs) make it look to us like a foreign language.

Far more resemblance can be seen between (c) and (b), written three hundred years earlier, mainly because the words are familiar (though oddly spelled). Even here, however, you will notice major differences: (b) uses the possessive pronoun *her* where we use *their*, and the object pronoun *hem* in place of modern *them*; it also inflects its verbs to distinguish between singular and plural, which we gave up doing long ago: *stood* and *schinede* are singular; *weren* and *dredden* have the *-en* ending that makes them plural.

The inflections we have lost

The noun

All the original case endings have been lost. (Neither of the two inflections we have now is original.)

The pronoun

The *thou*, *thee*, *ye*, *thy* and *thine* forms of the second person singular and plural have all been lost. These are now written indiscriminately as *you* and *yours*.

> Singular: nominative or subject case: *thou*
>   *Thou* seydest this, that I was lyk a cat.
> Singular: accusative or object case: *thee*
>   I love *thee* wel.
> Plural: nominative or subject case: *ye*
>   Now herkneth . . . *ye* wise wyves, that kan understand.
> Plural: accusative or object case: *you*
>   Ye know what was commanded *you*.
> Singular: genitive or possessive case (before consonants): *thy*
>   I trowe thou woldest loke me in *thy* cheste.
> Singular: genitive or possessive case (before vowels): *thine*
>   Keep *thyn* honour, and keep eek myn estaat.
> Plural: genitive or possessive case: *your*
>   Dishonour not *your* mothers.

Grammatical gender

The masculine, feminine, and neuter endings of adjectives, demonstratives, and definite and indefinite articles have all been lost. Once nouns had lost their gender, there was nothing for these words to agree with.

The verb

Most of the three hundred or so old strong verbs have been lost, and all new ones entering the language since the seventeenth century have been given the regular *-ed* ending of the weak verb. For example, we say *I telephoned* rather than *I telephane; I have telephoned* rather than *I telephene.*

The endings for the second and third person singular of the verb that lent such flavour to the writings of earlier centuries have also disappeared:

> *Dost* thou think, because thou *art* virtuous,
> There shall be no more cakes and ale?

> Time *hath*, my lord, a wallet at his back,
> Wherein he puts alms for oblivion . . .

> Allas! Whiche folie and whiche ignorance mysle*deth* wandrynge
> wrecchis fro the path of verray good!

The replacement of this old *-eth* ending with *-s* has left us with a grammatical illogicality:

* plural nouns end in *-s*, yet take plural verbs that do not:
  e.g. *Comedies make us laugh*;
* singular nouns do not end in *-s* yet take verbs that do:
  Tragedy makes us cry.

Activity

> After the Conquest, influenced by the French practice of using *tu* to indicate familiar relationships and *vous* to show respect, the distinction between *thou*, *thee*, and *you* took on another use. *Thou* and *thee* were used to address friends and inferiors; *ye*, *your* and *you* were reserved for acquaintances and people of higher rank.
>
> 1 Write a letter to someone in the familiar *thee* and *thou* forms of the past, inviting them to dine with you. Then reply to this letter, rejecting the invitation, using the more distant *you* and *ye* forms. Remember that *thou* takes an *-st* ending (*thou knowest/dost/ thinkst/findst*, etc.), *he, she* and *it* take an *-eth* ending (*hath/knoweth/ doth/thinketh/findeth*, etc.), while the endings going with *I, you, we,* and *they* are written as today.
>
> 2 Discuss whether English is the poorer for the loss of these older pronouns.

Inflections remaining in modern English

Nouns

Only two inflections have survived to the present day, both in an altered form:

1 the *s* that marks the genitive or possessive case: the man*'s* house;
2 the *s* that marks the plural: house, house*s*.

Even these may not last for ever, since, strictly speaking, neither is really necessary for clear understanding of what is being said. If someone writes,

He goes to his mother house for dinner every day

we understand him; if people talk of 'three pound ten' instead of 'three pounds ten', their meaning is not obscure.

▓ *Adjectives*

We still retain the comparative and superlative forms (technically called *degrees*) of the adjective. Adjectives with one or two syllables are given the inflections -*er* and -*est*. Adjectives with three or more syllables are preceded by *more* and *most*. For example:

	Comparative	**Superlative**
fast	faster	fastest
near	nearer	nearest
interesting	more interesting	most interesting

Exceptions		
good	better	best
bad	worse	worst

▓ *Pronouns*

The personal and relative pronouns are still inflected.

Personal pronouns
Nominative (subject) case: I, you, he, she, it, we, they
Accusative (object) case: me, you, him, her, it, us, them
Genitive (possessive) case: mine, yours, his, hers, its, ours, theirs

Relative pronouns
Nominative (subject) case: who
Accusative (object) case: whom
Genitive (possessive) case: whose

▓ *Verbs*

In Old English, as we remarked above, verbs were inflected to show
a person,
b tense.

Only the *s* of the third person singular now remains, having supplanted the old -*eth* ending current throughout Middle English. Found everywhere in Chaucer – *telleth*, *saith*, *doth*, etc. – and still fairly common in Shakespeare, it had disappeared for ever by the end of the seventeenth century.

Will this remaining -*s* also disappear, leaving us one day with the kind of perfectly regular verb system George Orwell thought could happen only in a totalitarian State? Will it make any difference to our understanding of a sentence if it does?

Disadvantages of the loss of inflections

As Bodmer points out in his *Loom of Language*, the loss of inflections has forced 'the introduction of roundabout expressions involving the use of particles such as *of, to, more than, most*, or of a special class of verbs some of which (e.g. *will, shall, can, may*) have more or less completely lost any meaning unless associated with another verb.' This has increased the number of monosyllables in a language that was already monosyllabic in character.

Some linguists accept the streamlined efficiency of modern English yet still mourn the flexible movement and rhythm given to prose and verse by the old inflections. One of them writes:

> . . . on the grounds of lilt and flow . . . I claim that the straightforward sentence 'The good lads went to the black mill' is inferior to the Chaucerian version, 'The goode lads wenten to the blake melle'*, where the three sounded final *-e* inflexions stand respectively for a plural adjective, a weak adjective after a definite article, and a dative noun (melle = *to* the mill).

Advantages of the loss of inflections

The loss of inflexions makes learning the language much easier, both for English schoolchildren and for foreigners. Only the following inflections are absolutely necessary in English today:

1 *-s* for the third person singular of the present tense of the verb (e.g. *sees*), or for the plural form of nouns (e.g. *glasses*);
2 *-ed* for the past tense verbs (e.g. *ordered*);
3 *-t, -en,* or *-ed* for the past participle (e.g. *burnt, eaten, disturbed*);
4 *-ing,* which can be added to the end of verbs to make present participles;
5 the different forms of the verb *to be: am, are, is, was, were, (have/has/had) been, (will) be;*
6 irregular noun plurals like *sheep, men, women,* and *children;*
7 the dozen or so common strong verbs mentioned below (page 64).

(We can get round the possessive apostrophe *s* by writing 'of the [something or other]', and round the *-er* and *-est* of comparatives and superlatives by writing 'more' and 'most'.)

Consider by contrast the plight of the French, who still have number and gender to cope with. They speak their language very fluently but find it difficult to write down correctly, since fifty per cent of its inflections exist only on paper and are never pronounced. Take the simple verb *aimer*, to love: the forms *j'aime* (I love), *tu aimes* (you love), *il/elle aime* (he/she loves), and *ils aiment* (they love) are all spelled differently but are pronounced exactly the same, while the infinitive *aimer* sounds exactly like the second person plural, *vous aimez*.

* The *-e* on *goode, blake,* and *melle* should be sounded as an extra syllable.

Activity

Read the following extract from Orwell's *Nineteen Eighty-four* and discuss whether the loss of all remaining inflections would be good or bad.

The grammar of Newspeak had two outstanding peculiarities. The first of these was an almost complete interchangeability between different parts of speech. Any word in the language could be used either as verb, noun, adjective, or adverb . . . The word 'thought', for example, did not exist in Newspeak. Its place was taken by 'think', which did duty for both noun and verb. No etymological principal was followed here: in some cases it was the original noun that was chosen for retention, in other cases the verb. Even where a noun and verb of kindred meaning were not etymologically connected, one or other of them was frequently suppressed. There was, for example, no such word as 'cut', its meaning being sufficiently covered by the noun-verb 'knife'. Adjectives were formed by adding the suffix '-ful' to the noun-verb, and adverbs by adding '-wise'. Thus, for example, 'speedful' meant 'rapid' and 'speedwise' meant 'quickly' . . .

The second distinguishing mark of Newspeak grammar was its regularity. With a few exceptions . . . all inflexions followed the same rules. Thus, in all verbs the preterite and the past participle were the same and ended in '-ed'. The preterite of 'steal' was 'stealed', the preterite of 'think' was 'thinked', and so on throughout the language, all such forms as swam, gave, brought, spoke, taken, etc., being abolished. All plurals were made by adding '-s' or '-es' as the case might be. The plurals of 'man', 'ox', 'life', were 'mans', 'oxes', 'lifes'. Comparison of adjectives was invariably made by adding '-er', '-est' ('good', 'gooder', 'goodest'), irregular forms and the 'more', 'most' formation being suppressed. The only classes of words that were still allowed to inflect irregularly were the pronouns, the relatives, the demonstrative adjectives, and the auxiliary verbs. All these followed their ancient usage, except that 'whom' had been scrapped as unnecessary, and the 'shall', 'should' tenses had been dropped, all their uses being covered by 'will' and 'would' . . .

The vexed question of grammar

Prescriptivists (people who like rules) believe you must know grammar in order to write good English. Others believe that learning grammar stifles creativity.

Look at these conflicting views and decide for yourself which (if either) is true. In order to do so, you need to know a little about grammar.

What is grammar?

Grammar is an umbrella term that covers two aspects of language:

1 the structure and function of individual words;
2 the arrangement of those words within a given sentence. (This second aspect is sometimes called *syntax*.)

The grammatical exercises that prescriptivists want all students to do are called *parsing* and *clause analysis*. Parsing is based on the structure and function of individual words; clause analysis on the arrangement of words into clauses within a sentence.

Parsing

When we parse, we:

1 examine each word in a sentence;
2 put it into its own particular category of the 'parts of speech';
3 explain what its function is (i.e. how it relates to other words in the sentence).

The parts of speech

Every word in the English language belongs to one of the categories of the 'parts of speech'. There are eight of these categories: nouns, pronouns, adjectives, verbs, adverbs, prepositions, conjunctions, and the definite and indefinite articles *the* and *a*.

A word of advice

Don't be put off by these technical terms. You have been using the parts of speech since you were a toddler and you can handle them all with ease. All you have to do is learn their names.

A good way to learn the different parts of speech is to think of how we pick words up when we are small, beginning with the first kind of word we learn to use: the *noun*.

Nouns

Definition: A *noun* is a word that is used to name any person, animal, thing, idea, state, or quality.

The first words we learn are nouns – the names of people and of objects: *mummy, daddy, teddy, doggy, biccy* (biscuit), *jink* (drink) – simply because people and objects are the most important things in our lives. When we learn their names we acquire power over them to a certain extent: we can ask for things, call people's attention to us, generally start to function in society.

Kinds of noun

* **Common:** a name common to all members of a large class of people, animals, or things: *man, cat, table, town, friend, word, sentence, apple, fig, leaf.*
* **Proper:** the name peculiar to a particular person, place, or thing; it is given a capital letter to distinguish it from names held in common by many other people and things): *Tiffany, New York, 'The Catcher in the Rye', the Empire State building, Friday, August, Concorde.*

* **Collective:** a name denoting a collection or group of people, animals, or things, regarded as a whole: *jury, committee, government, Cabinet, crowd, team, herd.*
* **Abstract:** the name of a quality, state of mind, physical condition, idea, or action: *attractiveness, intelligence, weariness, Capitalism, belief.*

Activity

Pick out the thirty-six nouns in this extract, counting each only once.

As he waited for his helping of blueberry pancakes with fresh cream and Winsconsin cheddar, the thought of dieting brushed feebly at his mind like an old remorse. He was aware that just eating a little of what he did not fancy would sooner or later do him good in the sexual chase. This idea had been brought sharply into focus at a fellow-publisher's party the previous year. Somebody's secretary had told him that what he wanted was all right with her on the understanding that he brought his block and tackle along. Five days later, sipping a half-cup of sugarless milkless tea to round off a luncheon of a lightly boiled egg with no salt, a decarbohydrated roll resembling fluff in plastic, and a small apple, he made up his mind for ever that, if it came to it, he could easily settle down to a regime of banquets and self-abuse. He sent his plate up now for a second helping of pancakes and put three chocolate mints into his mouth to tide him over. Outside every fat man there was an even fatter man trying to close in.

Kingsley Amis, *One Fat Englishman*

Nouns used as adjectives ─

▓ *Pronouns*

Definition: A *pronoun* is a word that stands in place of a noun, to save us saying the same noun twice: *she, he, they, it, we, you.*

Like nouns, certain pronouns are picked up early – *me* in particular, since our own needs and wants are the most important things in the world to us when we are small. However, some pronouns confuse two and three year olds greatly: daddy, for instance, can be *I* when he's talking and *you* or *he* or *him* when mummy is. This is very puzzling, and is the reason why children come out with sentences like 'Him didn't go to work today' and 'I can see she's bad'. The difference between *I* (the subject case) and *me* (the object case) also takes some time to grasp. *Me* is used indiscriminately in the one or two-word 'sentences' that are all toddlers are capable of at first. Utterances such as 'Me!' or 'Me biscuit!' have to do duty for more complete constructions like 'I want a biscuit'.

Kinds of pronoun
* **Demonstrative:** *this, that, these, those, the former, the latter* (as in, 'I've had enough of this')
* **Distributive:** *each, either, neither* (as in, 'I would be happy with either')
* **Emphatic:** *myself, yourself, his/herself, ourselves*, etc. (as in, 'Do it yourself')
* **Reflexive:** *myself, yourself, him/herself, ourselves*, etc. (as in, 'He hurt himself')

* **Indefinite:** *one, some, any, someone, anybody, everybody*
* **Interrogative:** *who, which, what* (as in, 'Who are you talking about?')
* **Relative:** *who, which, what, that* (as in, 'The book which you ordered has arrived')
* **Personal:** *I, you, he/she, it, we, you, they*
* **Possessive:** *mine, yours, his, hers, ours, theirs*

Adjectives

Definition: An *adjective* is a word that describes (or qualifies) a noun or pronoun e.g. a *lucky* break; the *happy* hour.

Once we have mastered nouns, adjectives soon follow: children have strong feelings about the people and things they are surrounded by, and since adjectives can express their feelings about them, they pick them up quickly: 'Nice mummy', 'Good daddy', 'Naughty teddy', 'Bad dog'.

Note: nice, beautiful, and *good* are obviously descriptive words and most people would have little difficulty in assigning them to the category 'adjective'. Others, like the first five kinds of adjective listed below, are less easy to recognize because they don't pick out any obvious features. For example, 'I want that book, not this': here, *this*, and *that* are clearly singling out/defining/describing which book is wanted and so can be only adjectives. The same is true of distributive, interrogative and numeral adjectives below, all of which qualify or describe the nouns they precede.

Kinds of adjective

* **Demonstrative:** *this, that, these, those* (as in, 'I want that book')
* **Distributive:** *each, every, either, neither* (as in, 'Either knife will do')
* **Interrogative:** *which? what?* (as in, 'Which kind of book do you prefer?')
* **Numeral:** *one, two,* etc.
* **Indefinite:** *all, many, several*
* **Possessive:** *my, your, his, our, their*
* **Qualitative** (showing what kind): *male, English, middle-class*

Activity

Pick out the adjectives (thirteen, or fourteen if you include the number) in the following extract. Count each only once.

verbal noun

THE GENTLE TOUCH . . .

I love touching, affectionate physical contact, massage, and all things tactile/kinaesthetic. Other pursuits: dance, walking, cinema, therapy.

Friendly, Affectionate Man, 35, seeks similarly Warm, Affectionate, Sensual Woman for these plus warm but unpossessive friendship, loving sex, and mutual support. London. Letter with telephone no. – and photo?

Verbs

Definition: A *verb* is a word that indicates an action or a mental or physical state, e.g.:

Sue Ellen *shot* JR. She *was* drunk.

Verbs expressing action are another part of speech that children pick up early. Again, they learn them because there is something in it for them; verbs get them what they want: *wee-wee, go, want, give, get down* ('doing-words' as primary school teachers often call them) quickly become part of every toddler's vocabulary.

But not every verb is a 'doing-word'. In the group of sentences that follows, only the first expresses action:

Sue Ellen *shot* JR.
She *wished* she had not. (*expresses feelings*)
She *felt* ill. (*expresses a mental and physical state*)
She *seemed* confused. (*expresses how she appeared to others*)

In addition, there is a category called auxiliary (i.e. helping) verbs, which some people have difficulty in accepting as verbs at all. These are the verbs *to be*, and *to have*, together with the incomplete verbs *shall, will, may, do*, e.g.:

I *have* seen, I *am* going, I *shall* go, she *will* go, we *may* call, *do* you want us to bring anything?

Children are slower to acquire non-action verbs like the above, and it is a clear sign of maturing intelligence when one appears in the vocabulary. One mother I know, chatting away as usual to her small son, asked him what he would like for lunch and was startled to hear him answer, 'I really don't mind'. She suddenly realized he was no longer a baby, but a person.

Kinds of verb

English verbs divide into two main classes: *strong* and *weak*.

* **Strong verbs** form their past tense and past participle by changing the vowel of the stem: *ride, rode, ridden; break, broke, broken; think, thought, thought; hide, hid, hidden; do, did, done; see, saw, seen; eat, ate, eaten; catch, caught, caught; spin, span, spun; bring, brought, brought; swim, swam, swum*, etc.
* **Weak verbs** form their past tense and past participle by adding the inflection *-ed* to the stem: *walk, walked, walked; prove, proved, proven*. Since weak verbs are far more common in English, toddlers frequently try to put weak endings on strong verbs: 'It hurted me'; 'He bited me'; 'I holded it'.

They also have two voices: the active voice and the passive voice.

When the subject of the sentence is doing the action, the verb is said to be in the **active voice:**

Shug *sang* the blues.

When the subject of the sentence is having something done to him or her or it, the verb is said to be in the **passive voice:**

Squeak's songs *were sung* in a little tiny voice.

Small children cannot cope with the passive voice and may still be trying to sort it out when they are nine or ten.

Activity

> Pick out the verbs (thirteen in all) in the following extract:
>
> – The kidney! he cried suddenly.
> He fitted the book roughly into his inner pocket and, stubbing his toes against the broken commode, hurried out towards the smell, stepping hastily down the stairs with a flurried stork's legs. Pungent smoke shot up in an angry jet from a side of the pan. By prodding a prong of the fork under the kidney he detached it and turned it turtle on its back. Only a little burned. He tossed it off the pan on to a plate and let the scant brown gravy trickle over it.
>
> James Joyce, *Ulysses*

▓ *Adverbs*

Definition: An *adverb* is a word that limits or modifies (i.e. tells us more about) the meaning of any part of speech except a noun or pronoun. Adverbs can therefore modify:

1 adjectives: *almost* eighteen; *very* nice; *fairly* cheap; *awfully* expensive; *rather* ill.
2 other adverbs: she jogs *quite* frequently; he *nearly* always goes with her.
3 prepositions: *close* by the lamp.

So, if you're not sure sometimes what part of speech you're dealing with, and it's got more than three letters, it's probably an adverb.

Kinds of adverb

* **Time:** *now, then, soon, yesterday, recently, always, never, till*;
* **Place:** *here, there, inside, outside, above, below, between*;
* **Manner:** *slowly, quickly, angrily, calmly, eagerly, badly, well*;
* **Degree:** *very, fairly, reasonably, almost, quite, too*;
* **Number:** *once, twice, firstly, secondly* (etc.), *finally, again*;
* **Certainty or uncertainty:** *certainly, surely, tentatively, perhaps, not*;
* **Interrogative:** *How? When? Where? Why?*

Adverbs of manner, degree, and certainty express complex mental judgements and so are too sophisticated for very young children to handle. Their minds are focused exclusively on physical things.

Activity

> 1 Discuss which of the above adverbs
>   **a** you would not expect toddlers to use
>   **b** you would expect to be in their vocabulary.
>   Try to suggest reasons for this.
>
> 2 Pick out the adverbs in the following extract. (There are seven if repeated words are counted only once. *Over* is a preposition.)

A few light taps upon the pane made him turn towards the window. It had begun to snow again. He watched sleepily the flakes, silver and dark, falling obliquely against the lamp-light. The time had come for him to set out on his journey westward. Yes, the newspapers were right: snow was general all over Ireland. It was falling on every part of the dark central plain, on the treeless hills, falling softly upon the Bog of Allen and, farther westward, softly falling into the dark mutinous Shannon waves. It was falling, too, upon every part of the lonely churchyard on the hill where Michael Furey lay buried. It lay thickly drifted on the crooked crosses and headstones, on the spears of the little gate, on the barren thorns. His soul swooned slowly as he heard the snow falling faintly through the universe and faintly falling, like the descent of their last end, upon all the living and the dead.

James Joyce, *Dubliners*

▨ *Prepositions*

Definition: a *preposition* is a word that shows the relationship between one noun and another noun or pronoun in a sentence. Prepositions are generally small words like *on, by, to, in, down, out, round*. Very young children find it difficult to handle most of them, and may even treat *on*, as in 'It's on the table' and *in*, as in 'Put it in the box' as verbs (e.g. 'In', said loudly as toys are put away in the box).

The technical definition of a preposition – 'a word that shows the relationship between two nouns (or pronouns) in a sentence' – doesn't seem to mean much as it stands. Translate it into terms of real life, however, and there's all the difference in the world between going *to* the pub and coming away *from* it; between being *below* or *above* something; between having a fascination *with* something and having it *for* someone.

Note: some prepositions consist of two prepositions, often combined to form one word, e.g.: *into, throughout, upon, from behind*.

By the time they are three, most children can handle nouns, pronouns, adjectives, verbs, and adverbs because they are what grammarians call *content words*: words that carry information about people and things and actions in real life; things that can be grasped with the senses. Children find it much harder to use prepositions, because prepositions refer to the grammatical relationships between words in a sentence. They are *structure words* as opposed to content words: small pieces of language like *to* and *on* that glue sentences together and help them to mean what they mean without having any independent meaning of their own. For this reason, being new to grammar, you will probably find them harder to recognize too. Further information about the role of these two kinds of words in the construction of sentences will be given at the end of this section, under *The role of 'glue' words in sentence construction* (page 94).

Not understanding prepositions, toddlers leave gaps where they should be: *Tom come me* or *Tom come my house* instead of *Tom come **to** my* *house.* They can cope with words that relate to physical things, but such abstract mental concepts as the relationship between them is still beyond their grasp. Andrew Wilson in *The Foundations of Language* explains why:

> Children deal with language by stripping it of inessentials, as we should do in writing a telegram.
>
> The child faced with *Daddy is eating cake* may produce, if he is at that stage, *Daddy eat cake.*
>
> To take an actual example, quoted by Brown and Bellugi (1964), a mother's sentence *No you can't write on Mr Cramer's shoe* was reduced by the child to *Write Cramer's shoe.*
>
> In both examples the child selects the grammatically important items, nouns, verbs, and adjectives, what are called 'content' words, because they carry high 'information' content. He leaves out, on the other hand, structure words – words whose grammatical function is more important than the meaning they carry – such as auxiliary verbs, determiners*, prepositions, and conjunctions. There is no object or process 'on' in his world.

▨ Conjunctions

Definition: A *conjunction* is a word used to join single words, phrases, or sentences, e.g. bread *and* butter; he tried *but* he failed; she left home *then* came back.

Children have little trouble with simple conjunctions, using them to string sentences together in a continuous stream:

'And we had our dinner and then we washed up and then Mummy said I could go out and play and I played with Tracey and we played with our dollies . . .'

Kinds of conjunction

Grammarians divide conjunctions into two categories:

- ❖ **Co-ordinating conjunctions:** these join two or more main clauses: She was poor *but* she was honest.
- ❖ **Sub-ordinating conjunctions:** these join a dependent clause to a main clause: She was poor *because* she was honest.

Activity

> In the extract from *The Foundations of Language* quoted above, prepositions (eight in all) are unmarked.
>
> Pick out these prepositions, counting each only once.

* Auxiliary verbs are verbs like *have* and *might*, which help to form the tense of other verbs, e.g. *I might have broken my leg*, where the main verb is *broken*. Determiners are words like *the*, *a*, *some*; they determine that a noun is to follow.

■ *Articles*

Definition: the *article* is a kind of adjective.

Kinds of article

There are two articles: the definite and the indefinite.

- The **definite article**, *the*, is used to refer to some specific person or thing or event on which attention is being focused: Pass me *the* paper, please.
- The **indefinite article**, *a*, is used when any one of a group of objects, not some particular one, will do: e.g. Pass me *a* paper, please.

Like prepositions, these two little words are by-passed by children in the very early stages: verb plus object constructions (e.g. *Want drink*) are used in preference to verb plus article plus object (e.g. *Want a drink*). However, *a* is soon picked up, to be followed later by the more discriminating definite article, *the*.

■ *Summary*

Here is the same information again in tabular form:

Nouns are the names	of people:	*Adam, Eve, man, woman*
	of animals:	*snake, worm*
	of places:	*garden, Paradise*
	of things:	*tree, fruit*
	of qualities:	*goodness, evil*
	of states of mind:	*innocence, guilt*
	of actions:	*temptation, eating.*

Pronouns are substitutes for nouns: *he, she, they, it, this, who.*

Adjectives describe nouns: *beautiful* garden, *subtle* serpent, *flaming* sword.

Verbs express	actions:	they *ate*
	states of mind or being:	they *felt* guilty, they *suffered*.

Adverbs tell you more about:
1 verbs: the manner in which actions are performed: *beguilingly, quickly, angrily*
2 other adverbs: the degree of intensity of that manner: *fairly* quickly, *very* angrily, *most* beguilingly
3 adjectives: *quite* nice, *mildly* annoyed, *fairly* attractive
4 prepositions: *far* from Heaven, *close* to Hell.

Prepositions show relationship between two things in a sentence:
Adam was *in* the Garden.
Later he was driven *from* it.

Conjunctions join two words, two phrases, or two sentences: *and, or, but, then.*

The versatility of the parts of speech

Many words can function as several different parts of speech. Consider the word *fast*, for example, in the following sentences:

Young men like to drive *fast*. (Adverb qualifying *drive*)
Fast cars attract higher insurance premiums. (Adjective describing *cars*)
Lent is a religious *fast*. (Noun)
These days, few people bother to *fast*. (Verb)

In the same way, you can *back* a horse (verb), ride on a horse's *back* (noun), go *back* (adverb), and enter by the *back* door (adjective).

Activity

> 1 Write sentences in which the word *round* appears as each of the following: noun, adjective, verb, adverb, preposition.
>
> 2 Explain what part of speech the word *cans* is in the following sentence by the philosopher J. L. Austin: 'Are cans constitutionally iffy?'
>
> 3 Say what part of speech the word *more* is in the following sentences:
>   a Tell me more.
>   b I need more time.
>   c You couldn't have hurt him more if you had tried.

Shakespeare even turned the adverb *backward* into a noun:
in the dark backward and abysm of time.

Old sayings turn conjunctions into nouns and verbs:
If ifs and ands were pots and pans there'd be no need for tinkers.
Don't but me.
But me no buts.

Even pronouns can be turned into nouns in phrases like *her indoors* and *she who must be obeyed*.

Activity

> Write down what you notice about the 'adjectives' in the two sets of headlines below:
>
> a Roux cleans up in kitchen-sink drama
>   Britain loses £500m Tornado fighter deal
>   Deng dispels ill-health rumour
>   Dons told exam row must end
>   Fireman dies in explosives van blast
>
> b Explosives van warning
>   Explosives van warning inquiry
>   Explosives van warning inquiry report
>   Explosives van warning inquiry report denial

The prescriptivist approach to the parts of speech

Prescriptivists have to accept what has been done to the language in the past. They object, however, when we do the same kind of things today. Our habit of turning nouns into verbs at the drop of a hat annoys them greatly, not so much because the resulting structures are inelegant (though they are), but because they blur the clear outlines of the individual parts of speech. We must be guided by the grammar book if we want to keep English pure, they claim. Besides, if it is left in the hands of ordinary people, they perpetrate all kinds of foulness upon it, like turning nouns into verbs in the crudest way:

'Bag it and bin it and we'll win it.' (Margaret Thatcher)
'Eyeball us today.' (notice outside garage)
'I waste-basketed it.' (secretary)
'Children must be enthused with a love of learning.' (Kenneth Baker)
'It will be televised next week.' (announcer)
'We are exiting the old year.' (chairman of ICI)
'Let me example that for you.' (Severn Water Authority official)
'Your wine is being room-temperatured.' (waiter)

Summary: what part of speech a word is is determined by its function in the sentence it happens to be in.

How parsing works

To show how parsing works when it is applied to an actual sentence, here is an example from Knight's *A Comprehensive English Course.*

Oh	**interjection**	expressing an emotion (here, surprise)
The old	**adjectives**	here describing or qualifying the noun 'postman'. 'The' is generally given the additional title of Definite Article.
postman	**noun**	here the name of a person.
very	**adverb**	here limiting or modifying another adverb, 'carelessly'.
carelessly	**adverb**	here modifying the verb 'dropped'.
dropped	**verb**	here describing an action, making an assertion.
some	**adjective**	here qualifying the noun 'letters'.
most	**adverb**	here modifying the adjective 'important'.
important	**adjective**	here describing the noun 'letters'.
letters	**noun**	here the name of a thing or object.
and	**conjunction**	here joining 'letters' and 'parcel'.
a	**adjective**	qualifying 'parcel'. 'A' or 'an' is usually given the additional title of Indefinite Article.
parcel	**noun**	here the name of a thing or object.
just	**adverb**	here modifying the preposition 'near'.
near	**preposition**	here showing relation between 'parcel' and 'you'.
you	**pronoun**	here used instead of noun 'man' or 'Smith', i.e. the person addressed by the speaker.

T. W. Knight, *A Comprehensive English Course*

Activity

> **1** To test your understanding of
>   **a** the parts of speech
>   **b** parsing
>
>   write the following sentence vertically down the side of a page: 'The wretched Council very stupidly built some nasty houses and a really ugly school close by us.'
>
> **2** Opposite each word indicate:
>   **a** what part of speech it is;
>   **b** what work it's doing in the sentence.
>
> *Note:* if you find any difficulty with this task, it will probably be with the prepositions and the adverb, which are structure rather than content words, and so more difficult to grasp. If you can't decide what part of speech each word is, and it's comparatively short, it will probably be a preposition. If it's slightly longer, it's probably an adverb.

A knowledge of parsing is essential for clause analysis. Since the dependent clauses you would be asked to analyse have the same function as the single nouns, adjectives, and adverbs met in the parts of speech, it is obvious that you need to have done some parsing before going on to clause analysis.

However, true as this last argument may be, it begs an important question. Parsing may indeed be essential for clause analysis. The question is, 'Is clause analysis essential for the understanding and writing of good English?' Read what follows and make up your own mind.

Clause analysis

Clause analysis is the process of breaking down complex sentences into their constituent parts: the independent main clause, the dependent or subordinate clause, and the phrase.

Key words

> *Independent main clause:* a group of words that carries the main idea of a sentence. It always has a subject and a main verb.
>
> *Dependent clause:* a group of words that adds extra information about the subject in the independent main clause. It also always has a subject and a main verb.
>
> *Phrase:* a word or group of words that adds further information about the main clause or the dependent clause. Phrases either have no verb at all, or have a verb in the form of a present or past participle.

Before we can look at clause analysis proper we must discover what clauses are and what they do in a sentence. There are only two kinds of clause, and only one kind of phrase, so the task should not be too difficult.

The independent main clause or simple sentence

The structure that lies at the heart of every sentence we speak or write is known as the independent main clause.

When children first begin to talk they use one-word utterances: 'Mummy,' 'Daddy,' 'Teddy,' and so on. Since these single words are ambiguous ('Daddy', after all, might mean either 'I want daddy' or 'I want daddy to go away'), they soon learn to add verbs to their nouns: 'Want Daddy', 'Smack Tommy', and so on. In other words, they learn to speak in sentences, for at their most basic, this is all that sentences are: nouns (or pronouns) and verbs, for example:

Manus broods. Yolland yearns. Maire hopes. Jimmy Jack dreams.

A subject-verb structure like these has two names: the *independent main clause* and the *simple sentence*.

It is called *independent* because it can make sense without the help of another clause, e.g.:

Owen changes.

It is called *main* because when it forms a complex sentence with the help of a dependent or subordinate clause, it makes the main, or most important, statement, e.g.:

Manus changes [*imc*] when he learns what Lancey intends to do [*dsc*].

It is called a *simple sentence* because its structure is simple; it consists of only one clause.

Here are are some further independent main clauses/simple sentences:

S	V	S	V	S	V
Owen	translates.	Yolland	is unhappy.	Something	will be eroded.
Doalty	larked about.	Bridget	laughed.	The English	were puzzled.

Not all independent main clauses are as short as this, of course. Most have objects or other groups of words that extend their meaning. We can call these *completers* for convenience. Below are some examples:

Subject	Verb	Object	
Yolland	loves	Maire.	

Subject	Verb	Object	
Maire	forgets	Manus.	

Subject	Verb	Completer	Object
Manus	tries	to insult	Yolland.

Even when they have completers like these, however, simple sentences still consist of only one clause, because they have only one subject and only one verb.

▨ *The punctuation of simple sentences*

Some people have difficulty in recognizing where a simple sentence ends, particularly in examples like the following:

1   Paul went home. He entered the house silently.

They argue that *he* should be included in the first sentence here by putting a comma rather than a full-stop after *home*. Readers, they claim, won't know what the pronoun *he* refers to if it's put into a separate sentence from the noun it stands for – *Paul*.

In fact, readers **will** know who *he* refers to because the preceding sentence – *Paul went home* – will have told them. The second sentence doesn't exist in a vacuum, cut off from what has gone before.

2   William wanted to bring Gyp home. Mrs Morel said she should come at the Christmas.

In 2, they again argue for a comma rather than a full-stop. Having been taught in primary school to start a new sentence only when they change the subject, they refuse to start a new one here. The pronoun *she* in the second clause, they point out, refers to *Gyp* in the first. The subject is therefore the same, and so the two statements should be linked by a comma rather than separated by a full-stop.

Here, those who argue for a comma have misinterpreted the description of a sentence as a 'complete statement'. They interpret 'complete' to mean 'containing everything that is said about the subject', when what it really means is 'grammatically complete in containing a subject and a verb'. If we took these two arguments to their logical conclusion, no one would ever be able to start a sentence with a pronoun, which is clearly absurd.

Note: putting a comma rather than a full-stop between sentences is the most common punctuation error. If you have this habit, try to stop it now.

Activity

> Insert full stops between the simple sentences below.
>
> **1** Annie and Leonard are friends as well as lovers their marriage is a very happy one.
> **2** The physical attraction between Arthur and Beatie is very strong they get carried away one night.
> **3** Clara was unhappy in her marriage to Baxter Dawes she was unhappy with Paul for another reason.

Key words

> *Simple sentence:* a sentence made up of one independent main clause.
>
> *Compound sentence:* a sentence made up of two independent main clauses, usually joined by a conjunction.
>
> *Complex sentence:* a sentence consisting of at least one independent main clause and one dependent clause.

▓ *Simple/compound sentences*

When two or more simple sentences are joined together by the co-ordinating conjunctions *and, so, but*, and *then*, the resulting structure is known as a **compound sentence**. (*Co-ordinating conjunctions* are so called because they join two clauses of equal value.) For example:

Mrs Morel washed up and [she] put the children to bed.
Walter ate his dinner then [he] got washed and [he] went out.

When we use the term 'simple sentence' in future, therefore, you should understand it to include compound sentences also, since they are nothing but simple sentences joined together.

Activity

> Read the following paragraph and follow the instructions below.
>
> Hugh knows what is going on. He ignores it. He is self-indulgent. He is the ablest man in Ballybeg. He is to blame for his people's plight.
>
> 1 Re-write these four simple sentences as two longer ones, using only the coordinating conjunctions *but* (twice) and *so* (once). You may use an *and* before the *so* if you wish. You will need to change the order of the third and fourth sentences.
>
> 2 Explain why the two longer sentences are to be preferred to the four shorter ones. You should have three reasons, concerning:
>   a the psychological effect it has on you (the way you feel about it);
>   b the logic of what is said (how does joining the sentences help to convey the meaning?);
>   c the style.

▓ *The semi-colon in compound sentences*

Strings of independent main clauses joined by coordinating conjunctions are simplistic in style and monotonous to the ear. One or two are acceptable in a sentence; more than this should be avoided by the use of the semi-colon. The semi-colon is a stop that lets you have your cake and eat it. It marks the end of an independent main clause/simple sentence, but it saves you from having to bring the sentence to an end. You can therefore join two simple sentences on the same subject into one longer compound sentence, which has the additional advantage of preventing your style from being too abrupt. For example:

Hugh is an educated man; he speaks Irish, Latin, English, and Greek.

To join two sentences that were not on the same subject with a semi-colon would be as illogical as joining them with a conjunction. For example:

Hugh is an educated man; Maire wants to go to America.
Hugh is an educated man and/but Maire wants to go to America.

Semi-colons wouldn't suit the rambling style of a child's story, but they add force and sophistication to writing on more serious themes. For example:

At last Mrs Morel despised her husband. She turned to the child; she turned from the father. He had begun to neglect her; the novelty of his own home was gone.

Activity

> Read the pairs of sentences below, then follow the instructions below:
>
> 1 a Paul cannot give himself completely to Clara but Baxter can.
>   b Paul cannot give himself completely to Clara; Baxter can.
> 2 a Clara wants Paul's body and she also wants his mind and heart.
>   b Clara wants Paul's body; she also wants his mind and heart.
> 3 a The episode involving the swing tells us about Paul and Miriam's attitudes towards life and sexuality and so is highly symbolic.
>   b The episode involving the swing is highly symbolic; it tells us about Paul and Miriam's attitudes towards life and sex.
>
> 1 Which of the statements in the above pairs seems to you to carry the greatest authority and weight?
>
> 2 Why do you think this is so?

▧ *A classic pattern for the semi-colon*

There is a classic pattern for the use of the semi-colon, indicated below:

Noun in the first imc/ss	Semi-colon	Pronoun in the second imc/ss
Clara is passionately in love with Paul;		*she* pursues him around the factory.
Miriam despises Paul's relationship with Clara;		*she* thinks he debases himself by indulging in a purely physical relationship.
Paul is frightened of both his women;		*they* want to possess him, body and soul.

Activity

> Join the following imcs/sss into compound sentences **where appropriate**:
>
> 1 Mrs Leivers is very religious. She elevates ordinary things onto a very high plane.
> 2 Paul loves painting. He hopes to be a famous artist one day.
> 3 Clara is a feminist. She feels bitter towards men.
> 4 Paul worked in a hosiery factory. The countryside was beautiful.
> 5 Miriam hated maths. Her mother was very intense.

▧ *Uses of the simple sentence*

Simple sentences figure largely in instructions.

Activity

> Read the alternative sets of instructions below, then carry out the activities that follow.

A Before you start to light the boiler, the electricity should be switched off. When this has been done, the thermostat should be checked to see if it is at the right setting to bring the heating on when the boiler is lit. Next, the control knob should be turned to 'pilot' and fully depressed. A match can now be inserted into the special holder provided and applied to the burner while you count to 30. When 30 seconds have passed the knob can be released and turned to 'On', after which the electricity can be switched on again. All that remains to be done then is for the thermostat to be adjusted to the desired temperature.

B Switch off the electricity at the socket. Set the room thermostat to high. Turn the control to 'pilot', depress fully, and apply a match to the burner. Check that the pilot is lit and count to 30. Turn control knob to 'On'. Switch on the electricity and adjust the thermostat.

1 Say which set you found clearer and easier to understand.

2 Explain why, being careful to mention:
a the transformation of dependent clauses into independent main clauses;
b the change from the passive to the active voice of the verbs.

(If you don't remember what the passive voice is, see under the heading *Kinds of verb* on page 64.)

Because they tell people quickly and clearly what they mean, simple sentences are good attention-grabbers. People who want to persuade us to buy their products know this, too. An advertiser buying space in a newspaper, for example, has to make a big impact in a small space. So he or she chooses short simple sentences.

**Letraset
was invented on a train.**

**John Dankworth
composes music on trains.**

**Peter Barkworth
reads scripts on a train.**

**This advertisement
was conceived on a train.**

**The only thing
ever created in cars is a jam.**

British Rail advertisement

The complex sentence

Complex sentences are those that contain two different kinds of clause:

1 an independent main clause that makes the main statement;
2 a dependent/subordinate clause that adds something extra to that statement.

They are called *complex* because their structure is more complex than that of independent main clauses.

▨ *The dependent or subordinate clause*

There are two important facts to note about the dependent/subordinate clause:

1 It **resembles** the independent main clause in one respect: it, too, always has a subject and a main or finite verb (one that is not a participle ending in -*ing* or -*en*, or an infinitive i.e. the verb stem plus *to*: *to write, to think,* etc.)
2 It **differs from** the independent main clause in one respect: it is always introduced by a subordinating conjunction such as *although, because, if, when, until, unless*. For example:

> Although Clara loved Paul [*dsc*], she went back to her husband [*imc*].

Remove *although* from the head of the dependent/subordinate clause and place it at the beginning of the independent main clause, and you will cause them to exchange their functions: the dependent/subordinate clause is now the independent main clause and vice versa:

> Clara loved Paul, although she went back to her husband.

A second difference, related to the first, should now be apparent: any clause introduced by a subordinating conjunction must necessarily be incomplete, and is therefore
  a *dependent* on the independent main clause for the completion of its meaning, and
  b *subordinate* to it in value or importance.

Activity

Distinguish the dependent/subordinate clauses from the independent main clauses in the following sentences:

Maire refuses to marry Manus, unless he will get a proper job.
Because he prefers the past, Hugh ignores the real world.
Hugh drinks so that he can escape reality.
When Manus teaches her to speak, Sarah finds her identity.
She has hope until he abandons her.
Although he knows the language well, Manus refuses to speak English.

▓ *The function of dependent/subordinate clauses*

Independent main clauses/simple sentences are used to make unqualified assertions and statements. Dependent/subordinate clauses allow us to say much more about the circumstances surrounding the statements made in the independent main clause. With their help we can talk about:

* **when** events happened:
  After Paul fell in love with Miriam, he neglected his mother.
* **why:**
  Paul gave Miriam up *because* he wanted to reassure his mother.
* **how:**
  Paul behaved towards Miriam *as if* she were a stranger.
* **what** concessions are being made:
  Paul treated Miriam as if she were a stranger, *although* his conscience pricked him sorely at times.
* **what** limits are being set:
  Paul held himself aloof from Miriam *until* her attraction for him proved too strong.
* **what** conditions are being imposed:
  Paul threatened to break off with Miriam *unless* she gave herself physically to him/*if* she did not agree to give herself physically to him.

▓ *The three different categories of dependent clause*

Clause analysis does not ask you simply to distinguish between independent main and dependent clauses. It asks you also to assign each dependent clause to the particular category to which it belongs: *Noun*, *Adjectival*, or *Adverbial*.

Note: you are not expected to learn the difference between the three kinds of dependent clause (unless, of course, you would like to). This is because knowing whether you were writing a noun, adjectival, or adverbial clause would help you neither to write well yourself nor to appreciate the prose style of anybody else. You are, however, asked to learn the difference between independent main clauses, dependent/subordinate clauses, and the phrase, because knowing this will help you to do both.

1 The noun clause

The *Noun clause* has just the same function as the single noun: it acts as the subject or object of a verb. For example:

> **Single noun:** Yolland told Maire of his *love.*
> **Noun clause:** Yolland told Maire *that he loved her.*
> **Single noun:** Jimmy Jack's *madness* is obvious.
> **Noun clause:** It is obvious *that Jimmy Jack is mad.*

In both cases here the noun clause is equivalent to the noun: *that he loved her* is the thing he told her; it is just as much the object of the verb *told* as *love* is in the first example. In the same way, *that Jimmy Jack is mad* is equivalent to a fact; it is as much the subject of the verb *is* as the single noun *madness* is in the first example. Both clauses are equivalent to *things*.

There are four different kinds of noun clause:

1 Noun clause as subject

This usually precedes the independent main clause, e.g.:

That Albert loved Shug was obvious.
What Celie wanted was love.

2 Noun clause as object

This usually follows verbs like *say, think, wonder, know, ask, hear*; they are introduced by conjunctions like *that, what, how, where*.

Celie said *that Albert had changed*.
Shug asked *how Celie liked the song*.

3 Noun clause as complement

This completes verbs of incomplete predication, such as *seem*, and the verb *to be*:

It seems *that Albert had been hiding Nettie's letters*.
That was *what Shug discovered*.

4 Noun clause in apposition

This is almost always introduced by *that*, and can be recognized by the fact that it spells out what the noun in the imc means:

Shug's idea *that God was a 'It'* was radical.

that God was a 'It' is the idea. The noun and the noun clause mean the same thing and have the same relationship to the rest of the sentence.

Note: a verb of incomplete predication is simply one that is unfinished until a statement (or complement) is added to it. For example:

It was (verb of incomplete predication) *a wet morning* (complement).

In practice, life is too short to worry about distinctions such as these (although sorting out the various kinds does give more scope for logical thinking than most English exercises).

Activity

> Pick out
> **1** the independent main clauses,
> **2** the noun clauses in the following sentences. (If you can distinguish those of subject, object, complement, and apposition you will be showing double brilliance, but to recognize the noun clause is the important thing.)
> **a** Sugar knew what was in Celie's mind.
> **b** Harpo believed that Sophia was a bad wife.
> **c** Celie didn't know where Nettie had gone.
> **d** His behaviour to Shug was what Celie disliked.
> **e** Celie didn't ask Mr if she could leave.

    f What Sofia said about Harpo's bullying was true.
    g That Harpo loved Sophia was obvious.
    h Women had to learn the rule that they must not talk back to men.
    i The beating was what she had expected.

Note: if you are doubtful about a noun clause, ask yourself if it could be replaced by a single noun. You will find that it often can, as in (a) and (c), for instance.

2 The adjectival clause

This has the same function as the single adjective: to describe the subject or object of the sentence. For example:

> **Single adjective:** Sugar was an *independent* woman.
> **Adjectival clause:** Nobody controlled Sugar, *who went her own way.*
> **Single adjective:** Celie's Pa was an *evil man.*
> **Adjectival clause:** Celie's Pa was a man *who abused his children.*

Activity

Pick out
1 the imcs,
2 the adjectival clauses in the following sentences:
    a Squeak had the kind of skin that looked yellow.
    b Albert's Pa hated Sugar, who was coal-black.
    c Albert cleaned up his house, which had been filthy for months.
    d They went to Shug's room, where they could be alone.
    e The frog that Albert gave Celie was green.
    f Nettie was a child who managed to escape.
    g Sofia had several sisters, who were called the 'Amazons'.

3 The adverbial clause

Like the single adverb, this can modify adjectives and other adverbs as well as verbs. Adverbial clauses are easy to recognize, however, because they always begin with one of the following subordinating conjunctions:

* as, because, since (introducing adverbial clauses of **cause**):
  As/because/since she loved Harpo, Sofia waited for him.
* as . . . as, than (introducing adverbial clauses of **comparison** or **degree**):
  Harpo ate *as much as he could.*
  Harpo ate *more than two men ate.*
* although, however (introducing adverbial clauses of **concession**):
  Although he couldn't make Sofia 'mind' him, Harpo loved her.
  Harpo couldn't make Sofia 'mind' him, *however hard he tried.*
* if, unless (introducing adverbial clauses of **condition**):
  A man was not a man *if he could not rule his wife.*
  A man was not a man *unless he could rule his wife.*
* as, as if (introducing adverbial clauses of **manner**):
  Albert warned Celie to do *as he told her.*
  He treated her *as if she were a slave.*

● where, wherever (introducing adverbial clauses of **place**):
Celie could not go *where she pleased.*
(Compare with the noun clause
Celie did not know *where Nettie had gone.*
The adjectival clause describes the kind of places Celie cannot go to;
the noun clause tells us what piece of information she doesn't know.)
● so that (introducing adverbial clauses of **purpose**):
Celie made herself wood *so that she wouldn't feel pain.*
● so that, so . . . that (introducing adverbial clauses of **result**):
The rock injured her forehead, *so that it bled.*
Celie controlled her emotions *so well that she seemed indifferent to
pain.*
● when, whenever, since (introducing adverbial clauses of **time**):
When Celie saw Shug's picture, she felt a gleam of hope.
Whenever she looked at Shug she became aware of her own ugliness.
Celie had thought of nothing but Shug *since she came.*

Note: some people have difficulty in recognizing independent main
clauses in complex sentences like these because they are often so short
that they don't seem to make much sense on their own. *It is obvious,
Yolland told Maire,* and *He treated her,* for example, don't seem to do
what independent main clauses are supposed to do – make sense on their
own. To overcome this problem, remember that:

1 such clauses are **grammatically complete** (they have a subject and a verb),
and

2 they are as long as they need to be to do their job in these particular
sentences.

Activity

> The advertisement on the following page contains eighteen clauses,
> four of which are adverbial and fourteen adjectival. List them under
> appropriate headings. (Remember that some adverbial clauses are
> headed by two subordinating conjunctions which may be separated
> from each other by other words, e.g. *as good as.*)

▧ *The punctuation of complex sentences*

The stop to use between an independent main clause and a dependent
clause is the comma. That is, if you need a stop at all, for the trend in
writing today is towards lighter punctuation, with fewer stops. Consider
the following examples:

A Until he met Miriam Paul was happy.
Because she loved him she was jealous.
B Paul was happy until he met Miriam.
She was jealous because she loved him.

Most people would put a comma between the main and dependent
clauses in the sentences in A, but not in B. But even in A it is not really

These are the pans that were used for the meal that was made from the recipe that featured a cream sauce that dried on the plates that went into the washer that has a powerful triple spray that gets things so sparkling clean that it doesn't matter how dirty the pots and pans are that go into the exceptionally quiet machine that has five fully automatic programmes that include two for economy that makes running costs so low that it's no more expensive than washing by hand that is a feature of the dishwashers that come with a Free Five Year Parts Guarantee and Free Installation Check that give such peace of mind that it's no wonder people say ...

"Thank you Hotpoint"

necessary, unless you feel that a comma would add emphasis to or alter the movement of your sentence.

Activity

> 1 Write out each pair of sentences, putting a comma in the ones in A and leaving the ones in B without one.
> 2 Now do the same thing in reverse.
> 3 Discuss the difference made to
>   a the movement,
>   b the emphasis of each sentence.

For most purposes it might be best to adopt the rule: 'Use a comma only where failure to do so might alter completely the meaning of the sentence, or make it very confusing to read' – as in the following examples:

  a If a pregnant woman smokes her baby may suffer damage of some kind.
  b However you may feel I'm wrong.
  c One day we decided to visit another town in the mountains.
  d The passengers who were in the front of the train were seriously injured.
  e All the students who had been in the examination hall at the time were interviewed by the police.

Activity

> 1 Write out each of these sentences twice, putting in a comma the second time. What difference does this make to each of the sentences?
> 2 If a comma were to be placed after the word 'Campbell' in the sentence below, what difference would this make to the trio's living arrangements?
>
> Designer Colin Davenport, former lover of actress Janie Campbell who now lives with Hollywood director Stewart Baker, has issued a summons in the West Land County Court.

▓ *More complex complex sentences*

So far, the complex sentences we have looked at have had only one independent main clause and only one dependent clause. They can however have more than one of each. *Multiple complex sentences* consist of **one** independent main clause and several dependent clauses, each of which is dependent on the one that came before. For example:

> Sugar said [*imc*] that God would be pissed off [*dnc*] if someone didn't notice the colour purple [*d.adv.c*] when walking in the fields [*d.adv.c*].

Composite sentences consist of **two** independent main clauses and one or more dependent clauses. The independent main clauses may come together at the beginning of a sentence –

> Shug loved Celie [*imc*] but she also loved Germaine, a young man [*imc*] who had nice buns [*d.adj.c*].

■ *The handling of complex and composite sentences*

It is complex and composite sentences like these that sometimes make writing hard to read. If writers do not make the connection between their main and their dependent clauses clear, their readers may be confused. This is particularly likely when one clause cuts across another, as in the example below:

(Shug loved Celie) but (she also loved Germaine, a young man) (who [she said] had nice buns).

Here, yet another main clause – 'she said' – comes between the two parts of the adjectival clause 'who had nice buns', complicating the sentence considerably.

In sophisticated writing, clauses often cut across each other like this. A dependent adverbial clause, for instance, is often put between the subject and the verb of the independent main clause, like this:

Harpo, *when he forgot about being boss*, was very happy with his wife. The Queen Honey Bee, *because she was emotionally frail*, depended on Celie.

Albert, *when he realized Celie's true worth*, wanted to marry her again, 'in spirit'.

The phrase

Both complex and simple sentences may well contain one or more phrases as well as dependent clauses. Phrases can consist of one word – *however, nevertheless, recently, fortunately, today*, etc. – or several: *of course, on the other hand, in contemporary society, on a good day, on the whole, little by little*, etc. You should be able to see that phrases differ in one important respect from independent clauses: they do not have a main (or finite) verb, as in *Paul **gave** Miriam up*. What phrases sometimes have instead are *participles*: either *present* participles ending in *-ing*, like the ones below –

talking about poetry, making haycocks, cooking chicken, burning bread, breaking off relationships, eating cherries

– or *past* participles ending in *-ed, -en, -t*, or *-k*, like those that follow:

the umbrella broken, the wages collected, the bread burnt, the chicken cooked, the meal eaten.

Other past participles can also be formed from a combination of the two kinds above:

having painted the picture, having won the prize, having looked at the rose bush, having burned the bread

▦ *The phrase and economy*

Phrases use fewer words than clauses and move at a faster pace – qualities that make them valuable to journalists who need to cram much detail into a small space. For example:

> Blond-haired Betty, mother of Wayne, two, and Darren, four, a keen dancer and part-time Avon lady, said today . . .

Activity

1 Compare the alternative versions of the same ideas that follow.

Although he was repentant, he was jailed for five years.
Although repentant, he was jailed for five years.

Wilson, who is a member of the hard left, has been defeated in the Council elections.
Wilson, a member of the hard left, has been defeated in the Council elections.

The glass making firm of Carterton Brothers, who are based in Birmingham, is gearing up to mount a fierce defence against the £1.16 billion take-over bid which has been made by the industrial conglomerate ORT. They will preface this defence with the early publication, in just over a week, of their pre-tax profits, which are sharply higher for the six months to the end of September.

Birmingham glass maker Carterton Brothers is gearing up to mount a fierce defence against the £1.16 billion take-over bid from industrial conglomerate ORT. They will preface this defence with the early publication, in just over a week, of sharply higher pre-tax profits for the six months to end September.

2 a Re-write the following paragraph using phrases instead of clauses wherever possible.
(You will have to alter the sentence structure and leave out words where necessary.)

Paul Leonard Newman was born sixty-one years ago in Cleveland. He was the son of a Jewish sporting-goods store owner, and was raised in the affluent suburb of Shaker Heights. He has appeared in forty-seven films and directed five. He has been nominated for an Oscar six times, and last year was awarded an honorary one recognizing his career and his 'personal integrity and dedication to his craft'. He lives with Joanne Woodward, to whom he has been married for twenty-eight years, in a 200-year-old carriage house in Westport, Connecticut. He is a champion racing-driver. He has also founded a successful food business. He is a political activist, and he is noted for his philanthropy.

   b Assess whether your alterations have improved or worsened the quality of the piece as journalism.

■ *Misuse of participles in phrases*

Beware of *dangling* or *unattached participles* that have no proper subject to go with, and so attach themselves to the wrong one. For example:

Crossing the road, a bus ran him over.
(As he was . . .)
Aged seven, both his parents died.
(When he was seven . . .)
Being a little girl of eight, her father ran off with another woman.
(When she was a little girl . . .)

Activity

> Pick out the phrases in the following extract from *Sons and Lovers*:
>
> 'You brazen imp!' she exclaimed, rushing and scuffling for the comb, which he had under his knees. As she wrestled with him, pulling at his smooth, tight-covered knees, he laughed till he lay back on the sofa shaking with laughter. The cigarette fell from his mouth, almost singeing his throat. Under his delicate tan the blood flushed up, and he laughed till his blue eyes were blinded, his throat swollen almost to choking. Then he sat up. Beatrice was putting in her comb.
>
> D.H. Lawrence, *Sons and Lovers*

Why clause analysis went out of fashion

Fifth form students used to hate analysing clauses for two main reasons:

1 Dependent clauses were sometimes hard to distinguish from one another. Consider for example the following dependent clauses, all beginning with the same subordinating conjunction, *where*:

  a Sugar went *where she pleased.*
  b Celie often didn't know *where she was.*
  c Celie took Shug to the house *where she was born.*

In (a) the clause is modifying the verb *went* – Where did she go? Where she chose – and so is an **adverbial clause**.

In (b), the clause is acting as the equivalent of a noun: it is an object, the thing that Celie didn't know, and is therefore a **noun clause**.

In (c), the clause is describing or identifying the particular house where Celie was born – Which house did they visit? The one where she was born – and so is an **adjectival clause.**

2 There seemed to be no real point in the exercise. What good did it do to identify clauses as noun, adjectival, or adverbial, they asked, and when they left school and became teachers themselves, they decided to have nothing more to do with it. The result was a conflict over the teaching of English that has raged ever since.

Activity

> Try to identify the different clauses in the following sentences, all involving the subordinating conjunction *that*:
>
> **a** Celie told Albert that he looked like a frog.
> **b** She liked the purple frog that he made for her.
> **c** He changed, so that she grew to like him.

The usefulness of parsing and clause analysis

How far do grammatical exercises in parsing and clause analysis help students:

a to understand complicated sentences written by other people,
b to write well themselves?

Breaking a sentence down into the different kinds of clause it contains will tell us something about its construction but little about its meaning. For that, a more practical approach is needed, as Wydick demonstrates below.

> Look at the following example of the kind of writing that gives us difficulty in real life:
>
> > In a trial by jury, the court may, when the convenience of witnesses or the ends of justice would be promoted thereby, on motion of a party, after notice and hearing, make an order, no later than the close of the pretrial conference in cases in which such pretrial conference is to be held, or in other cases, no later than ten days before the trial date, that the trial of the issue of liability shall precede the trial of any other issue in the case.
>
> The subject matter of that passage is not profound or complicated, but the passage is hard to understand. It consists of a single sentence, eighty-six words long, containing five pieces of information. It tells us that:
>
> 1 in a jury case, the liability issue may be tried before any other issue;
> 2 the judge may order this if it will serve the convenience of witnesses or the ends of justice;
> 3 the order may be made on a party's motion after notice and hearing;
> 4 in a case with a pretrial conference, the order must be made before the end of the conference; and
> 5 in a case with no pretrial conference, the order must be made at least ten days before the trial date.
>
> The passage is hard to understand for two reasons. First, the single-sentence format caused the author to distort the logical order of the five pieces of information. The first thing the readers want to know is what the passage is about. It is about the trial of the liability issue before the other issues. But the readers do not discover that until they have climbed through a thicket of subsidiary ideas and arrived at the last twenty words of the sentence. Second, the single-sentence format strains the readers'

memories. The subject of the sentence ('court') appears at word seven. At word thirty-two, the verb 'make' finally shows up. Part of the object ('an order') comes next, but the critical part remains hidden until the readers arrive, breathless, at word sixty-eight. By then they have forgotten the verb and must search back in the sentence to find it. The remedy is simple. Instead of one long sentence containing five thoughts, use five sentences, each containing one thought. Here is one way the passage could be rewritten:

> In a jury case, the court may order the liability issue to be tried before any other issue. This may be done if the court finds that it would serve the convenience of witnesses or the ends of justice.
>
> The order may be made on motion of a party, after notice and hearing. In cases where a pretrial conference is held, the order must be made before the end of the conference. In other cases, the order must be made at least ten days before the trial date.

Wydick, *Plain English for Lawyers*

Activity

Rewrite the two passages below by using Wydick's method of breaking one long sentence down into several shorter ones. Remember to arrange your sentences in logical order. (You will need to add words here and there, and cut out others which are no longer needed.)

a By establishing a technique whereby the claims of many individuals can be resolved at the same time, class actions serve an important function in our judicial system in eliminating the possibility of repetitious litigation and providing claimants with a method of obtaining enforcements of claims which would otherwise be too small to warrant individual litigation.

b While there are instances in which consumer abuse and exploitation result from advertising which is false, misleading, or irrelevant, it does not necessarily follow that these cases need to be remedied by governmental intervention into the market place because it is possible for consumers' interests to be protected through resort to the courts, either by consumers themselves or by those competing sellers who see their market shares decline in the face of inroads based on such advertising.

Wydick, *Plain English for Lawyers*

It should be clear to you by now that, as in any clash of extreme opinions, the truth lies somewhere in the middle ground. Grammar exercises *per se* help us neither to write well ourselves nor to comment sensibly on the writing of other people. A working knowledge of the different kinds of clauses and their arrangement within sentences will however help us with both.

The grammar every student should know

The parts of speech: Nouns, Pronouns, Adjectives, Verbs, Adverbs, Prepositions, Conjunctions, the Definite and Indefinite Articles.

The main or finite verb: A finite verb is one that shows number (singular or plural), person (*I, you, she,* etc.), and tense (present or past – *think, thinks, thought*).

The present participle: The part of the verb that ends in *-ing,* e.g. *eating, drinking, sleeping, waking.*

The past participle: The part of the verb that ends in *-en, -t, -ed* e.g. *forgotten, broken, learnt, destroyed.*

The independent main clause: A group of words that contains a subject and a main verb and so can make a complete statement without the help of another clause. Independent main clauses are also known as simple sentences.

The dependent clause: A group of words that gives further information about the main clause; it contains a main verb but cannot stand alone because it is introduced by a subordinating conjunction.

The phrase: A group of words that adds information to a sentence. It often does not contain a verb at all, but when it does, it is always in the form of a present or past participle.

The simple sentence: A sentence that consists of a single independent main clause.

The compound sentence: A sentence that consists of two or more simple sentences joined together; usually by conjunctions such as *and, but, so, then.*

The complex sentence: A sentence that consists of one or more independent main clauses, and one or more dependent clauses.

The subject of a sentence: The person (or thing) by whom the action of the verb in the main clause is performed.

The object of a sentence: The person (or thing) for, or to, or on whom the action of the verb in the main clause is performed.

Knowledge of all of these is important, but knowledge of the independent clause, the dependent clause, and the phrase is essential. The skilful handling of these three structures is what gives informative writing its clarity and force, and literary writing its style. We shall look at this next.

Grammatical characteristics of good writing

■ *The length of clauses within sentences*

Consider the two sentences below:

1 Most experts agree that for conveying complex factual information, particularly to the general public or to young people, short sentences are best.
2 Most experts agree that short sentences are best for conveying complex factual material (a) to the general public, (b) to young people.

Talking point | Which of these two structures did you find easier to read? Why? |

Many authorities on writing claim that short sentences are best for conveying factual information. 'We preach that a good average sentence length in public information documents is fifteen to twenty words', the British *Plain English Campaign* declares, and its American counterpart agrees: 'Write short sentences with an average of no more than twenty words.' This advice is backed up by an even higher authority: an official booklet issued to the staff of the Cabinet Office: 'Use short sentences. For writing to civil servants, aim to average fifteen to twenty-five words. For the public, average fifteen to twenty.'

To test the readability of a piece of prose, the American Campaign for Plain English uses the *Flesch Reading Ease Test*. They take a representative sample of 100 words from the piece, then assess it mathematically.

Activity

1 Read the following passage from an A level textbook, then run the Flesch test on it. (The instructions are given below.)

Acceptability is concerned with the attitudes of native users of the English language to particular forms of usage. If one form of usage is 'acceptable' to substantial numbers of such users, then the grammatical description of the language must take that into account. For example, 'I don't want nothing' is acceptable to large numbers of people as a very emphatic statement of what somebody does not want. Such an emphatic use of double negatives must feature in a description of English grammar, although 'prescriptive' grammarians might argue that such double negatives ought not to be used, since they are illogical.

Step 1 Count the words in the piece of writing.
Step 2 Count all the syllables in the words.
Step 3 Count the sentences. Count as a sentence each full unit of speech marked off by a full stop, colon, semi-colon, dash, question mark or exclamation mark.
Step 4 Calculate the average number of syllables per word, dividing the number of syllables by the number of words.
Step 5 Calculate the average number of words per sentence, dividing the number of words by the number of sentences.
Step 6 Find your readability score as follows:
* Multiply the average sentence length by 1.015.
* Multiply the average word length by 84.6.
* Add the two numbers together.
* Subtract this sum from 206.835. The balance is your readability score, on a scale from 0 to 100.
  To be considered plain English, a text must score a minimum of 60. The higher the score, the more readable the passage will be.

2 How accessible for A level students do you find the extract?

The same criterion of brevity is also cited by journalist Peregrine Worsthorne:

> As a general rule, when considering post-war non-fiction texts, the grammarians say this about the number of words per sentence:
> 0–14: staccato, or 'sergeant-major' English
> 15–24: good English
> 25–37: long-winded
> 38 upwards: intolerably verbose, legalese.

He is dismayed to find that, judged by these criteria, two of his favourite writers, Bernard Levin and Auberon Waugh, have average sentence lengths of 26 and 36 respectively, putting them into the 'long-winded' category. How can this be, he wonders, when they write so well? The answer is that length in itself has very little to do with whether a sentence is good or bad. A sentence may contain well over fifty words, yet be easily understood at a first reading. Even lawyer Richard Wydick, who believes that long sentences make legal writing difficult to read, has no objection to them per se. He offers a qualified guide to clarity:

> 1 In most sentences, put only one main thought.
> 2 Keep the average sentence length below twenty five words.
>
> *Do not misinterpret this guide.* The first part says that *most* sentences should contain only one main thought. It does not say that *every* sentence should contain only one main thought. The second part says that the *average* length of your sentences should be below twenty-five words. It does not say that *every* sentence should be twenty-five words or less. A succession of short, simple sentences sounds choppy:
>> Defence counsel objected to the question. She argued that it called for hearsay. The Court overruled the objection, and the witness was allowed to answer.
>
> You need an occasional longer sentence in which two or more main thoughts are joined:
>> Defence Counsel objected to the question, arguing that it called for hearsay; the Court over-ruled the objection, and the witness was allowed to answer.
>
> Wydick, *Plain English for Lawyers*

For writing that seeks to convey anything more than facts, even more allowance needs to be made. When talking about such things as ideas and feelings, attitudes, values, and beliefs, writers must be free to qualify or enlarge upon their statements with as many subordinate clauses as they feel necessary. As long as the connection between the clauses is clear, so will be the meaning of the sentences.

■ *The clear arrangement of clauses within complex sentences*

The key to good writing in general therefore lies not so much in brevity as in the skilful handling of clauses *within* long sentences. If

a the meaning of the main clause is well expressed,

b the connection between the main clause(s) and any dependent clauses and phrases is clear,

c the relation of each dependent clause and phrase to all other dependent clauses and phrases is clear,

then it is a good sentence, regardless of its length. Take, for example, the following sentences from a piece by Bernard Levin:

> But Stoppard fills the pool with a flood of laughter apparently conceived for its own sake, and only when his audience has drowned in the pool, weak with a total surrender to joy, does he permit the hideous creatures from the deep to come crawling to the surface. Freezing an audience's laughter with a stroke of horror is a familiar playwright's device, and not a particularly difficult one for a technically accomplished writer to handle, but Stoppard goes further; he shifts the whole structure bodily into the horror, and so deftly that we do not even realize we are moving until we are there.

These sentences are obviously well over the twenty word limit, yet are easily grasped at first sight. Now compare Levin's sentences with those of another well-known journalist, Alastair Forbes:

> I am pretty sure that the mere 2,000-plus other, mostly West End and Grub Street, consumers to whom John Murray has made available the present 125,000 words long specimen of Frank Giles's journalism (boasting a Good Housekeeping Seal from that most admirable of Gray's Inn Road literary editors, the late lamented Jack Lambert) will suffer no such cardiac arrhythmia,* not even on the early page where the avowedly colour-blind autobiographer asserts that the naked near-albino Duke of Windsor (for whom, and his 'quiet, dignified, and composed . . . never anything but stately wife', he then felt an 'infatuation') had absolutely no hair on his body, even in the places where one would most expect it to be.

What makes the Forbes passage so difficult to read? The solitary main clause, *I am pretty sure*, has five dependent clauses and three lengthy phrases hanging on to it, yet it is not the number of the clauses but the lack of clear connection between them that confuses the reader. Dependent clauses and phrases grow out of one another as each new thought strikes the writer. The result is that they cut across one another, blurring the train of thought. For example, the writer begins by saying, 'I am pretty sure that

* Cardiac arrhythmia is a term used to describe any deviation from the normal rhythm of the heart.

the mere 2,000-plus other, mostly West End and Grub Street, consumers', then doesn't complete his statement by adding the verb – 'will suffer no such cardiac arrhythmia' – for another thirty-seven words. Instead he introduces a lengthy adjectival clause – 'to whom John Murray has made available the present 125,000 words long specimen of Frank Giles's journalism' – and a lengthy phrase in brackets – '(boasting a Good Housekeeping Seal from that most admirable of Gray's Inn Road literary editors, the late lamented Jack Lambert)'.

So thirty-seven words come between the subject ('consumers') and its verb, and by the time readers have ploughed through the thicket of dependent clause and phrase, they've lost the thread of what the sentence was about.

Talking point

> Can you find a similar splitting apart of subject and verb later in the passage?

Activity

> 1 Run the Flesch test on the two passages above and record their scores.
>
> 2 Basing your answer on the Forbes passage, what advice would you give to inexperienced writers on the handling of dependent clauses? (Children, by the way, prefer the main statement of a sentence to come first: 'Pat your tummy then rub your nose', not 'Before rubbing your nose, pat your tummy'.)

▨ *The match between complex vocabulary and complex sentences*

Generally speaking, the longer a writer's sentences are, the more elaborate and obscure his or her vocabulary is likely to be. You can prove the truth of this statement by working a calculation based on what is called the Fog Index. As with the Flesch Test, a sample of prose of as near as possible 100 words is chosen, starting at the beginning of a sentence and finishing at the end. The following steps are then taken:

Step 1 Count the exact number of words and divide by the number of sentences.

Step 2 Add to the total the number of words of three or more syllables. Do not count proper names, compounds (e.g. shock-horror) and suffixed words (e.g.publish[ing]).

Step 3 Multiply the grand total by 0.4. The resulting score is the Fog Index.
Readability levels indicated by Index scores:
1–10: readable by any school-leaver
14–16: readable by the average sixth-former
18 upwards: too hard for most people to read.

Activity | Calculate the Fog Index of the Levin and Forbes extracts.

▓ *The role of 'glue' words in sentence construction*

According to Wydick,

> . . . in every English sentence there are two kinds of words: working words and glue words.* The working words carry the meaning of the sentence. In the preceding sentence the working words are these: *working, words, carry, meaning,* and *sentence.* The others are glue words: *the, the, of,* and *the.* The glue words do serve a purpose: they hold the working words together to form a proper English sentence. But when you find too many glue words, it is a sign that the sentence is badly constructed.

To see what Wydick is getting at, consider the following sentence:

Please send clean clothes and money to me at the Palace Hotel Bath.

The content or working words here are *send, clothes, money, Palace Hotel, Bath.* Strip the sentence down to these content words, as you would when sending a telegram, and it will still communicate its meaning clearly:

Send clothes money Palace Hotel Bath.

If a sentence cannot communicate as clearly as this when reduced to its content words, then, Wydick suggests, it must be badly written. To verify the point, consider the following:

If you want to write well, the thing to aim at is to use as few structure words as possible.

Reduced to its content words this would never make an intelligible telegram:

You want write well thing aim use few structure words possible

The thing to do therefore is to rewrite it more succinctly:

To write well, use few structure words.

Activity | Rewrite the sentence below using as few structure words as possible/fewer structure words. (As you can see, it's easy to use six words where three will do). Since sentences that contain large numbers of words will be long ones, make this your subject and begin, 'Long sentences . . .'

The fact that there is a large number of words in a sentence does not necessarily mean that it will be difficult to read.

---

* Referred to as 'content' and 'structure' words in the section on Prepositions, page 66, and in the rest of this section.

▧ *Constructions that create structure words*

Three constructions in particular can lead to the build-up of unnecessary structure words in a sentence. They are:

1 the false subject
2 the use of abstract nouns
3 the passive voice

1 The false subject

Consider the following sentences:

> **a** The thing that makes sentences difficult to read is the number of long constructions that they contain.

This is not a long sentence, but it contains almost as many structure as content words. The writer's mistake was to begin the sentence with a false subject: *The thing*. Having done so, he or she is forced to use three clauses stuffed with structure words to finish it off:

> . . . that makes sentences difficult to read
> is the number of long constructions
> that they contain.

Had the writer begun the sentence with the true subject –

> Long constructions . . .

and followed it immediately with its verb and object –

> make sentences . . .

then the rest of the sentence –

> difficult to read

would have fallen naturally into place, and the sentence would have been both shorter and crisper to read.

> **b** In the case of teachers, they are very badly paid.

In this example the opening phrase, *In the case of*, is again redundant. The subject – *teachers* – should come first, tightening the sentence up:

> Teachers are very badly paid.

Activity

> Rewrite the following sentences, using fewer structure words.
> Remember to throw out false subjects such as *it* or *there is*, and to put the true subject first:
>
> 1 It has been twice that I have telephoned the shop to complain.
> 2 In older people, drink changes their personalities.
> 3 She was pregnant, and it was not very far away that her baby was due.
> 4 In a recent survey it shows that crime is on the increase.
> 5 There are two factors that have contributed to this rise in crime: poverty and unemployment.
> 6 There is a lack of wisdom in the way some people spend their money.
> 7 Sentences are not necessarily verbose just because they contain a lot of words.

2 The use of abstract nouns

Good writers use concrete subjects and active verbs: their sentences are full of **people**, **doing** things.

Poor writers use abstract nouns instead of people, causing structure words to proliferate. Wydick explains:

Base verbs* v derivative nouns and adjectives

At its core, the law is not abstract; it is part of a real world full of people who live and move and do things to other people. Car drivers *collide*. Plaintiffs *complain*. Judges *decide*. Defendants *pay*. To express this life and motion, a writer must use verbs – action words. The purest verb form is the base verb, like *collide, complain, decide,* and *pay*. Base verbs are simple creatures. They cannot tolerate adornment. If you try to dress them up, you squash their life and motion. Unfortunately, that is done all too easily. The base verb *collide* can be decked out as a derivative noun, *collision*. Likewise, *complain* becomes *complaint*, *decide* becomes *decision*, and *pay* becomes *payment*. Lawyers love to ruin base verbs. Lawyers don't *act* – they *take action*. They don't *assume* – they *make assumptions*. They don't *conclude* – they *draw conclusions*. With too much of this, legal writing becomes a lifeless vapour. When a base verb is replaced by a derivative noun or adjective, surplus words begin to swarm like gnats. 'Please *state why you object* to the question' comes out like this: 'Please *make a statement of why you are interposing an objection* to the question.' The base verb *state* can do the work all alone. But to get the same work out of *statement*, you need a supporting verb (*make*), an article (*a*), and a preposition (*of*). The derivative noun *objection* attracts a similar cloud of surplus words.

Do not conclude from this that derivative nouns and adjectives are always bad; sometimes you need them. But do not overuse them in place of base verbs. You can spot the common ones by their endings: -*ment*, -*ion*, -*ance*, -*ence*, -*ancy*, -*ency*, -*ant*, and -*ent*. When you spot one, stop to see if you can make your sentence stronger and shorter by using a base verb instead.

Wydick, *Plain English for Lawyers*

---

3 The passive voice

The *active voice* is a grammatical term to indicate that the subject of a verb is actually doing the action:

The lawyer [subject of this sentence] *believed* his client [the object of this sentence].

The *passive voice* on the other hand is used to show that the subject of a verb is suffering the action – i.e. having it done **to** him:

* By *base verb* Wydick means the main stem of the verb, to which endings are added; the infinitive, without the *to*, e.g.: *(to) write, talk, think, feel,* etc.

The client [subject of this sentence] *was believed* by his lawyer [the object of this sentence].

Again, Wydick has an interesting note on this:

The active voice v the passive voice

When you use the active voice, the subject of the sentence acts: 'The union filed a complaint.' When you use the passive voice, the subject of the sentence is acted upon: 'A complaint was filed by the union.'

The passive voice has two disadvantages. First, it takes more words. When you say 'the union filed a complaint', *filed* does the work by itself. But when you say, 'a complaint was made by the union', the verb *filed* requires a supporting verb (*was*) and a preposition (*by*).

The second disadvantage of the passive voice is its detached abstraction. With the active voice, the reader can usually see who is doing what to whom. But the passive voice often leaves that unclear:

It is feared that adequate steps will not be taken to mitigate the damages that are being caused.

Who is doing the fearing? Who is taking the steps? Who is causing the damages? We cannot tell because the actor in each case is hidden in the fog of the passive voice.

The passive voice has its proper uses. First, you can use it when the thing done is important, and the one who did it is not:

The summons and complaint were served on 19th January.

Second, you can use it where the actor is unknown or indefinite:

The ledgers were mysteriously destroyed.

Third, you can use it to place a strong element at the end of a sentence for emphasis:

In the defendant's closet was found the bloody coat.

Fourth, you can use it on those rare occasions when detached abstraction is appropriate:

All people were created with a thirst for knowledge.

But elsewhere, use the active voice; it will make your writing stronger, briefer, and clearer.

Activity

Rewrite the following sentences
1 replacing abstract nouns with people and things;
2 using the active voice.

The first is done for you as a guide:
   a The general opinion was that the money should be spent on the improvement of the leisure centre. (8 structure, 7 content words)
   Most people wanted to spend the money on improving the leisure centre. (8 structure, 4 content words)

b It should be noted that the closing date for entries is 1st April.

c A request was made by many of the students for a ban on smoking in the refectory.

d It is hoped that it will be possible for us to finish the work by Easter.

e A government inquiry should be made into the running of old people's homes.

f Early application is advisable.

g It is the opinion of many critics that Shakespeare is the greatest writer who ever lived.

h Literary criticism was held by F. R. Leavis to be a branch of moral philosophy.

▓ *Summary*

To keep your sentence constructions clear, forceful, and brief:

* Use phrases instead of clauses wherever possible: *Having written the book she sent it to the publisher*, rather than, *After she had written the book she sent it to the publisher*.
* Avoid putting lengthy clauses or phrases between the two halves of another clause or phrase.
* Avoid false subjects.
* Use the active voice of verbs.
* Use concrete subjects instead of abstract nouns: *Most people want*, instead of *There is a general desire for*.
* Use one word instead of several wherever possible: *because* instead of *due to the fact that*; *if* instead of *in the event of*; *about* instead of *with reference to*.
* Avoid what Wydick calls 'throat-clearing' – pompous little phrases that add nothing to the sentence but superfluous words:
  it is important to add that
  there is little doubt that
  it is obvious that/obviously
  it is clear that/clearly
  it may be recalled that
  it is interesting to point out
  actually
  in point of fact

The appropriate versus the correct

There are people who cannot bear to hear English spoken 'incorrectly' and who write to the BBC to tell them so. Their complaints about grammar focus on the following points:

1 When to use *I* or *me* in phrases such as *you and I*, or *you and me*.
2 Whether words like *none* and *a number* should take a singular or a plural verb.

3 Whether or not we should split infinitives, i.e. to say *to boldly go* rather than *boldly to go* or *to go boldly*. (Infinitives in Latin could not be split because they were a single word rather than two, as in English: *amare*, for example, as opposed to *to love*. Grammarians who were keen on Latin therefore ruled that infinitives shouldn't be split in English – the sort of thing that gets grammar a bad name.)

4 Whether we should say *different than*, *different to*, or *different from*.

5 Whether we should say *I wish I was* (the indicative mood used for making definite statements of fact), or *I wish I were* (the subjunctive mood used for expressing wishes and hopes).

6 Whether it is correct to end a sentence with a preposition: should it be *Who did you give it to?*, or *To whom did you give it?*

7 When to use *who* and *whom* in sentences such as *Who were you talking to last night?* Is *who* correct here, or should it be *whom*?

8 When to use *shall* and when to use *will*.

9 Whether it is acceptable to use sentences without verbs; newscasters, for example will often say something like, '*And now over to Michael Fish at the London Weather Centre*', instead of, '*And now we are going over to Michael Fish at the London Weather Centre*'.

In the 1940s, complaints like these might have been taken seriously. Announcers read the news in 'cut-glass accents' like that of the Queen today and wore evening dress to do so, even on the radio. In an age when 'common' accents are used as a matter of course in the media and four-letter words have found their way even into poetry, such formality is not only dated, but doomed.

That does not mean that all rules and conventions have been abandoned, of course. It is taken for granted that essays, scholarly articles and books, serious journalism, and so on should continue to be written in formally correct, conventional English. (Think of the difficulties foreign readers would have if they were not.) Creative writers, advertising copy-writers, TV and radio script-writers on the other hand are allowed to break the rules whenever they want to on the grounds that it is sometimes necessary to do something 'wrong' in order to get it 'right'. Copy-writers can happily use incomplete sentences in their advertisements, serious novelists can use unconventional sentence structure, punctuation, and spelling to get the effect they want. The phrase to remember is 'appropriate for the purpose'.

Breaking the rules in advertising

Consider the following advertisement. It breaks two writing conventions:

1 It breaks one complete sentence into fragments, treating each fragment as if it were a sentence in its own right, e.g.:

    A belt-drive semi-automatic turntable;

2 It treats each of these non-sentences as a separate paragraph, defying the convention that all points on the same subject should be grouped together to form one coherent whole.

There's a Compact Disc Player with front-loading motorized disc tray, track select and skip function.
(1 in either direction.)
A belt-drive semi-automatic turntable.
A twin cassette deck with auto tape switching and Dolby noise reduction.
A 3-band synthesized digital timer with 21 pre-sets, no less.
And, (wait for it) a ferocious 35 watts RMS per channel amplifier feeding high quality two-way speakers with flat, square bass drivers.

Activity

1 Write out the advertisement in one long, formally correct sentence.
2 Explain what, if anything, has been lost by doing so.
3 How far do you think that acceptance of the paragraphing used in such advertisements might damage:
   a a writer's ability to present a carefully worked out argument;
   b the general public's ability to read one?

Advertisers also fracture conventional sentence structure with their treatment of the dependent/subordinate clause. In the Volkswagen advertisement opposite, for instance, the copy-writers deliberately ignore the rule that a dependent clause cannot stand alone. They detach it from its independent main clause by a full stop and leave it to masquerade as a sentence in its own right. For example:

Will we never learn that cars are virility symbols? That spoilers, for instance, should jut out the back looking mucho macho?

Activity

Consider the treatment of sentence structure in the rest of the advertisement and carry out the activities suggested below.

1 What convention regarding conjunctions are the copy-writers breaking in line 7? Are they justified in doing so?
2 Lines 9–10 and lines 11–12 consist of a phrase followed by a dependent adverbial clause. What is 'incorrect' about these 'sentences'?
3 Find three further examples of dependent clauses being used 'incorrectly' as complete sentences.
4 Find one example of a phrase being used as a sentence in its own right.
5 Explain what the copy-writers are satirizing in the first two sentences. Why do they drop into fake Spanish?
6 What reason do they give for Volkswagen's refusal to follow this trend?
7 Explain the appeal being made to male readers in the use of the phrase 'virility symbol' in the last sentence (it has a double meaning).
8 How does this relate to the mocking of such things in the first two sentences?
9 Re-write the advertisement in conventionally constructed sentences.
10 Compare your version of the advertisement with the copy-writers' and say how far you think the original version's unconventional sentence structure is justified by results.

Trust Volkswagen to put a spoiler where no one can see it.

Will we never learn that cars are male virility symbols?

That spoilers, for instance, should jut out the back looking mucho macho?

Believe us, if that's where they worked best that's where we'd put them.

But our engineers insist that on the Golf they work better closer to the road.

Underneath the car where they deflect the turbulent airflow away from the axles.

Thereby easing drag so the Golf has the best aerodynamics in its class, cd 0.34.

Which, in turn, helps the Golf go faster and further on less fuel.

Which, in turn, means it needs, and gets, better direct-acting servo brakes.

Which we hope shows why we make such a fuss over a little thing like a spoiler.

Everything on a Volkswagen has to work. Everytime.

Again and again.

Frankly, gentlemen, isn't that what the ladies really look for in a virility symbol?

THE NEW GOLF PRICES FROM £4,597 MODEL ILLUSTRATED GL £6,696, EXCLUDING NUMBER PLATES AND DELIVERY. FURTHER INFORMATION FROM VOLKSWAGEN SALES ENQUIRIES, YEOMANS DRIVE, BLAKELANDS, MILTON KEYNES, MK14 5AN. TELEPHONE: (0908) 679121. EXPORT AND FLEET SALES, 95 BAKER STREET, LONDON W1M 1FB. TELEPHONE: 01 486 8411.

Breaking the rules in literary writing

Creative writers (from whom copy-writers probably stole their ideas in the first place) had begun to shatter language conventions early in the century. Lawrence's novel *Lady Chatterley's Lover*, first published in 1928 (though not in England), used language obscene enough for the book to merit prosecution in 1961. Earlier, in 1922, James Joyce's *Ulysses* upset readers as much by the originality of its style as by the explicit nature of its content – vivid descriptions of every aspect of life from eating through going to the lavatory to masturbating and making love. Sometimes the words would flow in an unbroken torrent, with no full-stop for several pages: at others they would be arranged in sentence fragments, with full-stops everywhere they should not be.

Activity

In the two extracts from *Ulysses* that follow, Joyce is trying to capture the way in which thoughts grasshopper through our minds. Something we see or hear reminds us of something else, which sparks off another memory or thought, which makes us think of still another. Read the extracts and then carry out the activities suggested below.

a Yes because he never did a thing like that before as ask to get his breakfast in bed with a couple of eggs since the City Arms hotel when he used to be pretending to be laid up with a sick voice doing his highness to make himself interesting to that old faggot Mrs Riordan that he thought he had a great leg of and she never left us a farthing all for masses for herself and her soul greatest miser ever was actually afraid to lay out 4d for her methylated spirit telling me all her ailments she had too much old chat in her about politics and earthquakes and the end of the world let us have a bit of fun first God help the world if all the women were her sort down on bathing suits and low necks . . .

b Ba. What is that flying about? Swallow? Bat probably. Thinks I'm a tree, so blind. Have birds no smell? Metempsychosis. They believed you could be changed into a tree from grief. Weeping willow. Ba. There he goes. Funny little beggar. Wonder where he lives. Belfry up there. Very likely. Hanging by his heels in the odour of sanctity. Bell scared him out, I suppose. Mass seems to be over. Could hear them all at it. Pray for us. And pray for us. And pray for us. Good idea the repetition. Same thing with ads. Buy from us. And buy from us. Yes, there's a light on in the priest's house. Their frugal meal. Remember about the mistake in valuation when I was in Thom's. Twenty-eight it is. Two houses they have. Gabriel Conroy's brother is curate. Ba. Again. Wonder why they come out at night like mice. They're a mixed breed. Birds are like hopping mice . . .

1 The first passage is a glimpse into the mind of a woman as she lies drowsily in bed; the second depicts the thoughts that go through the

mind of a man as he walks in the environs of Dublin. Discuss how far the sentence structure and punctuation of each passage is appropriate,

a for describing the kind of thoughts that go through our minds when we're alone,

b for revealing the thinker's gender. (The stereotypical view pictures women as emotional, spontaneous, and impulsive; men as more rational, controlled, and detached.)

Depicting character in this way has been called the *stream of consciousness technique*, because all we are given is the flow of the characters' thoughts and feelings as they live from minute to minute. Just how original and brilliant an achievement it was in 1922 can be seen if you compare it with this more conventional account of a character's thoughts in E. M. Forster's *A Passage to India* (completed in 1924):

And, unlocking a drawer, he took out his wife's photograph. He gazed at it, and tears spouted from his eyes. He thought, 'How unhappy I am!' But because he really was unhappy another emotion soon mingled with his self-pity: he desired to remember his wife and could not. Why could he remember people whom he did not love? They were always so vivid to him, whereas the more he looked at this photograph the less he saw. She had eluded him thus, ever since they had carried her to her tomb. He had known that she would pass from his hands and eyes, but had thought she could live in his mind, not realizing that the very fact that we have loved the dead increases their unreality, and that the more passionately we invoke them, the further they recede. A piece of brown cardboard and three children – that was all that was left of his wife. It was unbearable, and he thought again, 'How unhappy I am!' and became happier.

Activity

Forster's method of presenting character is not inferior to Joyce's; it is simply different. Consider this difference carefully, then answer the questions below.

1 What distinguishes the sentence structure and punctuation of the Forster passage from those of Joyce?

2 Which character or characters do you feel closer to after reading the different passages – those of Joyce, or that of Forster? Can you say why?

3 Try to write the thoughts that go through the head of the Forster character as you think Joyce would have written them. How will you deal with the fact that he's looking at a photograph? What will you have to leave out?

4 Has the passage lost anything of importance by being rewritten in this way? If so, what?

Below is an extract from Russell Hoban's novel, *Riddley Walker*. In this passage, Riddley and his friend Lissener, more intuitive and sensitive than most of their fellows, visit a ruined nuclear power station:

The lite wer coming from behynt some girt mouns of rubbl unner where the over head ben barmt out. It cudntve ben no moren a cuppl of candls or lanterns jus a feabl glimmer and the jynt shadders wivvering on the stanning walls and broakin stoan and rubbl and what ever over head wer lef. The jynt shadders wer from girt machines o they wer guvner big things and crouching all broakin but not dead they cudnt dy there wer too much Power inthem . . .

Lissener hispert me, 'What is it? Be they terning be they moving?' I hispert back, 'It's broakin machines they ain't moving.' It wernt nothing like when you dig up old rottin machines ourt of the roun these wer in ther parper working place nor nothing rottin they wer some kynd of iron dint rot it wer all shyning all catching that shaky glimmer . . . Tears begun streaming down my face and my froat akit. Lissener hispert, 'What's the matter?'

I hispert back, 'O what we ben! And what we com to!' Boath of us wer sniffling and snuffling then. Me looking at them jynt machines and him lissening ther sylents.

Hoban never actually tells us that his characters are living in a world left desolate by nuclear war, but the language he gives them to speak quite clearly shows that civilization and knowledge as we understand them have broken down. Does his book offer any support for the idea that correct writing is the basis of a civilized society?

Finally, the use of 'incorrect' grammar to create convincing characters. Here is an extract from Alice Walker's novel *The Color Purple*, which contains the following solecisms:

* the omission of the *-s* from the ending of the third person singular ('Sofia say' instead of 'Sofia says');
* the omission of the main verbs from many sentences ('What that?' instead of 'What is that?');
* the omission of the *-ed* ending of the past tense of the verb ('We kill them off' instead of 'we killed them off');
* the omission of the *-en* ending of the past participle ('she beat' instead of 'she was beaten');
* the omission of the subject from many sentences ('look like her old self' instead of 'she look like her old self');
* the use of the object or accusative case of the pronoun instead of the subject or nominative case ('Us outnumbered' instead of 'We (were) outnumbered');

> Sofia say to me today, I just can't understand it.
>
> What that? I ast.
>
> Why we ain't already kill them off.
>
> Three years after she beat* she out of the wash house, got her color and her weight back, look like her old self, just all time think bout killing somebody.
>
> Too many to kill off, I say. Us outnumbered from the start. I speck we knock over one or two, though, here and there, through the years, I say.
>
> (*beaten)

The uninflected use of the verb *to be* is the other major grammatical 'error' that runs through the book: *I/she/they/us be*, rather than *I am*, *she is*, *they are*, etc.

Activity

> 1 Write out the passage in conventionally correct grammar.
> 2 Explain what has been lost in your translation.

It is easy to justify 'bad' writing like the above: it gives authenticity to both character and situation. It is also possible to defend 'bad' writing by advertisers: cleverly done, it entertains, and it helps the economy by persuading us to buy.

There is a hidden paradox here, however: if writers are to be free to experiment with the language like this, must the rest of us be content to follow the norms? Perhaps originality can flourish only where there are rules still left to break. If colloquialisms, obscenities, and slang were in general use, how could writers use them to make their points? If Standard English (with slight variations) had not been the norm in America and England, how could Alice Walker have created Miss Celie, or Russell Hoban his Riddley Walker? If everyone wrote in sentence fragments, how could Joyce have achieved his stream of consciousness technique or advertisers their hard sell? The concept of appropriateness may itself be an argument for teaching 'correct' English, for everyone in a society as developed as ours must be able to use the vocabulary and grammatical structures appropriate to formal contexts – even if only to talk to the DSS. People who cannot speak or write in formal terms and structures find it hard to function in formal situations. Their ability to use language appropriately is therefore limited and they are disadvantaged.

Activity

> Read the passage below, then discuss the question that follows.
>
> Modern scientific language study has rendered the notion of one correct English untenable. We are used to wearing different clothes for different occasions, and with language many of us are used to doing something similar. The little boy in a Liverpool playground who says to his assailants 'Geroff, youse' (a perfectly grammatically regular plural of 'you' in his speech) is using language likely to work there. If he had said something with a distinctively Standard English flavour it would have been counter-productive. There is no one correct language; there is only

language appropriate or inappropriate to particular circumstances, and education should aim to produce language users likely to select and use such language effectively.

How far do you agree with the ideas expressed by the writer of this piece? In your opinion, should Standard English and dialect forms be given equal treatment in schools? (Note that failure to 'talk proper' is still a rich source of humour in British plays, films, and television sit-coms.)

Spoken English

Written versus spoken English

In educational circles, speech has always been considered less important than writing. The probable reasons for this include the following:

1 Teachers don't have to teach children to speak; they do have to teach them how to write, however, and so writing seems more valuable and more prestigious.
2 Higher education is largely delivered via textbooks and its social importance adds prestige to the written language.
3 Great literature reaches most people in the form of books and lends its dignity and value to the written language.
4 Most spoken English is uttered 'off the cuff', spontaneously, and so is less formal, less tidy, and grammatically less well-structured than writing – and teachers in higher education dislike work that is untidy, disjointed, and ungrammatical.

This last reason for disparaging speech only appeared in the 1950s, when the introduction of the tape-recorder into academic life alerted us to what conversation really sounds like. As Trudgill and Hughes put it:

> When even highly educated people are chatting together with friends, their speech is very different from textbook conversations. They begin a sentence, then change their mind; they hesitate, then start again, differently; they muddle one grammatical structure with another. They omit various words, forget others, replacing them with *thingy* or *whatsit*; if necessary they will invent words just for the occasion. In a relaxed atmosphere they do not feel constrained to speak carefully, to plan what they are going to say . . .
>
> Hughes and Trudgill, *English Accents and Dialects*

This point is illustrated by the three-way conversation about the writing of dialogue that follows. (A dot in brackets (.) is used to indicate a micropause, where speakers pause very briefly.)

> **T.D.** When writers try to er any good dramatist sets out to show how um people talk in ordinary in real life but it's interesting to see how they usually clean up the messy er aspects of talk when they start to actually um write it down (.) all the ums and errs the missing verbs and bits of bad grammar they all get tidied up and turned into correct English because as soon as you see them on paper they look terrible (.) they sound fine because that's how we talk when we speak but

they look terrible (.) we know the-the-the listeners would understand it but it um doesn't look (.) comprehensible in um writing just because it's um er-er it doesn't look well organized so writers always try to clean it up (.) or have done till recently anyway.

R.P. (*to T.P*) Do you do that?

T.P. Er well (.) the problem with writing um dialogue is (.) when (.) when I (.) first (.) start to write dialogue I er well I don't write it (.) that's the point I hear it at-at-at first in my head (.) and er (.) but then (.) the thing is that um you've got to er you've got to have it in a form (.) you've got to convey it to (.) it's got to be spoken by actors (.) and um (.) and you um if you gave actors something they couldn't read they wouldn't have anything (.) and er (.) most plays anyway are er are er published if you don't write it down in a if you don't tidy it up the publisher is er will do um (.) so what er (.) that's-that's what-what um what the what the playwright does is to um (.) is to write it down in a er (.) correctly if you like and er when the er (.) when the (.) what the cast (.) that's what actors are for they er they put all the speech er mannerisms back on into the um dialogue otherwise we wouldn't bother going to the theatre we'd just read the play instead if you see what I mean . . .

Activity

1 Clarify what T.P. has said by translating the speech into written English.

2 Explain what major difficulty you encountered in translating the speech into writing.

3 Discuss the differences between the sentence structures in the transcript and your written version of it. (The list of features of spoken English given in question 5 may help you to do this.)

4 Make your own recording of a spontaneous conversation between two or three people (it doesn't matter what it's about).

Play it back a couple of times to get the general drift, then write it out *just as it is*. Use the following markers:

a (.)(micropause), (1.0) (one second), (2.0) (two seconds), etc., to show where and for how long a speaker pauses;

b a row of dots at the end of unfinished utterances to show they are incomplete;

c *err* and *um* to indicate where speakers utter these filler sounds to give themselves time to think;

d dashes to indicate repeated words or sounds, e.g. *er-er-er*; *that-that*.

5 Look carefully at your transcript and see if it contains any of the following features:

a unfinished sentences left to dangle in the air, e.g. *. . . so I didn't . . . ; It was just that . . .*

b interrupted constructions (sentences that are dropped half-way through in favour of another), e.g. *So I think that perhaps it's . . . What I'm trying to say is I think it's wrong.*

c non-standard uses of grammar, e.g. *We was playing records*; *He done that riff I showed you.*

d omissions (the leaving out of part of the sentence construction), e.g. *I'm trying to say I think it's wrong*, where the written construction would be *I'm trying to say **that** I think it's wrong.*

e contractions, e.g. *don't, won't, can't, haven't; she's, they've, we'd*, etc.

f hesitation indicators such as *er* and *um*; repetitions of words, or filler sounds, e.g. *a-a-a-; the-the-the.*

g informal language, e.g. the colloquial *bloke, guy, booze, great, stuff like that*, or slang such as *heavy, wicked, safe.*

h fillers such as *sort of, you know, I mean.*

Talking point

Below are two passages of speech. One is of an educated person reflecting on his academic experience, the other is spoken by the character Len in Harold Pinter's play *The Dwarves*. Read both extracts, then discuss how close Pinter's dialogue is to ordinary speech.

A He (.) seemed of course he had that kind of n er I-I'm er I-I er I-I er-er are you northern by any chance I was going to say that kind of northern (1.0) er (.) scepticism or at least questioning mind (1.0) which er (.) but of course he would mislead you with that he er he gave you the impression that he only er you know he gave you the impression that he was (.) sceptical and at times sceptical and nothing else (2.0) but I think he er (1.0) I think he appreciated the course there you know (.) from one or two things he said when I bumped into him.

B What you are, or appear to me to be, or appear to be to you, changes so quickly, so horrifyingly, I certainly can't keep up with it and I'm damn sure you can't either. But who you are I can't even begin to recognize, and sometimes I recognize it so wholly, so forcibly, I can't look, and how can I be certain of what I see? You have no number. Where am I to look, where am I to look, what is there to locate, so as to have some surety, to have some rest from this bloody racket? You're the sum of so many reflections. How many reflections? Is that what you consist of?

The Pinter extract is clearly more organized and rhythmic than ordinary speech. It has to be, for the sake of the audience. Would you want to sit through a play in which the characters expressed themselves like the speaker in A? As T.S. Eliot remarked, '. . . an *identical* spoken and written language would be practically intolerable. If we spoke as we write we should find no one to listen: and if we wrote as we speak we should find no one to read. The spoken and written language must not be too near together, as they must not be too far apart'.

In spite of appearances, then, spoken English is not just a looser, messier version of the written language. It is a different medium, with rules and conventions of its own – rules that speakers follow unconsciously, unaware of what they are doing. The most important of these are looked at below.

Unconscious rules governing spoken English

Spoken English is often criticized for its disjointed and incomplete sentence constructions, and for its repeated use of 'filler' words such as *like, sort of, I mean, you know,* and *know what I mean?*

Research, however, shows that speakers use both of these features in a highly patterned and rule-bound way.

Sentence structures peculiar to speech

How can disjointed sentence structures make meaning clearer for listeners, when in written English they have exactly the opposite effect? Consider the following pair:

a I'm very interested in irony – how to read it without becoming confused.

b I'm very interested in how to read irony without becoming confused.

Sentence (a) is clearly a disjointed sentence if measured against conventional written structures.

1 The second half of the sentence does not fit logically on to the first half: *how to read it* shows that the speaker is not interested in irony itself – only in the process of learning how to read it.

2 It does not fit grammatically, either. The first half of the sentence finishes with a noun, *irony*, and to be in proper apposition to it (that is, to match it in construction), the second half of the sentence should begin with another noun such as *technique*, not with the noun clause *how to read it*, e.g.:

I'm very interested in irony – a technique I find rather confusing.

According to Quirk, people use sentence structures like these a lot, both in real life and in plays that try to represent real conversation. He calls the technique of breaking apart the two halves of the sentence 'disjuncture', and points out that it has a very useful purpose: it foregrounds or draws attention to a certain item or items of information that readers might find hard to grasp in a longer, more conventionally flowing sentence. In a sentence like (a) above, *how to read it* stands out more clearly and makes a greater impact on the mind than it does in (b).

Quirk's research supports this idea. Students reading for English degrees at University College, London, were asked to assess which of the following versions of the same information they found easier to understand:

a He's doing research on the mineral resources of various parts of the Commonwealth – the procedures for assessing, the methods of surveying and the techniques for exploiting them.

b He's doing research on the procedures for assessing, the methods of surveying and the techniques for exploiting the mineral resources of various parts of the Commonwealth.

Interestingly, the group that were given sentence (a) absorbed on average sixty per cent of the information; the group given sentence (b) absorbed on average only forty per cent.

Speakers also use incomplete structures to foreground the most important items of information. Like the senders of telegrams (see the comments on 'glue' or structure words, page 94), they leave out any words that are not necessary for understanding and so concentrate listeners' attention on the ones that are. Writers of telegrams generally leave out prepositions, however: little grammatical words like *to, from, up, down, over, behind, across, on, in* and so on. *Send money Monaco Hotel Athens,* they write, not, *Send money to me at the Monaco Hotel, Athens.*

Sports commentators in contrast use prepositions all the time, because they have to tell their listeners where people and things are in relation to one another:

Becker to Edberg
the ball goes into touch
a good pass from Lineker to Platt.

They have to use adverbs also, to make their listeners see:

Graf low over the net.

What we seldom find is subordinate adverbial clauses beginning with conjunctions like *when, where, because, unless,* etc. If commentators took the time to use lengthy subordinate clauses the next piece of action would be over before they could begin to describe it. And subordinate clauses would *sound* wrong in a sporting context, too: too *literary* as well as too leisurely. Raw physical effort is what commentators try to communicate, a world away from conventional written style. We do find a lot of phrases, however – both prepositional and adverbial.

A construction like *Lineker forward to Platt* shows perhaps the most common technique for shortening constructions – the leaving out of the verb. In conventional written English, *Lineker forward to Platt* would be written, *Lineker passes forward to Platt.*

Speaking to interested and knowledgeable listeners drinking in every word, the commentator can foreground just the important items – player

(*Lineker*), direction (*to*), and receiver (*Platt*). He doesn't have to mention passing because everybody understands that that is what's going on. Sometimes the adverb is left out too and we get the even simpler construction *Lineker to Platt, Platt to Gascoigne . . .*

Verbs that commentators leave out very frequently are the *is* and *are* forms of the verb *to be* :

a as main verbs (*he is/they are*)
Barnes on the right wing now (instead of *Barnes **is** on the right wing now*)

b as auxiliaries helping to form the present continuous tense of another verb (*is/are* moving):
Fashanu moving towards goal now (instead of *Fashanu **is** moving towards goal now*)

The impersonal method of introducing a subject with the verb *to be* – *There is/are/was/will be*, etc. – is also ignored by commentators. They bring things into existence by simply mentioning them: *A tie-break of course if Cash evens the score with this one* (instead of ***There will be** a tie-break . . .*)

On the other hand, the verb *to be*, in the impersonal construction *it is*, (shortened to *it's*), is often used instead of the longer constructions used in writing: *It's Barnes now for England* rather than *Barnes **is about to/is getting ready to take the penalty** for England*.

Sometimes commentators leave out whole phrases and clauses by using prepositions in a way peculiar to themselves. In *Pip's Pride is showing good speed **from** Petardia* for example, *from* takes the place of a phrase such as *Pip's Pride is showing good speed **in beating** Petardia* or a clause such as *Pip's Pride is showing good speed **and is ahead of** Petardia*.

Even nouns, those vital content words, are sometimes dropped for the sake of speed: *There are still two to play* (instead of *There are still two **holes** to play*).

So are pronouns, together with linking *and*s: *Waqar comes in . . . bowls him!* Written conventionally, this would be *Waqar comes in, **and he** bowls him!*

Activity	1 Record two minutes of racing commentary from Radio 5. Make a written transcript of it.

2 Give examples of any of the following features you have found in your transcript.

* Use of present rather than past tense (to add drama, life, excitement)
* Heavy use of prepositions and adverbs (particularly the adverb *now*)
* Frequent use of prepositional and adverbial phrases
* Omission of verbs (particularly forms of the verb *to be*)
* Omission of pronouns
* Infrequent use of subordinate clauses
* Infrequent use of conjunctions such as *and*.

■ *The role of fillers in speech*

Fillers have a twofold use in spoken English:

a They forge a friendly link between speakers and listeners. Quirk's students disliked the use of *you know* and *you see* from the style point of view, but found it *friendlier, more informal*, and so to be preferred in contexts where style was not important.

b They have several specific functions in a sentence; as Crystal points out:

> they have a grammar of their own, being inserted at different places in the sentence according to the nature of the job they have to do.
>
> Thus, *you know* is often used:
>
> 1 at the beginning of a sentence, to soften the force of a statement: compare the abrupt *You should be more careful* with the more sympathetic *Y'know, you should be more careful.*
> 2 in the middle of a sentence, to introduce an explanation or illustration of what has just been said: *He's just got a new BMX – you know, one of those tough little bikes . . .*
> 3 at the end of a sentence, as a kind of tag question to check that the listener has understood what is being said: *He's bought a BMX – you know?*
> 4 to mark the boundary between one topic and another: *you know, I've been thinking about that.*
>
> Crystal, *English Today* magazine

Talking point

> Discuss the use of *you know* in the following two sentences.
>
> John's bringing his – you know – flatmate.
>
> She's left that bloke she was living with – you know.

You see and *I mean* are two other important fillers with specific speech functions, as Britt Erman has shown in her book *Pragmatic Expressions in English*. Her research reveals that English speakers use *you see*:

1 after a summarizing remark, or at the end of an explanation:
   . . . and that's how the monkey got its tail, you see;

2 when someone is justifying a previous claim:
   so that's why I left, you see.

They use *I mean*, amongst other things, to clarify or justify something previously said: *I mean, how else could she have known?*

Where the prescriptive grammarian is irritated by such phrases, Crystal values them as 'facilitating mechanisms': for him they are:

> . . . the oil which helps us perform the complex task of spontaneous speech production and interaction smoothly and efficiently. They give the speaker an opportunity to check back, to plan ahead, and to obtain listener reaction. They give the listener an opportunity to keep up and to react.
>
> Crystal, *English Today* magazine

Conversation

Key words

Speech-act: a unit of purposeful speech in a social context.

Discourse: a longer period of speech made up of individual speech-acts.

The kind of *discourse* we call *conversation* is paradoxical: it *seems* spontaneous and natural, yet it is governed by unspoken rules and conventions. We cannot even begin to speak to someone, for instance, until we've checked that they are able and/or willing to give us their attention – usually by greeting them with their names, if known:

> Peter, did you finish that essay?

or by introducing ourselves by our names, if not:

> Hello! I'm [name], your local Liberal Democrat candidate . . .
> Good morning! [name] speaking. I'm ringing about . . .

We would be considered brusque and rude if we plunged straight in without such preliminaries.

Once we have introduced ourselves to each other, however, a whole new set of rules comes into play.

▓ *Opening a conversation*

There are several conventional ways of opening a conversation:

a The request

> Excuse me, but could you tell me something about the food here?
> Sarah, could you fill me in on what happened in the meeting this morning?

(Don't confuse requests like this with questions asking for some form of *yes* or *no* answer. The speakers aren't asking whether it's *possible* for their interlocutors to tell them these things – they know they can. They're requesting them to do it – a form of indirect command.)

b The question

> Did you watch *Neighbours* last night, Alison? What did you think about the rabbit?

c The offer

> Shamin, I've just watched that video you were talking about last week. It was good.

(The speaker is 'offering' or volunteering a conversational topic here – showing that he or she wants to talk.)

▓ *Turn-taking*

Once we have got a conversation going, further conventions come into play:

1 Listeners know when a speaker is coming to the end of an utterance because they hear the voice begin to fall.
2 Often the person who is speaking decides who shall be given the next turn. He or she shows this by such devices as
    a mentioning the person's name;
    b looking at the person enquiringly;
    c talking about a subject that the person is known to be well-briefed in.

(a) and (c) are often combined in a phrase such as, *You've done a lot of work on this, Bob, haven't you?*

If the current speaker doesn't pick anyone out, the next turn goes to whoever gets in first, or manages to shout everybody else down. If nobody offers to say anything after the current speaker has finished, after a moment or two's silence he or she is free to speak again.

▓ *Relevance*

When new speakers take up their turns, convention demands that what they say shall be relevant to what has previously been said. New topics cannot be opened up until properly introduced.

▓ *Introducing a new topic*

When they want to introduce a new topic, speakers use conventional signalling phrases like *incidentally*; *by the way*; *apropros of what we've just been talking about*; *that reminds me*; *well, I think we ought to move on to another point*; *is there anything else you'd like to bring up?* etc.

▓ *Positive feedback*

Positive feedback (technically *back-channel feedback*) is the term for the signals that listeners send to speakers to assure them that attention is being paid and their message is getting through. These signals can range from non-verbal noises, through one word responses (*Quite, Really?*) to short questions. (Requests for clarification of a point can be included under this heading.)

a Encouraging phrases
Really? You don't say! No! How interesting. I know.

b Non-verbal signs
Uh huh, Mmm, plus a wide range of expressive noises.

c   Paralinguistic features

Changing facial expressions, head tilts, shakes and nods, etc.

In the same way, speakers have mechanisms for checking that people are listening to them:

* They try to make eye contact with their listeners, changing their position if necessary to do so.
* They look enquiringly at their listeners and check on their facial expressions.
* They try to keep their listeners involved by using phrases like *you know?*, *right?* and *do you see/know what I mean?*
* They use gestures and changing facial expressions to hold their listeners' attention; research shows that something of this kind occurs at five- to seven-second intervals in conversation between adults.

Key word

> *Paralinguistic features*: the range of gestures, facial expressions, and tones of voice that accompany conversation. *Body language* is the popular name for unspoken paralinguistic features.

▓ *Closing a conversation*

Unspoken rules also govern how we close a conversation. To get up abruptly and walk away without a word would signal anger and/or dislike. We soften the break by signalling our intention to leave several moments before we actually go. Mechanisms include:

Body language

Shifting from one foot to the other and half turning away if we're standing up; shifting about in our chair and/or moving forward on to the edge of the seat if we're sitting down; starting to collect books or bags or other belongings together, etc.

Conventional phrases

Well, it's been lovely talking to you; *Oh well, can't stand here all day, I suppose*; *I've really enjoyed our chat, we must get together again soon/meet for lunch*, etc.; *Well, if there's no other business I think we can call it a day*, etc.

▓hildren's versus adult conversation

Children pick up the unspoken rules of conversation much as they learn to talk – by listening to adults and imitating them. Before they have had time to learn, however, they can be awkward conversational partners for adults used to observing the rules.

Children will do any or all of the following when they talk to other people:

* plunge straight into a conversation with a statement (instead of the conventional request or question or offer): *I've got new shoes.*
* fail to give the person to whom they are talking their turn to speak, for instance by asking two questions in a row, or by cutting across what somebody else is saying: *Are you washing your car?* [no pause for answer] *Is it a new one?*
* fail to give positive feedback; they will just stand there, staring;
* fail to involve their listeners by using questions like *you know?*, gesture, etc.
* fail to soften the ending of a conversation by the use of conventional mechanisms; they just walk away.

Activity

> 1 Find a child aged between three and five (visit the local playgroup if you don't have one in your family circle) and record or note down the conversation he or she has with an adult or teenager.
>
> 2 Make notes also on any paralinguistic features noticed. Does the child use gesture, facial expression, and so on?
>
> 3 Make a transcript of your recording or write out your notes in full.
>
> 4 Discuss any ways in which the child's conversation breaks the rules of adult conversation.

Note: the kind of role-models a child has plays a very important part in developing conversational skills. The child of self-confident, articulate parents has an inbuilt advantage here.

Male and female conversation

> Men and women use much the same grammar and vocabulary in English, although each sex uses certain kinds of words and structures more frequently than the other. Most men, for instance, use more swear-words than most women, whilst far more women than men use such emotive adjectives as *super* and *lovely*, exclamations such as *Goodness me!* and *Oh dear!*, and intensifiers such as *so* and *such* (e.g. *It was so busy*).
>
> Crystal, *The Cambridge Encyclopedia of Language*

Greater differences emerge, however, when we look at the way in which men and women operate in male-female conversation.

Pamela Fishman claims that, just as women do all the chores around the house, so they do all the chores – the 'shitwork' – in mixed-sex conversation. After listening to fifty-two hours of taped talk between men and women, she came to the conclusion that women made all the effort and that men joined in only when 'offered' a topic that interested them – after which they would take control and do all the talking. Her thesis is supported by Spender's transcript of a conversation at a social gathering:

> Female: Did he have the papers ready for you?
> Male: Mmm.
> Female: And were they all right . . . was anything missing?
> Male: Not that I could see.
> Female: Well, that must have been a relief, anyway . . .
> Female: I suppose everything went well after that?
> Male: Almost.
> Female: Oh. Was there something else?
> Male: Yes, actually.
> Female: It wasn't X . . . was it? . . . He didn't let you down again?
> Male: I'd say he did.
> Female: He really is irresponsible, you know, you should get . . .
> Male: I'm going to do something about it. It was just about the last straw
>   today. How many times do you think that makes this week?
>
> Spender, *Man-Made Language*

Notice how the woman spends all her time talking about matters that relate to the man, and how he resists all her efforts to draw him out until he chooses to respond – after which he interrupts her in mid-sentence and then proceeds to dominate the conversation.

Women restrict their own opportunities for expression, Fishman argues, by concentrating on the development of male topics. They are required to be 'linguistically available' to men, to listen to them and to keep the conversation going. Women who go against this convention by holding their own in conversations with men are made to suffer for it:

> Women who consistently and successfully control interactions are criticized by men and are likely to be called 'bitchy', 'domineering' or 'aggressive'.
>
> Fishman, quoted in Spender, *Man-Made Language*

In case you should think this is merely female prejudice, Crystal reports that

> Women have been found to ask more questions, make more use of positive and encouraging 'noises' (such as *mhm*), use a wider intonational range and a more marked rhythmic stress, and make greater use of the pronouns *you* and *we*. By contrast, men are much more likely to interrupt (more than three times as much in some studies), to dispute what has been said, to ignore or respond poorly to what has been said, to introduce more new topics into the conversation, and to make more declarations of fact or opinion.

Most interpretations of these differences refer to the contrasting social roles of the sexes in modern society. Men are seen to reflect in their conversational dominance the power they have traditionally received from society; women, likewise, exercise the supporting role that they have been taught to adopt – in this case, helping the conversation along and providing men with opportunities to express this dominance.

However, Crystal is prepared to see shades of grey where Fishman and Spender see only black and white. He points out that each sex can be found to adopt the other's linguistic practices in different contexts.

> Men do not always hog the conversation; women are not always content to encourage them and draw them out.
>
> The danger . . . is that in the process of criticizing old sexual stereotypes, researchers are in danger of creating new ones.

Activity

> Try to observe (as unobtrusively as possible) a mixed-sex conversation, and assess whether:
>
> 1 it supports what Fishman claims about
> a women contributing more speech-acts than men;
> b men making longer contributions than women;
> c men interrupting women more;
>
> 2 women
> a use more paralinguistic features than men;
> b give more positive feedback than men.

The relative values of spoken and written English

In theory, written English scores over spoken English in two ways:

1 it is more carefully constructed, formally punctuated, and so more clear;
2 it is 'frozen' on the page and so can be read:
 a at the reader's own pace;
 b as many times as is necessary to grasp the meaning.

Before the invention of recorded sound it was also the only way of passing information on to people who were not there to hear you speak, to later generations, and to people in other parts of the world.

In practice, spoken English is usually easier to understand, partly because it is usually accompanied by the features described immediately below.

Suprasegmental features of spoken English

Key words

> *Suprasegmental features*: communicative activities in conversation which accompany language, but which are not themselves part of language, e.g. stress, pitch, and intonation. (*Segmental features* are the actual segments of language – vowels and consonants. *Supra* means *above, beyond*.)

Compared with a piece of written English, spoken English seems muddled and unclear. In practice, however, speech is almost always more immediately understandable. Speakers can use meaningful looks, winks, smiles and frowns, discreet coughs, and disparaging sniffs to show what they're really thinking, but more importantly, they can use the suprasegmental features called *stress*, *rhythm*, and *intonation*. We can separate these features from one another in order to examine them, but in reality they are inextricably linked and work together to get their effects.

Stress

Stress is the pronunciation of one particular syllable of a word with slightly more force than the other(s). In the following examples this syllable is marked by the symbol ●.

■ Word stress

1 English words have one syllable which is naturally stressed more than others, e.g.:

    ●   ●   ●
   brother   garden   happy

2 When prefixes and suffixes are added, the stress remains on the same syllable in many cases, e.g.:

   ●   ●   ●
   happy   unhappy   happily
   ●   ●
   pretty   prettier

3 Notice that some word families have a shifting stress pattern:

   ●   ●
   triangle   triangular
   ●   ●
   hexagon   hexagonal
   ●   ●   ●
   politics   political   politician
   ●   ●   ●
   photography   photographic photographer

4 Generally speaking, English prefers the stress to fall close to the beginning of a word, either on the first syllable or, if that is a prefix, on the second.

Activity | Write out the following words, and mark the accented syllable in each word by placing a large dot above it:

pencil   big   bigger   biology   biological

Changes in word stress
Words have a natural forward stress in English but there are two instances where the stress changes.

1 **–*teen* words**
When we count, or when there is a following noun, we stress the first syllable:

twelve   thir•teen   four•teen   fif•teen   six•teen

I've got ni•neteen hamsters.

However, when the number stands alone, we stress the *–teen*:

She's six•teen.

Turn to page seven•teen.

2 Contrastive stress

When we want to correct what someone says or contrast our opinion with theirs, we can break the normal pattern by stressing the syllable that we think gives the correct information:

A: She was look•ing happy tonight.

B: She looked un•happy to me.

The fact that the accent in *unhappy* falls on the first rather than on the usual syllable shows the native English listener that the negative idea in *un* is the important one here.

▧ *Sentence stress*

In a sentence, we normally stress *content words* such as nouns, verbs, adjectives, and adverbs more than the *structure* words that hold sentences together (words like articles, prepositions, and auxiliary verbs such as *was* and *had*.) Thus in the sentence

Sign• here• at the bot•tom of the doc•ument.

the content words *sign, here, bottom*, and *document* are stressed, while the structure words *at, the*, and *of the* are not.

Contrastive stress may also be used, and a different sort of word stressed when we want to make a point:

I said in• the cupboard, not on• it!

<table>
<tr><td>**Activity**</td><td>To find out for yourself how different sentence stress can also indicate meaning, write out the following sentence three times, labelling the sentences (a), (b), and (c).

John could only see his wife from the door.

1 In sentence (a), mark the word that would be stressed if the speaker meant that John could not hear his wife from the door.

2 In sentence (b), mark the word that would be stressed if the speaker meant that John could not see the other person or persons in the room.

3 In sentence (c), mark the word that would be stressed if the only place John could see his wife from was the door.</td></tr>
</table>

Rhythm

Rhythm is created by our perception of prominent stresses in speech. English is said to be an *isochronous* or *stress-timed* language – that is, one in which stressed syllables are equally spaced in time, with the unstressed syllables reduced to fit between them. (Compare this with French, in which all syllables, stressed and unstressed, are equally spaced, thus giving a much more staccato rhythm.)

Because English speakers stress content or lexical words and leave structure or grammatical words unstressed, the same number of stresses can be found in sentences like the following:

    •   •
He told his mother.

    •   •
He sent it to his mother.

As Quirk points out, if these sentences were spoken by the same person under the same conditions, they would have the same number of stresses and take the same amount of time to say. *Sent it to his* would be said more quickly than *told his*, to make the intervals between the stresses roughly the same length.

Rhythm in speech is spontaneous and natural, whereas in some kinds of poetry there is a preconceived pattern. When a regular beat occurs in speech, the effect is oddly poetic. This example came from a conversation between friends:

Many a dish I've washed there, and many a bed I've made.

On the whole, however, rhythm plays only an incidental part in everyday communication. It has more to do in persuasive speech, in the language of advertising, and in poetry.

Intonation

Key words

> *Pitch:* the degree of highness or lowness in the voice, similar to the placing of different notes in music.
>
> *Intonation:* the rise and fall in the voice due to varying the pitch. When we describe an accent as 'sing-song', this is because we hear very clear rising and falling intonation patterns in it.
>
> *Tone units:* segments of spoken English, roughly corresponding to units of information.
>
> The *tonic syllable:* the syllable within a tone unit on which the strongest stress falls.
>
> The *onset:* the first prominent syllable in a tone unit; the voice begins to rise on the onset then rises further towards the tonic syllable.

▓ *Tone units*

To clarify what *tone units* are, it may be useful to contrast the structure of spoken and written utterances.

Written English is made up of units with a clearly defined structure, called clauses and phrases:

In reality [*phrase*] because he needed them so much [*dependent clause*] Lawrence hated women [*main clause*].

Punctuation is added, to make the connection or lack of connection between the units plain:

In reality, probably because he needed them so much, Lawrence hated women.

Spoken English on the other hand is made up of groups of words with a less definite structure, called *tone units*. There are no punctuation marks to show where one tone unit ends and another begins; instead, they are separated by such things as brief pauses, obvious changes of pitch and/or loudness of voice, or the drawing out of the last sound in the unit.

Here, for example, is a short piece of spoken English. The boundaries of the tone units into which it can be divided are marked by thick vertical lines:

Farmers | in Southern France | have lifted | their blockade of railway lines | which has stranded thousands | of passengers | on trains | and at stations. | Trains are now running again | twenty four hours after groups | of farmers | erected | the barricades.

There may be several stresses in each tone unit, but one syllable always stands out more than the others – has *peak prominence* – because it is given a heavier stress. It is called the *tonic syllable*. The tonic syllables in the passage above are shown by ■.

The voice does not peak abruptly on this tonic syllable. The rise begins earlier in the tone unit, starting on a slightly less heavily stressed syllable, then rising with varying degrees of sharpness to a peak. (The stressed syllable on which the voice begins to rise is called the *onset*.)

Consider the following tone units, for example. The *onset* is shown by ▫ and the *tonic syllable* is shown by ■.

a | At an age when most punters have swapped |

b | the racecourse for the armchair |

Say (a) aloud and you should hear your voice begin to rise on *age*, then climb to a peak on *mo* before falling slightly to mid level on *have swapped.* Say (b) aloud and you should hear your voice rise on *race,* and go on climbing slightly until it reaches the tonic syllable, *arm,* before falling away to a much lower level.

The normal English intonation in a tone unit is therefore a rise followed by a fall.

Activity

for goodness sake	for the time being	at the present moment
bread and butter	heaven and earth	collapse into a heap

1 Write out the above phrases, marking the tonic syllable. Then say them slowly and carefully to yourself and listen for the fall in pitch from the syllable you have marked as the tonic syllable – the one on which the stress is strongest, or most prominent. Mark it with a downward line.

2 If you think there is an *onset* – that is, a stressed syllable on which the voice begins to rise towards the *tonic syllable* – mark this syllable with ☐ and a line rising towards the tonic syllable.

Remember, the stressed syllable on which the rise begins is called the *onset*.

▓ *General patterns of intonation in English sentences*

There are four intonation patterns in English speech:

1 falling, indicated by a downward arrow (↘);
2 rising, indicated by an upward arrow (↗);
3 rise-fall, indicated by a combination of the first two signs (⌒↘);
4 fall-rise, indicated by a combination of the first two signs (⌄↗).

Falling intonation

Falling intonation is the most common in English, simply by default; it's the one speakers use when they have no reason for using any other. It might be described as the *neutral* tone.

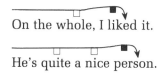

On the whole, I liked it.

He's quite a nice person.

The above examples show how English speakers drop their voices from high or medium pitch to low when they are coming to the end of what they have to say.

Since we spend a lot of time making simple factual statements like this, it is hardly surprising that the falling tone is so common in English speech.

By contrast, falling tones from a very high pitch can convey extreme exasperation coming to a head.

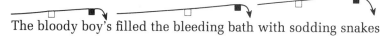

The bloody boy's filled the bleeding bath with sodding snakes

On a more practical note, speakers drop their voice on the tonic syllable in most questions beginning with a *wh-* word:

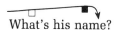

What's his name?

and in short responses to such questions:

Charlie Brown.

Rising intonation

Rising intonation is the next most common intonation. Broadly speaking, it is used:

    a to signal lack of finality; speakers are unsure of what they are saying and want to leave it open:

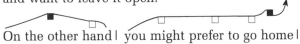
On the other hand | you might prefer to go home |

    b to signal that speakers haven't finished all they've got to say:

We need to build more houses | we need to provide more jobs | . . .

    c to ask declarative questions:

You're upset?

Rising and falling intonation

The next two intonations do not have such clear-cut uses as the ones just described, and individual speakers use them to express a variety of different meanings. Quirk discerns one or two patterns, however.

Rise-fall intonation

Quirk notes two main uses, both involving contrast:

1 To express an opinion contrary to the one uttered by a previous speaker:

She seemed unhappy | to me

2 To express a contrast with something that has been said or implied in the previous sentence:

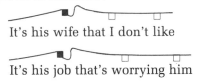
It's his wife that I don't like

It's his job that's worrying him

3 Knowles discerns a further use of the rise-fall: to hint at something instead of saying it outright, or to warn. Consider the following examples:

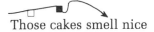
Those cakes smell nice

Uttered with a falling intonation only, this is a simple observation. Uttered with a rise-fall, it becomes a clear hint: 'I'd like one'.

Fall-rise intonation

1 The falling and rising intonation can be used to express doubt:

I'll do it if I can

2 It can also express a warning:

You'll fall

Uttered with a fall-rise intonation to a child doing something dangerous, this becomes an indirect command, 'Get off'; whereas uttered with a falling intonation it is a simple observation.

3 It is especially common on adverbs when they come at the beginning of sentences:

Hopefully, England will win.

Finally, we decided not to go.

Talking points

1 Which of the following is an invitation, which a command?

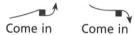

Come in   Come in

2 Which of the following versions of 'Goodbye' implies 'See you again', which suggests the parting is final?

Goodbye   Goodbye

3 Which of the following shows genuine gratitude, which sarcasm?

Thank you   Thank you.

4 Which indicates that the play was quite good, which that it was mediocre?

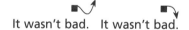

It wasn't bad.   It wasn't bad.

Activity

1 Decide which of the tonic syllables in the following have a rising, and which a falling intonation.

If you like| I'll go with you

On the whole| I prefer to wait

You're not leaving already [disappointment, not surprise]

What's his name

Please sit down [a persuasive request, not an order]

2 When you've decided, write down these sentences and indicate the rising intonations on the stressed syllable with this mark (⤴), and the falling ones with this (⤵).

Activity

> 1 Try to find or make a recording of someone
>   a speaking emotionally about their country or their religion;
>   b speaking angrily.*
>   Make a transcript of the recording.
>
> 2 Mark on your transcript every tonic syllable on which the intonation rises or falls. Do this by putting ■ above the tonic syllable, and an upward or downward facing arrow following it, like this: ■↗ ■↘.)
>
> 3 a Say the word *really* in such a way that you express the following attitudes:
>   interest
>   wondering surprise
>   indifference
>   anger
>   cynical disbelief (a sort of 'who-do-you-think-you're-kidding' attitude)
>   b Draw lines to show the intonation for each pronunciation (the overall shape made by the rise and fall of the voice).
>
> 4 Listen to a newsreader reading one item of news. What level does his or her voice start on, what level does it go to in the middle, and on what level does it finish?

empo

Key word

> *Tempo:* the speed or rate at which speech is delivered.

The rate at which speakers utter their words varies considerably. It depends on such factors as the amount of time available, the state of their emotions, the context in which they are speaking, and the audience they are speaking to.

Speakers tend to **speed up** their delivery when:

* time is running out;
* they are excited or enthusiastic about their subject;
* they fear someone will interrupt or disagree with them;
* they want to get an unpleasant item over with quickly;
* they realize they have made a gaffe or a mistake or have expressed themselves confusingly and hurry on to a new topic in the hope that their listener(s) will either fail to notice or simply forget;
* they think of another, more interesting topic and get rid of the old one as quickly as possible;
* they realize they've been droning on at a boring rate and over-compensate by then going too fast.

---

* If you can't manage a recording, use your imagination on the extracts from John F. Kennedy's or Bill Clinton's speeches in the section *Practical writing skills*, page 270.

Speakers tend to **slow down** their delivery when:

* they have a captive audience and no time constraints;
* the occasion is a solemn one;
* they are trying very hard to find exactly the right way of expressing their meaning;
* they want to impress their listeners with their importance.

Suprasegmental features of speech in written English

Written English may be better organized than speech, but it is not so warm, so vivid, or so immediate. To compensate for this, writers try to indicate effects of stress, pitch, intonation, loudness, rhythm, and tempo in their work. The headlines of tabloids like *The Sun* and *The Mirror* are often referred to as 'screaming'. Their large, bold capitals are the written equivalent of someone speaking at the top of his or her voice. They resort to capitals too to indicate stress:

The Sun says 'Let them go NOW!'

It is novelists who try hardest to capture the living quality of speech. They usually resort to italics to show stress:

> 'A large girl like you must wear clothes that *fit*; and Elfine, *whatever* you do, always wear court shoes.'
> Stella Gibbons, *Cold Comfort Farm*

Pitch, loudness, and timbre of voice are indicated by appropriate verbs and adverbs. Low pitch is conveyed by verbs like *growled, muttered, mumbled, dropped his voice half an octave, his voice sank to a whisper, he spoke in a low murmur/muffled whisper*, etc.; mid pitch by phrases like *said evenly/levelly, spoke in even tones*; high pitch by verbs like *cried, screamed, shrieked, shouted*, and by phrases like *spoke in rising tones*. Whether these devices add life and force or simply slow down the narrative depends upon the skill of the writer. At best, they seem contrived and clumsy when measured against the flow of living speech.

Summary

Spoken English is not an inferior version of written English but a different, parallel form. When we speak to one another we communicate as much through suprasegmental features as through the actual words we use. *Stress* is the most central of these suprasegmental features for the following reasons:

* it is perceived as a sequence of regular beats and therefore is the basis of *rhythm*;
* it requires some syllables to be pronounced with greater energy than others and consequently leads to changes in intonation.

Activity

> 1 To shape your thinking about the different qualities of speech and writing, discuss in pairs how you would prefer to learn a new subject – by correspondence course or by personal contact with a tutor. Explain your reasons.
>
> 2 Look again at the transcript of Ann Devlin's speech (page 108). In the light of what you have read in this section, explain why it would be easier to understand when listened to than when read.

An outline of speech development

▨ *0–8 weeks*

Babies start the process of learning to speak the moment they enter the world. They begin to cry and make little sounds referred to as *vegetative noises*, and this exercises the vocal organs and gives them practice in controlling the flow of air through mouth and nose – preliminary steps towards speech. Crying with lips stretched back and mouth wide open produces something that sounds like the vowel *a* (say *ant* and you'll see what I mean); smacking the lips together produces noises that sound rather like the consonants *p* and *b*. So, at a very early stage of their lives, babies have taken the first steps on the road to speech.

▨ *8–20 weeks*

Fortunately, babies don't just cry. They make quieter, lower-pitched, and more musical sounds called *cooing*, too, from roughly eight weeks of age. Cooing gives rise to a wider range of vowel and consonant-like sounds – *u*s, *k*s and *g*s, for example, the *ch* sound as in *loch*, and even a sophisticated rolled *r* sound like the one used in French and German. Somewhere between two and five months babies start stringing these sounds together into sequences like *kuu* and *guu* – the characteristic 'cooing' sound.

    So, during their first two months of life, babies use some of the sounds found in speech and vary the pitch and loudness of their voices. The noises that they make do not yet sound like speech, however. Two of the most important features of normal speech – intonation and rhythm – are still missing. Babies stop for breath at random intervals, and so their cooing lacks the normal rising and falling tones and stress-timed rhythm of adult speech.

▨ *20–30 weeks*

Over the next two and a half months the babies' vocal organs develop and they begin to try out new positions for their tongues. Friction sounds like *fff* emerge, and the trilled *r* that sounds like a 'raspberry'. Sounds begin to be combined into longer sequences (the first signs of *babbling*) and long glides from high to low pitch are heard, but adult intonation and rhythm are still missing and speech is still a long way off.

■ *25–50 weeks*

At roughly six months, babies begin *babbling* – stringing together long sequences of repeated sounds such as *bababab, dadadada.* From about nine months more varied patterns of babbling (*variegated babbling*) are heard, in which consonants and vowels change from one syllable to the next: *ada, maba,* and so on. *S* and *sh* sounds begin to emerge for the first time. The babble is jerky and erratic. Some segments will be loud, some soft; some high in pitch, others low. Speed too may vary from very fast to quite slow.

■ *36–72 weeks*

At about nine months comes a very significant change. The suprasegmental features of melody and rhythm – the things that make speech sound fluent and natural – occasionally make themselves heard. A phrase with a definite melodic shape emerges from a welter of meaningless babble, and parents are sure that the baby has spoken its first word. In reality it is still just practising its sounds, and the first word is still some way away.

By the end of this period, the characteristic melodic shape (or *tones*) of questions, exclamations, greeting, and naming can all be heard in the child's speech, but it is still quite meaningless. In Crystal's words, 'it has got "its act together", but it has yet to learn what the act is for'.

Nevertheless, the emergence of rhythm and intonation in children's speech is the first sign that real language will soon be heard. Up to this point, all babies, whatever their nationality, have gone through the same stages of development and have sounded much the same. Now, thanks to rhythm and intonation (rhythm, you will remember, arises from the perception of stress), they begin to sound increasingly different from one another. The babbling of English babies can be described as *tum-ti-tum*, that of French infants as *rat-a-tat*, whilst the utterances of Chinese children have a more sing-song quality.

Somewhere around 52 weeks of age, short utterances of one or two syllables begin to be heard. These are called *proto-words*. Because they are uttered with the rhythm and intonation of normal speech they sound deceptively like real words, but they are not. As far as the babies are concerned, the sounds mean nothing, and real words – language – must have meaning.

■ *12–18 months*

The first real words appear, combining sound and meaning. At first, one-word utterances are the norm: *teddy, gone, more,* and so on. Some, like *allgone* and *ready-steady-go* may look different, but as far as the child is concerned, they're single words. Most of these single-word utterances take the form of nouns (about sixty per cent) and verbs (about twenty per cent).

If prepositions like *in*, uttered very loudly, are heard, the child is probably using them as verbs: *(Put it) IN!*

Combined with intonation, these one-word utterances are remarkably effective in telling adults what children want. *Biccy* said with a rising tone, for instance, stands for 'Can I have a biscuit'. Uttered with a falling tone in answer to the question 'What do you want?' it's short for the declarative sentence, 'I want a biscuit'. In the same way, the single-word utterance *Dadda* can do duty for sentences that the child is not yet able to construct:

'Is that daddy?' (interrogative)
'It's daddy.' (declarative)
'Pick me up, daddy.' (imperative)

Crystal (*Listen to Your Child*) gives the lovely example of a child who murmured 'Allgone?' to himself on a rising tone before deliberately dropping his cup of drink on to the floor, and 'Allgone' on a satisfied falling tone afterwards.

Two-word utterances begin at around eighteen months of age. Typical examples are *coat off*, *kiss teddy*, *look car*. The brusque, abrupt quality of utterances like these have led some people to describe them as 'telegrammatic'. Like the senders of telegrams, children home in on the important content or lexical words and leave out the little structure words that make the connections between content words in adult sentences. But it is at this stage that children begin to learn how words work together in sentences, and structure words such as the following begin to appear:

* prepositions used as prepositions: *in there*; *on head*
* possessive pronouns: *my teddy*
* personal pronouns: *she cold*; *he gone*; *it there*; *me want.*

Children have trouble with personal pronouns at first. Confusion over the possessive case leads them to make mistakes like

This is hims car.   I can see shes bed.
Mys want to come in.   My finished now.

Confusion between the subject and object forms of the different pronouns leads to mistakes like the following:

Use of object case instead of subject case
Me want it.
Him did it.
Her gave me one.
Them's all gone now.

Use of subject case instead of object case
Let she do it.
I gonna push they over.

Inconsistent use
She like that, her do.

Understanding children who can speak only two-word sentences can be both difficult and frustrating. 'Car allgone' makes sense if father and child are waving mother off in the car together, but if the context doesn't help to explain a two-word sentence, its meaning may be far from clear. (Crystal gives the example of a mother who had difficulty in deciphering the cryptic utterance 'daddy's car'. In the end the child led her into the next room and showed her the overturned chair he had been sitting in: 'daddy's car'.)

▓ *The second year*

As children's experience of language grows, typical two-word utterances like *Kick ball* begin to expand. Subjects are added: *Man kick ball*, then adverbs that tell about time and manner and place: *Man kick ball now*; *Man kick ball hard*; *Man kick ball there*. A similar development can be seen in the sequence *Man sad. Man be sad. Man be sad now.*

It is in the second year too that the questions start. Before this, children had to rely on inflection alone to ask a question. When they get to two, they begin to use question words. *What?* and *Where?* are used on their own till about eighteen months, then combined with other words: *Where that? Where car? What that? What doing?* The question words *why*, *how*, and *who* emerge a little later, and *when* last of all. (Children have trouble with *when*, perhaps because time is such an abstract concept: they often mistake it for *where* in questions like 'When did he go?').

▓ *The third year*

In year three, further grammatical words like *in*, *a* and *the* appear, together with the verbs *is* and *do*. The telegrammatic structures characteristic of two-year-olds give way to sentences that are longer and more varied in structure:

Two-year-old	Three-year-old
Where daddy going?	Where will you put my presents in the morning?
Man kick ball.	The man is kicking that ball.
Push car.	Push the car in the garage now.

Children of three begin to use adjectives like *big* and *black*, and to put inflections on the end of these – e.g. *bigger*, *biggest* – and on the end of their nouns and verbs (see the section *The parts of speech*, page 61). They don't get everything right straight away, of course. Having worked out for themselves that the ending *-ed* is the way to make the past tense, they then proceed to apply it to irregular verbs too, giving characteristic forms like *wented*, *hurted*, *bited*, and *thinked*. They get their first attempts at irregular verbs wrong later on, in the same way: having gone through *thinked* my brother at three and a half came up with *thunk*.

As you might expect, the verbs that children put into the past tense first are the ones that express physical actions – verbs like *swallowed* and *wiped.* Those of a more abstract kind, like *stay*, *have*, and *see*, are put into the past tense rather later.

Towards the middle of the third year, children take a great step forward: they learn to use *and*. With its help they can join one thing to another:

> Lucy (*deciding which toys to take to bed with her*): And I want teddy, and that teddy, and my dolly, and Mr Happy, and that one, and –
> Mother: Hey, that's enough. There'll be no room for you!

They also learn that *and* can join one sentence to another, and then there is no holding them:

> I got a car and I got a gun and I got a game and we have a party and he gived me a big kiss and I was very tired.

Curiously enough, when they first start to use *and* they often choose to begin their sentences with it. 'And I close them', one two-year-old tot was heard to say to himself as he shut his toys away in their box.

In their third year children also start to get to grips with the auxiliary verbs *do*, *can*, *have*, and *will*. The acquisition of *have* is a great step forward in expression; with the different forms of *have* they can talk much more clearly, for instance about time. The two-year-old is limited to the two words *daddy gone*, for example, and this might refer to something that only happened fairly recently or to something that happened much further back in time. Once they have got the hang of auxiliary *have*, in contrast, three-and-a-half- to four-year-olds can make the time-scale clear by using the appropriate tense: either *Daddy went* (ordinary past tense), or *Daddy has gone* (perfect past tense). Similar progress is made when children start to use *is* as an auxiliary. Two-year-olds say *Teddy sitting*; three-and-a-half- to four-year-olds say *Teddy is sitting*. (The more abstract auxiliaries that help to express wishes, intentions, and obligations – verbs like *will/shall*, *would/should*, and *ought* – are not mastered until much later, between the ages of six and eight.) Three-year-olds often get auxiliary verbs wrong when they first begin to use them: the uninflected form *be*, for example, is often used instead of *is*, giving constructions like *Teddy be sitting*. Similarly, *has* and *is* are often confused at first, especially in the shortened forms we use in speech – *he's*, for example, and *it's*. These mistakes fade with practice, and by the end of their third year children are able to express themselves in an amazingly sophisticated way. Most of the parts of speech are now being used more or less correctly, as are pitch, intonation, and stress. Children are getting to be good conversationalists, too. Whereas two-year-olds talk as much to themselves as to other people, three-and-a-half- to four-year-olds interact with their parents and can sustain a genuine dialogue.

▓ *The fourth and fifth years*

By the time they reach their fifth year, most children are fluent speakers who can get through many sentences without making a single mistake. They do go wrong, of course, when they try out new expressions. They mix different constructions (e.g. *quite a very difficult one*); they use the wrong prepositions (e.g. *I'm bored at shopping*); put weak endings on strong verbs (e.g. *tooken* instead of *taken*). They may still be making mistakes like these at the age of ten or eleven, but the mistakes get fewer all the time and from the fifth year onwards, the most noticeable feature of children's speech is its increasing fluency. By the age of four and a half most children are composing quite sophisticated complex sentences with the help of subordinating conjunctions such as *if, what, when, because, that, where, before, after* and *while*. (*Since* doesn't come till the sixth year.) Listen to their talk, however, and you will find very few of the other connecting words and phrases that oil the wheels of adult conversation, and make the transition from sentence to sentence sound easy and natural: *well, for instance, like, say, instead, anyhow, at least, maybe, perhaps, probably, anyway, actually, unfortunately, for example, believe it or not, you know, I mean, I'm afraid, also, of course, well anyhow, at any rate, though, however, really,* and so on.

Only when they begin to use words like these to link their sentences into a continuous sequence will children's speech begin to sound like that of adults.

Talking point

> In the two following versions of the same conversation:
>
> **1** pick out the linking words that make the conversation run fluently and smoothly.
>
> **2** which is more like ordinary friendly conversation: (a), with linking words left in, or (b), with them all taken out?
>
> **a** Actually, I was thinking of buying a statue for the end of the garden. You know, about five feet high. They're expensive, I'm afraid, but they make a good focal point. Anyway, I'm going to see what I can find.
>
> **b** I was thinking of buying a statue for the end of the garden. About five feet high. They're expensive but they make a good focal point. I'm going to see what I can find.

No such linking words are found in the conversation of most four-, five-, and six-year-olds. One survey cited by Crystal found linking words beginning in year seven and increasing in number after the age of eight, but even twelve-year-old children used far fewer of these words than adults, and the words they did use were still simple: *now, then, so, anyway, though,* and *really.*

The distinguishing marker, then, between adult and childish speech is not the ability to talk fluently – five-year-olds are fluent talkers – but the ability to form sentences into smoothly-flowing, natural-sounding sequences with the help of a wide range of linking words.

Activity

Below are extracts in chronological order from the conversation of speakers of various ages, taken from Crystal, *Listen to Your Child*.

Point out the features that make their speech characteristic of their different age groups.

3 months
Michael: (*loud crying*)
Mother: Oh my word! What a noise! What a noise! (*Picks up Michael.*)
Michael: (*sobs*)
Mother: Oh dear, dear, dear! Didn't anybody come to see you? Let's have a look at you. (*Looks inside nappy.*) No, you're all right there, aren't you?
Michael: (*spluttering noises*)
Mother: Well, what is it, then? Are you hungry, is that it? Is it a long time since dinner-time?
Michael: (*gurgles and smiles*)

18 months
Child (*at breakfast table*): Bun. Butter. Jelly. Cakie. Jam.

21 months
Child (*coming in from garden*): Daddy-knee.
Mother: What's that, darling? What about daddy's knee?
Child: Fall-down daddy.
Mother: Did he? Where did he fall down?
Child: In-garden fall-down.
Mother: Daddy's fallen down in the garden! Poor daddy. Is he all right?
Child: Daddy-knee sore.
Mother: Daddy's fallen over and his knee's sore? I'd better come and see, hadn't I?

28 months
Child: Me want – Look! Balls. You like those balls?
Mother: Yes.
Child: Ball. Kick. Kick. Daddy kick.
Mother: That's right, you have to kick it, don't you?
Child: Mmm. Um. Um. Kick hard. Only kick hard . . . Our play that. On floor. Our play that on floor. Now. Our play that. On floor. Our play that on floor. Now. Our play that. On floor. No that. Now.
Mother: All right.
Child: Mummy, come on floor me.

3 years
Child: Hester be fast asleep, mummy.
Mother: She was tired.
Child: And why did her have two sweets, mummy?
Mother: Because you each had two, that's why. She had the same as you. Ooh dear, now what?
Child: Daddy didn't give me two in the end.
Mother: Yes, he did.

Child: He didn't.
Mother: He did.
Child: Look, he given one to – two to Hester, and two to us.
Mother: Yes, that's right.
Child: Why did he give?
Mother: Because there were six sweets. That's two each.

4 years 7 months

Susie: Oh, look, a crab. We seen – we were been to the seaside.
Baby-sitter: Have you?
Susie: We saw cr-fishes and crabs. And we saw a jelly-fish, and we had
    to bury it. And we – we did holding crabs, and we – we holded him
    in by the spade.
Baby-sitter: Did you?
Susie: Yes, to kill them, so they won't bite our feet.
Baby-sitter: Oh.
Susie: If you stand on them, they hurt you, won't they?
Baby-sitter: They would do. They'd pinch you.
Susie: You'd have to – and we put them under the sand, where the sea
    was. And they were going to the sea.
Susie: And we saw some shells. And we picked them up, and we heard
    the sea in them. And we saw a crab on a lid. And we saw lots of
    crabs on the sea-side. And I picked the – fishes up – no, the shells,
    and the feathers from the birds. And I saw a pig.

5 years 6 months

Dad: What do you want to play, then?
Lucy: I'll be the waitress and you have to eat in my shop. You come in,
    and sit down, and I can come and see you.
(*Dad acts his part obediently. Lucy walks over, clutching an imaginary
    notebook and pencil.*)
Lucy: Good afternoon.
Dad: Good afternoon.
Lucy: What do you want to eat?
Dad: Ooh, I'd like some cornflakes, and some sausages, please.
Lucy: We haven't got any sausages.
Dad: Oh dear. Well, let me see . . . Have you got any steak?
Lucy: Yes. We got steak.
Dad: I'll have some steak, then.
Lucy: O.K. 'Bye.

(The next two extracts are descriptive accounts rather than
conversation.)

9 years

At tennis, we learn different strokes each time, and then afterwards we
play games. When we get there, our teacher warms us up and gives us
a little game to play. Then she puts us into partners and she tells us the
strokes to do. The strokes I've been told are lob, smash, forehand,
backhand, slice, and serve, and there's several serves. The tennis is quite

> near, so it's not very long to walk back. The teacher understands me, and understands the way I think about tennis, and I think that tennis is fun and exciting.
>
> **12 years**
> The next two days were the weekend, which we spent with our French families, and on the Sunday we were going to a fair, and I was feeling very ill. I don't know why, perhaps it was the water or something, or food, or something I'd eaten, perhaps just heat stroke. Anyway, so we were all supposed to be going to a fair, and we went to the fair and it turned out that it had all packed up and we were far too late.

Children's brains are programmed to speak, but not to write, and fluent speakers take far longer to become properly fluent writers. When writing about things that have happened to them personally, even eleven-year-olds write in much the same style as children of seven speak: in short, declarative sentences strung together with *and*, *so*, and *and then*. Witness the following examples:

a

> Today it's my birthday and I had a spiaragrath and a airfix Bumper Books and I played with my spiaragrath and when daddy brought me to school hes going back and his going to play with my spiaragrath and today Gary is coming to tea and we will play subuiteo and football and with my spiaragrath and we might have a game at table soccer and Gary will have to go at about 8 o'clock and I will go and help him cary his things then I will go home and go to bed.
>
> David, aged 7

b

> Dear Mrs Smith,
> My monster is late because I did not finish it in English and I only had a cuple of lines to do and I finished it off in geography so my house tutor mister mordred taw it up and I had to take it home and do it. I hope you like it from Stephen Tolley yours faithily.
>
> Stephen, aged 11
>
> Quoted in Jones and Mulford, *Children Using Language*

Notice that the writers of these pieces describe the events:

* in the order in which they occurred;
* in short, blunt, declarative statements.

In (a) there is no logical connection between the events, and only the continuous use of *and* binds them together into some sort of whole. Older, more sophisticated writers might single out one event as more important or interesting than the others and deal with it first, going back to describe earlier ones later on. They might also put in the kind of asides and linking phrases that would express their feelings about the events – *I had to go in to get my tea then, unfortunately*. This writer is writing simply as he speaks, and all the things that might make the accounts more interesting if they were heard rather than read – changes of intonation, stress, and rhythm – are of course missing.

When asked to write about things outside themselves, nine- and eleven-year-olds use fewer conjunctions. This makes the writing sound more controlled, but at the same time rather monotonous and clipped:

a   On Thursday we went to have a look round the Tithe Barn. We went through the woods and we saw a grey squirrel which jumped from a branch to a very thick branch. The trees were not all out, but the flowers were. The Tithe Barn is on Cupfield Hall Farm. The outside of the barn is made of flint and stone, and the tiles are very uneven. A lot of the barn is the arridginal material. At the tops of the roof there were nests, the tiles had moss and grass growing on them. There were holes in the roof. It was very dark in there.
Mary, aged 9

b   What kind of world is a fish world? Imagine living in water all the time. There are many kinds of insect that crawl about the weeds and mud. Many are unearthly like creatures. Illustrated opposite is a caddis larvae made up of bits and bobs such as sticks and stones. Also there is the water scorpion which kills its enemys. First it kills them and then sucks out all the juices. Fish are streamlined for swimming. They breath by swallowing water and extracting the oxygen from the water and pushing it out through his gills.
Neil, aged 11

from Jones and Mulford, *Children Using Language*

This last piece does have a coherent logical structure – that of question and answer. Again, however, the techniques that more sophisticated writers use to weave clauses into longer, smoother sentences – subordinate clauses and linking words – are largely missing. For something much closer to adult writing, see the account written by a fourteen-year-old, below.

School trip to the South of France

After an exhausting eighteen hour journey by coach and ferry we arrived at Marseilles to meet the families we were going to stay with for the rest of the week. We were all called off the coach in pairs to be greeted by our very enthusiastic French families. We were kissed on the cheek twice by each person, a strange, but friendly experience! Despite the frenzied last minute practice of our French on the coach we found that, at first, all we could say was oui or non. However, over the next few days our French improved, especially when we realized we needed it to survive. The next day we set off early to the Camargue and St Marie de la Mer. At the Camargue, the landscape was very flat, marshy, and rather boring, until we spotted a group of pink flamingoes! Later on during the journey we saw herds of wild black bulls and the occasional white horse. In St Marie de la Mer we visited Arles and looked around two old Roman bull fighting rings, where bull fighting still sometimes continues.

Activity | Rewrite (a) above in a more sophisticated prose style. Make any alterations you see fit.

Accent and dialect

Key words | *Regional dialect*: a variety of English distinguished by its own characteristic features of vocabulary and grammar, spoken in a particular geographical region.

Standard English: the dialect (i.e. the vocabulary and grammar) used by well-educated people throughout the British Isles.

Ideolect: the linguistic system of an individual speaker (i.e. the speech habits peculiar to an individual speaker) within a particular dialect.

Regional accent: a variety of pronunciation peculiar to people who live in a particular geographical region.

Received pronunciation: a variety of pronunciation used by a small number of people throughout the British Isles who constitute a social elite.

Differences between accent and dialect

The first thing to note is that *dialect* and *accent* refer to distinctly different things. *Dialect* is the term used to describe the different kinds of vocabulary and grammar used by different groups of speakers. *Accent* refers to the way in which they pronounce words.

Thus, if you compared non-standard forms of the past tense like *I seen* and *I done* with the standard forms *I saw* and *I did*, you would be discussing *dialect*. If you compared the Lincolnshire word *frit* with its southern English counterpart *frightened* you would also be discussing dialect. But if you compared the way in which people in east London pronounce *things* (*fings*) and *well* (wɛʊ) with RP versions of the same words, you'd be talking about *accent*.

Regional dialects and Standard English

The second thing to note is the difference between *regional dialects* and the dialect known as *Standard English*. This is the dialect used by educated people throughout the country, whether they speak with a regional accent or not. It is the dialect in which all official documents, textbooks, instruction manuals, 'quality' newspapers and magazines are written, and the dialect that children are taught to use in school. It is also the form of English taught to foreigners, and therefore a model for English users world-wide.

Since Standard English is the written norm, we tend to think of regional dialects as deviations from it. In fact, each dialect has a stable grammar of its own, derived from the dialect of the Germanic tribe that originally settled the region in which that dialect is used.

Map, after Bourcier, from Lass, *The Shape of English*

What seem to be 'errors' when measured against Standard English may actually be usages unaltered since Anglo-Saxon times. Double negatives, for instance, such as 'I haven't got no time', are actually relics of Old English. It used to put a negating particle *ne* in front of the verb, and an intensifying word *noht* after it, in effect, saying the same thing twice, e.g.:

And ne bið ðǣr nænig ealo gebrowen mid Estum, ac þær bið medo genoh.

Literally, 'There is not there no ale brewed amongst the Esthonians, but there is plenty of mead.'

What many people do not know is that Standard English itself started out as 'only' a regional dialect – that of Anglo-Saxon Mercia, the south-eastern part of England. Together with the accent in which it was pronounced – *Received Pronunciation* – it spread outwards from the south-east into all areas of the British Isles.

Activity

> Below are some non-standard dialect forms (from Hughes and Trudgill, *English Accents and Dialects*). Divide a page into two columns labelled *Non-Standard English* and *Standard English*. Write out the non-standard forms in the appropriate column, then fill in their Standard English equivalents:
>
> Being on me own had never entered me head.
> We was forever having arguments.
> I hadn't got nothing to fall back on.
> Go to the pub is it?
> Where's it by? Over by here.

Standard English itself is not completely uniform throughout the country. Trudgill and Hughes (*English Accents and Dialects*) have shown that variations exist between north and south, for example, in the use of contracted negative forms:

North	South
I've not got it	I haven't got it
She'll not go	She won't go
Does he not like it?	Doesn't he like it?

But if there are variations within Standard English itself, there are many more between Standard English and regional dialect forms. A check-list of these variations is given below for those who might wish to do project work in this area.

Checklist of regional dialect variations

You may find dialect speakers using one or more of the following non-standard features:

1 Double or triple negatives where SE uses only one: *I didn't have no money* (I didn't have any money/I had no money/I hadn't any money), *I couldn't get none nowhere* (I couldn't get any anywhere)

2 *Ain't* where SE has *aren't*: *I ain't going* (I'm not going), *I ain't seen him* (I haven't seen him), *she ain't got it* (she hasn't got it)

3 *I aren't* where SE has *I'm not*: *I aren't going* (I'm not going)

4 *No* or *nae* in Scottish dialects, where SE would use *not* or *no*: *he's no nice* (he isn't nice), *I've nae got time* (I haven't got time), *I cannae come* (I cannot come)

5 The past participle where SE would use the past tense: *I seen it last night* (I saw it last night), *I done it yesterday* (I did it yesterday)

6 *Never* used to make the past tense negative, where SE would have *not*: *she said she'd come, but she never* (she said she'd come, but she didn't), *You did it. No, I never.* (You did it. No, I didn't.)

7 Omission of SE *-s* from third person singular of present tense of verbs:* *she go to see her mother every day* (she goes to see her mother every day), *he work in Norwich* (he works in Norwich)

* Mostly found in East Anglian, Afro-Caribbean, and southern American dialects, but one example – *don't* for *doesn't* – is said to be common among English speakers, including the upper classes.

8   Addition of non-standard *-s* to all persons of the verb: *I likes it. We sings it. You plays it.* (I like it. We sing it. You play it.)

9   Different relative pronoun patterns from SE: *that's the house what I told you about* (that's the house that/which I told you about), *that's the house as I told you about* (that's the house that/which I told you about), *that's the woman which I told you about* (that's the woman who/that I told you about), *that's the man which/what his wife left him* (that's the man whose wife left him)

10   Possessive case (*hisself* and *theirselves*) in reflexive pronouns where SE uses the object case (*himself* and *themselves*): *he shot hisself* (he shot himself), *they blamed theirselves* (they blamed themselves)
(It is SE that seems to be illogical here. It uses *myself, yourself,* and *ourselves,* but doesn't carry it through consistently. Dialect users are simply making things consistent.)

11   Double comparatives and superlatives where SE uses single: *he's more nicer than her* (he's nicer than her), *she's the most kindest person I know* (she's the kindest person I know)

12   Subject or object case of personal pronoun *they* (they, them) where SE would use the demonstrative pronouns *those* and *these*: *I don't like them cigarettes* (I don't like those cigarettes), *look at they pictures* (look at these pictures)

13   Unmarked plurals where SE uses *-s* in plural nouns of weight and measure: *she earned a thousand pound* (she earned a thousand pounds), *the river is two mile wide* (the river is two miles wide), *the pond was three foot long* (the pond was three feet long)
(This is a usage coming down from Middle English. Old English said 'a thousand *of* pounds/two *of* miles' instead of the simpler modern versions above. The plural of the possessive case was *-a*: *punda, mila,* and when this ending was eroded in the Middle Ages, it left us with the dialect forms *mile* and *pound* instead of SE's plural marker, *-s*.)

14   Different preposition patterns from SE: *she lives at London* (she lives in London), *I'm going up the market* (I'm going to the market), *he got off of the bus outside Smiths* (he got off the bus outside Smiths), *I bought it off of him* (I bought it from him), *she was attacked with a man* (she was attacked by a man)

15   Different adverb patterns from SE: *wait here while the light goes green* (wait here till the light goes green), *he read the paper while she was ready* (he read the paper till she was ready)

16   Adjectives where SE uses adverbs:* *he says it too quick for me* (he says it too quickly for me), *she did the tea nice* (she did the tea nicely), *it was built good* (it was built well)

This is by no means a complete list. In parts of the north-west they use *hoo* and *shoo* instead of SE *she* (a hangover from Old English *heo*) whereas speakers in a broad band from Shropshire down through Wiltshire into

---

*   Although Standard English users would never do this in writing, they frequently use constructions like 'The car's running smoother now it's been serviced' in casual conversation.

Dorset, Somerset, and Devon prefer *her*, accompanied by uninflected *be*, as in *Her be a real good sort, her be. Thou* is still used in large areas of the North, with *thee* as a variant; areas of Yorkshire and Lincolnshire contract SE contractions even further (*isn't – int, doesn't – dunt*); Liverpool goes in the opposite direction and extends *you* into *yous*; Bradford uses *were* for all persons of the past tense of *to be* (*I/you/he/she/it were*); and Geordie has its own version of the SE forms *didn't, doesn't, don't: divn't*. The north also has many dialect words not understood south of the Wash: there, children *laik* instead of *bunk off* from school; they *go on messages* rather than *run errands*, get their *tabs rattled* (ears boxed) for *chelping* (cheeking) their parents. There, tea is *mashed*, sulky people are called *mardy* and asked to *get out of the road* (out of the way); *bairns greet* (babies cry), and *yes* and *no* are *aye* and *nay*, *anything* is *owt* and *nothing*, *nowt*.

In spite of the homogenizing effect of television, regional dialects are still going strong. I hope they never die out.

| **Activity** | Conduct a research project. Your aim is to collect data which will help you to assess the truth of the claim that people at the lower end of the social scale are more likely to use non-standard grammatical forms than those above them. Your method will be a questionnaire. |

1 Select a cross-section of your local community to respond to your questionnaire. Include young as well as old, male as well as female, from the following categories:

Social class	Typical occupations
1	people from the higher professions (solicitors, doctors, university lecturers, architects, accountants, lawyers)
2	people from the lower professional and technical class (managers of banks and other business organizations, middle managers, engineers, aircraft pilots, fire brigade officers, teachers, nurses)
3a	people from other non-manual occupations (bank clerks, sales reps, supervisors, and other white-collar workers)
3b	skilled manual workers who have gained qualifications through apprenticeships, City and Guilds examinations, etc.
4	semi-skilled workers (farm-workers, postal delivery staff, telephone operators, etc.)
5	unskilled manual workers (kitchen hands, driver's mates, hospital porters, window cleaners, labourers, etc.).

Adapted from Selfe, *Sociology*

I, 2, and 3a are generally considered to be the 'middle classes', and 3b, 4, and 5 the working classes.

2 Try to identify some of the non-standard dialect forms in your own locality.

3 Construct
  a sentences that contain these non-standard forms,
  b equivalent sentences containing Standard English forms.

4 Write out these pairs of sentences at the head of a questionnaire. Underneath, set out the following questions. Your respondents can tick the appropriate box to indicate their answers to these questions:

  ◈ Would you yourself use this sentence?   Yes   No
  ◈ Would any members of your family use this sentence?   Yes   No
  ◈ Would any of your close friends use this sentence?   Yes   No
  ◈ Do you know anybody who might use this sentence?   Yes   No

  In case none of these applies, you should also include the question:

  ◈ Who do you think might use this sentence?

5 Conduct your research.

6 Assess whether your results confirm or disprove the claim that the lower down the social scale you go, the more likely you are to find people using non-standard forms.

7 Assess whether your respondents claim different practices for themselves and for their friends. If they do, speculate on their motives.

Regional accents and received pronunciation

Prescriptivists believe that regional accents are sloppy deviations from the 'correct' standard of pronunciation – *Received Pronunciation*. It is truer to say that they are based on the pronunciation of Middle English in their particular area, or even, in some cases, of Anglo-Saxon. In my own area of south Lincolnshire, *mister* is pronounced *mester* – a clear link with the earlier long vowel, combining the *a* of *apple* and the *e* of *egg*, in Old English *mæster*.

Linguists usually distinguish four main dialects of Middle English: Northern, East Midland, West Midland, and Southern. The Northern extended as far south as the Humber; West Midland and East Midland (including London) between them occupied the area from the Humber to the Thames, while Southern covered the area south of the Thames, together with Gloucestershire and Hereford. Although Kent was included in this area, it always retained individual features of its own, making it a distinct variety of southern English.

The most obvious division in Britain today is between north and south, and differences in pronunciation between these two areas can be traced back to the different dialects of Middle English. Old English *a*, for example, remained unchanged in the North and persists today in the Scottish forms *stane* and *hame*. South of the Humber, however, it was modified into *o*, giving southern *stone* and *home*. (The Lowland Scots dialect actually springs from the early Northern Middle English of the twelfth century, Gaelic having retreated to the Highlands and Islands.)

Similarly, *f* and *s* at the beginning of words in the Northern dialect were often turned into *v* and *z* in the Southern, giving *vor*, *vrom*, *vox*, instead of *for*, *from*, and *fox*. This difference can be seen in Modern English *fox* and *vixen*, the former coming down from the Northern and Midland dialects, the latter from the Southern. These differences can be seen in the dialect poetry of the Dorsetshire poet, William Barnes, the first verse of one of whose poems is given below, and in the speeches of Edgar, disguised as a peasant, in *King Lear*. These also reveal the grammar of the Dorsetshire dialect, in which 'I will' is contracted to 'chill'; 'I shall' to 'ice':

Chill not let go, zi, without vurther cagion.
Ice try wither your costard or my ballow be the harder.

The wife a-lost

Since I noo mwore do zee your feäce,
Up steärs or down below,
I'll zit me in the lwonesome pleäce,
Where flat-bough'd beech do grow;
Below the beeches' bough, my love,
Where you did never come,
An' I don't look to meet ye now,
As I do look at hwome.

William Barnes

Sometimes, variant forms of the same word occur in different dialects, one deriving from Old English, one from Scandinavian. *Ch*, for example, in the Southern dialect often corresponds to a *k* in the Northern, giving *bench/benk*; *church/kirk*.

On the other hand, Received Pronunciation (or RP) is the accent used by a small elite (somewhere between five and three per cent of the population). A random sample of the population of the city of Norwich, for example, produced one RP speaker out of sixty people interviewed. In contrast, a massive eighty per cent of the population speak with regional accents of varying degrees of strength, whilst the remainder speak some form of modified RP.

Activity

Go out into the major shopping centre/precinct of your locality and take a random sample of sixty passers-by. Assess the percentage that falls into the following categories:
⁕ pure RP speakers;
⁕ modified RP speakers;
⁕ speakers with regional accents.

RP is the voice of the upper classes, of authority and of power. It is used by Brigadiers and Generals, by judges and barristers, and by those who read the national news on radio and television. All accents, like all dialects, are the products of particular regions, and RP was originally the regional accent of the south-east of England – the Mercia of Anglo-Saxon times. When wealth, power, and culture became concentrated in the south-east (it had the port of London, the Court, and the universities of Oxford and Cambridge), the accent and dialect of the region came to be associated with these things. They suggested power, culture, and wealth. From the 1300s onwards, therefore, people with social ambition learned to speak in the style of the south-east, just as in the 1100s they had had to learn French. Two further factors then helped to spread RP and SE more widely:

1 the setting up of public schools in the south-eastern region in Victorian times. These took in boys from all over the country and sent them home speaking with a standardized accent that became the mark of the middle class.

2 the establishment of the British Broadcasting Company in 1927. Director-general John Reith set his organization the task of achieving 'the very best thing we could do' in both speech and writing, which in effect meant the use of immaculate SE and RP in all 'serious' programmes and the banishing of regional accents to the more trivial area of comedy shows. The experiment of having the news read in a Yorkshire accent by Wilfred Pickles during the Second World War outraged many listeners, and even as recently as 1987 an announcer with a Highland Scots accent was moved from the news-desk because some listeners complained that they couldn't understand a word she said.

Thanks to these two factors, McCrum remarks, Standard English and RP became '. . . the voice of the officer, administrative, and consular class throughout the Empire – the voice of authority.'

It became detached from the region which bred it and became instead the badge of a particular social class. No one can tell which part of the country an RP speaker comes from simply by listening to his or her voice, whereas most of us can recognize speakers from such regions as Birmingham, Newcastle, and Liverpool.

Talking point

1 The Lairds of many famous Scottish clans still live on estates that their ancestors have held for centuries. They claim to be Scottish to the core, yet they have no trace of a Scottish accent. Why?

2 Read the following poem, then explain why
   a listeners with RP accents and
   b listeners with regional accents
   react against having the news read in a regional accent such as that of Glasgow, below.

3 Discuss how Leonard manages to get across
   a what he sees as the arrogance of the RP speaker, and
   b his own feelings of resentment in reaction to it.

This is thi
six a clock
news thi
man said n
thi reason
a talk wia
BBC accent
is coz yi
widny wahnt
mi ti talk
aboot thi
trooth wia
voice lik
wanna yoo
scruff. if
a toktaboot
thi trooth
lik wanna yoo
scruff yi
widny thingk
it wuz troo.
jist wanna yoo
scruff tokn.
thirza right
way ti spell
ana right way
ti tok it. this
is me tokn yir
right way a
spellin. this
is ma trooth.
yoouz doant no
thi trooth
yirsellz cawz
yi canny talk
right. this is
the six a clock
nyooz. belt up.

Tom Leonard

That, broadly speaking, is the way in which prestige and social status came to be built into the pronunciation of the English language. Standard English and Received Pronunciation, once the dialect and accent of a particular region, are now enshrined as models of correctness for the whole nation.

Standard English and received pronunciation

The terms *Standard English* and *Received Pronunciation* are often confused with each other, perhaps because the use of Received Pronunciation almost always implies the use of Standard English. It would be strange indeed to hear someone speaking in a regional dialect using the sounds of Received Pronunciation – try saying 'Just walk up the streets and you'm out of Dudley' (the dialect of the Birmingham area) in the RP accent of a radio or television news-reader and it will sound ridiculous. Standard English, on the other hand, is spoken by many educated people whose voices reveal traces of the accent of the region in which they were brought up. Their accent is said to be a modified form of RP. One well known Professor of Linguistics speaks with a largely RP accent but still uses the flat 'a' vowels of his northern county, saying *bath*, *laff*, *path* instead of *barth*, *larf*, and *parth*. He sees no reason to change his accent any further in the direction of RP, but he does, like almost all well-educated people, use Standard English on all formal occasions.

Prescriptivists, who spend most of their time worrying about 'correctness', teach that regional dialects are inferior to Standard English. (Do they know that Standard English was itself originally 'only' a dialect?) This is largely because standards of correctness in our society are set by the written language, and most important writing uses Standard English vocabulary and grammar. (I know that many novels and plays contain characters who speak regional dialect with regional accents, and that Robert Burns and William Barnes wrote their best poetry in dialect – Barnes even put in marks to show how it should be pronounced in the Dorset accent – but for the most part novels are written in Standard English, and so is most poetry. There is very little important dialect writing in English.)

Even prescriptivists, however, if pushed, would have to admit that regional dialects add pungency and force to the language, and that the world would be blander and less interesting without them.

Talking point

> 1 Are speakers who use only Received Pronunciation likely to use regional dialect forms?
>
> 2 Do regional dialect users ever use full Received Pronunciation?
>
> 3 Do regular Standard English users ever have regional accents?
>
> 4 In the film musical *My Fair Lady*, Eliza, exquisitely dressed and using the purest RP, is made to say, 'It's my belief she done him in'. Explain why this is funny.

Dialect, accent, and social prestige

As George Bernard Shaw observed in *Pygmalion* in 1912, the moment an Englishman opens his mouth, some other Englishman begins to despise him. From the early 1900s until well into the 1950s, Received

Pronunciation was the badge of entry into middle and upper-class society. Listen to news bulletins from those days and you will hear a very formal, precise, and clipped English pronunciation, with the vowel *a*, for example, as in *that*, flattened to something closer to *e*: *thet*. Formality of speech was matched by formality of dress: announcers had to wear evening dress to read the news – even on the radio!

Things have changed a lot since then, thanks to the influence of American media stars with transatlantic accents, English working-class anti-heroes in books, plays, and films, and television personalities, chat-show hosts, and comedians speaking with accents as diverse as southern and northern Irish, Scots, Geordie, Scouse, and London. In media circles, RP stopped being king in the late 1950s. Regional accent and dialect were 'in', RP speakers 'out' – seen as either pompous, camp, or phony. Some people have taken the reaction against RP to such extremes that they show a kind of inverted snobbery. One well-known violinist, for example, has swapped his natural RP for the accent and dialect of a London street-market trader (Cheers, Nige). Even the younger Royals – Andrew and Edward and Diana – have 'ordinary' accents, very different from the *affected RP* of the Queen. (This is probably due partly to the media stars they mix with, partly to their need to play down their social status in a modern democratic state.) Outside media circles, however, Britain is still a remarkably snobbish country, and people are still frequently judged on the way in which they speak.

Some people argue that the link between accent, dialect, and social status is weakening, pointing out that Dukes have been heard to speak of 'flogging their Canalettos', like any barrow-boy. Others argue that they persist in all social circles, and that the key to prestige and social success is still smart clothes and a 'good' (i.e. as close to RP as possible) accent. (A television documentary in the 1980s revealed how a candidate for the Foreign Office was selected on the basis that 'with that voice, anyone would believe anything she said'. Her rival for the post clearly knew far more, but spoke RP flavoured with flat northern vowel sounds.) This idea is supported by Canadian research into the way in which people evaluate various dialects:

> . . . we know that there may be three 'rewards' for the speaker who upgrades his accent one or two notches towards his partner. These are: (i) an increase in perceived status; (ii) an increase in perceived favourability of personality (i.e. they like him more); and (iii) an increase in the perceived quality and persuasiveness of the content of the message (he seems more convincing).
>
> Howard Giles, *New Society*

The process of upgrading your accent to match that of the person you are talking to is *upward divergence of accent*. The opposite process, by which RP speakers might deliberately coarsen their accents to show friendship or the desire to make their interlocutor feel more comfortable, is known as *downward divergence*.

Accent, dialect, gender, and social class

Research seems to suggest that:

a   Men and women have slightly different attitudes towards the use of dialect forms and regional accents; women (perhaps because they have been trained by social pressure to conform to standard norms?) tend to seek what is called *overt prestige*, that is, prestige that fits in with socially approved norms of behaviour. On the other hand men, or at least men from the three bottom social classes, prefer *covert prestige*: the sort of respect and admiration of their peer group for standing out against those very ideals of respectability and good behaviour so important to their girlfriends and wives.

b   This difference shows itself more clearly at the border-line between upper working-class and lower middle-class – the point where those at the bottom of the lower middle-class have the least to lose, and those at the top of the upper working-class have the most to gain, in terms of social success. Both gender and social class, therefore, help to determine how people speak.

Activity

Devise some research of your own into attitudes towards language.

1   How could you discover whether people in your neighbourhood were self-conscious about using such words as *toilet* and *serviette*? A questionnaire? If so, would you ask only about specific words, or ask an open question such as, *Are there any words that you as parents would not like your children to use?/Are there any words that your parents do not like you to use (excluding swear words)?* (Before you start you might find it useful to read the short chapter on language – eighteen very small pages – in *Debrett's U and Non-U Revisited*, ed. Buckle, The Viking Press, New York.)

2   It is a well-known fact that some people assume a 'posh' accent when they answer the telephone. Ask a cross-section of people
    a   if they do this,
    b   why?
    Analyse and discuss your results.

3   How could you discover whether non-RP speakers upgrade their accent to match that of someone who speaks 'better'? Could the telephone help you here? Could you set up some kind of experimental situation in which you involve an RP speaker in conversation with someone with a 'less good' accent? Would observation of real-life situations serve your purpose better? Where might you find two such people interacting? A student talking to a Head Teacher or Principal? A customer asking for information in a very smart shop? Someone asking for a loan from a Bank Manager? (Students can get all kinds of help, including overdrafts, now. Take one of your friends, without telling them what you're up to, and see what happens.)

4 Check people's reactions to accent by getting two speakers to give the same short talk to a group who have no idea what you are trying to discover. Try to make your two speakers look and dress very much alike, but get one to speak in an accent as close to RP as possible, and the other in some kind of regional or urban dialect. Afterwards, ask the group which speaker struck them as being:

- more intelligent;
- more self-confident;
- more ambitious;
- more hard-working;
- more determined;

(assumptions usually made about RP speakers on the basis of their accent alone)

- more honest;
- more sincere;
- more friendly and warm;
- more likely to have a good sense of humour;
- more likely to make a good friend.

(assumptions usually made about regional dialect speakers on the basis of their accent alone)

5 Check whether people adapt their accent to fit formal and informal contexts by performing either or both of the following experiments:

Experiment A

1 Set up a small discussion group (four or five people) and either record it if possible, or make notes on the kinds of vocabulary and grammar used.

2 Introduce a tutor, counsellor, or other older person into the discussion to lift it on to a more formal plane. Again, record or make notes.

3 Assess whether any of the speakers changed their accent, grammar, and idiom in the second session.

Experiment B

1 Identify some of the non-standard (i.e. non RP) features of your local accent. (Hughes and Trudgill give thorough check-lists of all the major English accents and dialects if you need help with this.)

2 Set up a group of as many people as you think you can handle from the following social classes:
- Upper middle class
- Lower middle class
- Upper working class
- Middle working class
- Lower working class.

Ask them one by one to perform the following tasks, and record or make notes on each.

a Read out a list of words (a page from a dictionary will do) (WLS).

b Read out a passage from a book (RPS).

c Respond to some questions put to them in formal interview style (FS).

d Talk casually with the others involved in the experiment on the question of accents (CS).

Key: WLS = Word-List Style; RPS = Reading-Passage Style; FS = Formal Style; CS = Casual Style.

3 Analyse your results. You should find that accent and grammar diverge more noticeably from SE and RP standards the more relaxed and less formal the situation and task become.

4 Assess whether there was any noticeable difference between the accent and grammar of males and females in your group in any of the different styles.

6 a Read the advertisement for Trophy beer on page 153, then draw character sketches of
  ◈ the dialect speaker,
  ◈ the user of SE and RP
  as they seem to you.

b Assess how far their portrayed accent and dialect have influenced your opinions of each kind of speaker.

Talking point

In the light of what you have just read, which of the following attitudes seems to you to be the most sensible:

a Since Received Pronunciation is the most prestigious accent and Standard English has the most correct vocabulary and grammar, all children should be taught to use them all the time, regardless of their family background and the region where they live.

b Since Received Pronunciation and Standard English are really only dialects themselves, we should teach children who don't already use them to ignore them and carry on speaking in their own way.

c Since Received Pronunciation and Standard English are the forms of language that everyone is likely to meet in formal situations, children should be taught to use them so that they can be self-confident in such contexts. We should teach them to use different styles of speech for different audiences in the same way that we teach them to use different written registers for different readers.

d We should teach all children to write 'correctly' in Standard English, because this will help them to pass exams and to please employers, but we should leave their accents alone. The way you speak is a part of your personality, and as long as you're using Standard English, nobody will worry about your accent.

Bristol barmaid sings praises of locally-brewed Whitbread Trophy bitter:

"Nuthin' can touch moy lovely Bristol Bigheads fer flavour, natsa fact."

Whitbread 'Bighead' Trophy Bitter.
Brewed to understand the local tongue.

Trophy is brewed by local Whitbread breweries in Blackburn, Cardiff, Castle Eden, Cheltenham, Faversham, Kirkstall, Liverpool, Luton, Marlow, Portsmouth, Rhymney, Romsey, Salford, Samlesbury, Sheffield and Tiverton.

Translation:

("I firmly believe that the Trophy bitter brewed for the Bristol area has a taste superior to that brewed elsewhere.")

"Strewy nuff to say that every drarp a-Big'ead oi'm a-servin' 'ere's a-brewed special fer th'West Vingland."

(All Trophy 'Bighead' bitter sold in Bristol has, in fact, been brewed in and especially for the West of England.)

"An' we're much 'bliged ta Whitbread, thassall oi can say, a-coz wee 'preciate people 'oo 'preciates our e-fined tastes."

(Whitbread's policy of brewing Trophy to suit local tastes pleases us greatly. Peoples' tastes do vary from area to area, you know.)

"Aft trawl, snice to know yer understud."

(Whitbread's sensitivity in this delicate matter is touching, don't you think?)

"S'warm in 'ere, innit, wine chew get stuck inter one o'moy lovely Bristols?"

(But enough of this careless chatter. Allow me to pull for you a pint of our own local Trophy brew.)

The sounds of English

Look again at the Trophy advertisements and the Tom Leonard poem you met earlier and you'll see that combinations of ordinary letters can give you quite a good impression of the way regional speakers pronounce their words. A more exact method, however, is to use the symbols of the *International Phonetic Alphabet* (the IPA). These are based on the vowel and consonant sounds of Received Pronunciation, and give us a fixed standard against which the varying pronunciations of regional speakers can be assessed. In the columns below you will find

1   the individual symbols of the IPA,
2   a sample word in which RP speakers use the sound represented by that symbol,
3   the phonetic transcription of that word (i.e. the writing out of the word using phonetic symbols instead of ordinary letters).

Phonetic transcriptions, whether of single symbols or whole words, are always contained within two oblique lines. This indicates that the sounds represented by the phonetic symbols refer to the sounds of an actual language. Phonetic symbols enclosed within square brackets represent sounds in the abstract, not attached to a particular language.

Although they look very strange and intimidating at first, phonetic symbols have two advantages over ordinary spelling:

1   they don't change from word to word, as many ordinary letters do. In RP, *u*, for instance, is pronounced one way in *but*, another in *put*; however, the phonetic symbol for the sound in *but* is always the same: /ʌ/.
2   the phonetic spelling of a word is shorter and simpler than the ordinary spelling: *beach*, for example, uses five letters, but only three phonetic symbols: /bitʃ/.

Don't try to learn by heart all the phonetic symbols given below. Just go through them slowly and carefully, listening to the different sounds each makes. If you then do a little practice on each category in turn, starting with vowels, phonetic symbols will soon become familiar to you and you'll stop being frightened.

Single vowels

i as in RP	bead	/bid/		ɔ	board	/bɔd/
ɪ	bid	/bɪd/		ʊ	put	/pʊt/
e	bed	/bed/		u	shoe	/ʃu/
æ	bad	/bæd/		ʌ	cup	/kʌp/
ɑ	bard	/bɑd/		ɜ	bird	/bɜd/
ɒ	cod	/kɒd/		ə	about, porter	/əbaʊt/, /pɔtə/

Note: the one very common vowel sound that is not represented on its own in the table is the one that looks like an upside-down *e*: /ə/. This is a sort of all-purpose sound found in words like *another* (/ənəðə/), and the many different words that end in *ent* or *ant*: /prezənt/, /kleimənt/. It is called *schwa.*

Activity

> Copy out the following paragraph, replacing all the ordinary vowel letters – a, e, i, o, u – with phonetic symbols that represent the way the words would be spoken by an RP speaker. You will find that some symbols – ɑ and ɔ, for example – cut down the number of letters in the word by sounding like a vowel and consonant combined: *r* isn't needed in words like *yard* and *sort*.
>
> Whenever Willy was in trouble his thoughts turned towards planting seeds in his back yard. He resented his boss, was fed up with his work, and sad that Biff, his son, was just bumming along instead of planning ahead. For Willy, true success meant earning hundreds of dollars and winning respect from other men.

Not all the vowel sounds of RP can be represented by single vowels, however. When writing the paragraph above, for instance, I couldn't use words like *out*, *around*, *thousands*, and *go*, because the sounds in these words are made up of *combinations* of vowels, called *diphthongs*. Say 'go' aloud and you will hear your voice glide from the neutral *schwa* sound to the more rounded vowel represented by /ʊ/.

Key words

> *Diphthong*: two vowel sounds combining to produce one syllable of a word; during the pronunciation of the syllable the tongue moves from one position to another, causing a continual change in vowel quality: as for instance in the pronunciation of the syllable *a* in *late* during which the tongue moves from the position of *e* towards that of *i*.
>
> A *triphthong* combines three vowels sounds to form one syllable; e.g. fire (/faɪə/).

The full list of diphthongs is given below. Look carefully at each one, pronounce them, then do the practice suggested.

Diphthongs

eɪ	**pay**	/peɪ/		aʊ	**hound**	/haʊnd/
aɪ	**pie**	/paɪ/		ɪə	**beer**	/bɪə/
ɔɪ	**boy**	/bɔɪ/		ɛə	**bear**	/bɛə/
əʊ	**go**	/gəʊ/		ʊə	**cure**	/kjʊə/

Activity

> Write out the following paragraph, representing *all* vowels and diphthongs with phonetic symbols.
>
> Lynda did not know what to say to her husband. She sighed and took up her darning. If only Biff would stop his bumming around and settle down. Willy would be happy then, it would give him something to cheer about. He cared so much for Biff, and she could not bear to watch his slow drift towards death. It was pure torment to her.

Finally, look at the list of consonants. Apart from the fact that there are two different symbols for the two different sounds of *th*, these are quite straightforward and should give you little difficulty.

Consonants

p	**p**it	/pɪt/	ʃ	**sh**oe	/ʃu/
b	**b**i	/bɪt/	ʒ	mea**s**ure	/meʃə/
t	**t**ip	/tɪp/	h	**h**ot	/hɒt/
d	**d**id	/dɪd/	tʃ	**ch**arge	/tʃɑdʒ/
k	**k**ick	/kɪk/	dʒ	**g**in	/dʒɪn/
g	**g**ive	/gɪv/	m	**m**ouse	/maʊs/
f	**f**ive	/faɪv/	n	**n**ice	/naɪs/
v	**v**ine	/vaɪn/	ŋ	si**ng**	/sɪŋ/
θ	**th**umb	/θʌm/	l	**l**eaf	/lif/
ð	**th**is	/ðɪs/	r	**r**un	/rʌn/
s	**s**ome	/sʌm/	j	**y**acht	/jɒt/
z	**z**oo	/zu/	w	**w**et	/wet/

Activity

> Complete your practice of phonetic transcription by adding the symbols for consonants to the paragraphs about Willy and Lynda Loman. You will end up with something that looks like a foreign language.

There is just one other symbol to notice: the *glottal stop*: ʔ. This represents not a consonant, but a sound used instead of a consonant. Where RP speakers pronounce /t/ in the middle of a word like *butter*, for example, some non-RP speakers produce a sound at the back of the throat by closing the space between the vocal cords. Try producing it yourself:

1 say the word *letter*, taking care to pronounce the /t/; notice how it is produced at the front of the mouth, with your tongue high on the ridge above your teeth on /l/, and on the top of the teeth themselves on /t/;
2 now say the word again, being careful to keep your tongue away from your teeth; you will feel the movement in your throat that produces the *glottal stop*, and will find your tongue ending up below your bottom teeth.

The sounds of RP

There are variations of pronunciation within RP. At the top of the continuum is the most exaggerated form, *affected RP*. This is practised not only by the Queen and old-fashioned members of the aristocracy, but also by members of the upper middle-class who are very conscious of their dignity and importance. The connoisseur and art critic, Brian Sewell, often to be heard on Radio 4's *Loose Ends*, speaks a form of RP that can only be described as exquisite.

The Queen herself has moderated her accent only slightly to suit the informality of the times. Her pronunciation differs enormously from that of most of her subjects, /æ/, for example, being closer to /e/ in words like *that*.

Lower down the social scale, changes are taking place between the pronunciation of older, more conservative users of Received Pronunciation and younger, trendier ones.

One tendency is for younger speakers to turn diphthongs and triphthongs into monophthongs. Where older speakers have /ʃiə/ for *fire*, younger ones have /ʃɑː/. As a result, the distinction between the pronunciation of words such as *paw*, *pore*, and *poor* is being lost.

According to Trudgill and Hughes, this is particularly true of the single word *our*, which many young RP and non RP speakers now pronounce /ɑː/. (This is having the secondary effect of causing students to misspell *our* as *are*.) For some unknown reason, /a/ remains untouched in other words such as *hour* and *flower*.

Despite these variations, however, most RP speakers sound fairly similar in style and give little or no indication of what part of the country they come from. It is when we listen to regional speakers that the real differences are heard.

◼ifferences between RP and regional accents

The most obvious difference between the accents of north and south, for instance, involves the following two letters. Both are pronounced short in the north but long in London and the Home Counties.

1 *-a* as in *chaff*

North	South
/æ/	/ɑ/

Words containing *-a* that are pronounced differently include:

> path, laugh, grass, dance, grant, demand, plant, branch, example

Words containing *-a* that are pronounced the same include:

> gaff, raffle, gas, lass, maths, ass, mass, chassis, pant, romance, band, camp, shambles

Words containing *-a* that can be pronounced either way include:
> plastic, transport

Note: speakers with strong south-western accents either do not distinguish between long and short -*a*, or do it inconsistently. The Welsh use long -*a* in some words, e.g. *grarse*, but not in others, e.g. *dance*; the Scots and the Irish do not use long -*a* at all, unless imitating RP in the search for higher social status.

2   -*u* as in *bun, put*

In the south, this has two distinct forms, represented by the phonetic symbols /ʌ/ and /ʊ/. In the north, /ʊ/ only is used most of the time. This means that while southern speakers can distinguish between pairs of words like *put* and *putt*, northern speakers cannot.

North	South
/pʊt/	/pʊt/
/pʊtt/	/pʌtt/
/cʊd/	/cʊd/
/cʊd/	/cʌd/

Some older northern speakers, however, use a further -*u* sound never found in RP: /uː/. This allows them to distinguish between /uː/ and /ʊ/ in such pairs as book (/buːk/) and buck (/bʊk/), pronounced in the south as /bʊk/ and /bʌk/.

Activity

> 1 Look for characters with a London accent in TV programmes such as *Birds of a Feather*, *Minder*, or *Only Fools and Horses*, and listen to the way they pronounce the words *no* and *poor*. What vowel sounds can you find in them?
>
> 2 Now try to describe the sounds, using symbols from the table on pages 154–156.
>
> 3 Sometimes an RP diphthong is changed into a single other vowel in London and other south-east accents. Listen to the way they say *poor* and write it down in phonetic symbols.

Talking point

> Other letters to look at in regional accents are -*a* and -*i*. How does a cockney or an Australian pronounce -*a* in words like *lady*? (Where did the first main settlers in Australia come from?) How does a dialect user from East Anglia or the Bristol area pronounce the personal pronoun *I* and other syllables containing -*i*?

▨ Consonants in RP and in regional dialects

Except when they are speaking quickly, RP speakers pronounce most consonants. The exception is the letter /r/, which is dropped:

1   after vowels, as in *bar*, *carpet* (pronounced /kɑːpet/, /bɑː/);
2   before consonants, as in *car-port* (pronounced /kɑːpɔːt/).
   (It is still pronounced between vowels, however, as in car engine – /kɑːrˈenjɪn/.)

Note: when /r/ occurs in the middle of a word it is known as *inter-vocalic* /r/. When it occurs at the end it is called *post-vocalic* /r/.

The Scots, the Irish, people who live in Bristol and the south-west and in parts of Lancashire still pronounce post-vocalic /r/. Try to listen to MP Rhodes Boyson and you will hear *thurr* for *there* and *their*.

Non-RP speakers on the other hand often drop consonants altogether. A check list is given below.

Activity

> Explain the confusion that arises in this conversation between a Hebridean Scotsman and an English in-comer:
>
> 'Maybe we'd all have time to play at the peats if we had a cart [like him],' I pointed out.
> 'How would that help him?' demanded Erchy, looking puzzled.
> 'Well, having a cart means he can get his peats home in his own time. He doesn't have to carry them himself or wait for a lorry like the rest of us.'
> 'I'm not gettin' your meaning,' said Erchy, still puzzled.
> 'His peats – in his cart. He has a cart, hasn't he?' I repeated testily.
> 'He has two or three but I don't see how they'd help him get home his peats,' said Erchy.
> 'Miss Peckwitt's meanin' to say a carrrt,' interpreted Morag.
> Erchy's face cleared. 'Ach, is that it? I thought she was goin' mad herself talkin' about a cat helpin' him to get home the peats. Honest, you English folk do speak a funny language sometimes.'
>
> Lillian Beckwith, *A Rope in Case*

Many speakers with regional accents on the other hand do not pronounce the consonants found in RP. Some consonants are simply dropped:

1 /h/ Many speakers of regional accents drop their aitches. *Hat* and *at*, *heart* and *art*, *hit* and *it* are therefore pronounced the same. Exceptions to this rule are those who live in Newcastle and parts of the north-east, the Scots, and the Irish.

2 /ŋ/ Most regional accents do not pronounce /ŋ/ in the suffix *-ing*: instead we find singin', pronounced /siŋin/; walkin', pronounced /wɔːkin/. (This is said to be true also of members of the aristocracy, who talk of *huntin'*, *shootin'*, *and fishin'*.)

3 /j/ In the past, /j/ used to be used after /r/ and /l/ in words like *rude* and *Luke*: /rjuːd/, /ljuːk/.

   At the moment, /j/ is being lost after /s/, even in RP, so that we find *super* /suːpə/, for instance, side by side with *suit* /sjuːt/.

   People with regional accents drop /j/ more often than RP users: parts of the north have lost /j/ after *th*: e.g. *enthuse*. London has lost /j/
   * after /n/: /njuːz/ becomes /nuːz/;
   * after /t/: /tjuːn/ becomes /tuːn/;
   * and after /d/: /djuːk/ becomes /duːk/

(The same thing also occurs in many American accents.)

Speakers in a large area of eastern England have dropped /j/ before /u:/ after all consonants, so that pronunciations like those below are now the norm: *pew* /pu:/; *few* /fu:/; *beauty* /bu:ti/.

Some consonants are replaced by glottal stops: Trudgill and Hughes find that non-RP speakers use glottal stops in the following places:

1 at the end of words before a following vowel or consonant:
   that man – /ðæʔ mæn/;
   that apple – /ðæʔ æpəl/;
2 before an /n/: button – /bʌʔən/;
3 before an /l/: bottle – /bɒʔəl/;
4 before a vowel: better – /beʔər/

Some consonants are replaced by other, different consonants:

1 Cockney speakers substitute /f/ for the -*th* sound we find in *thought* at the beginning, in the middle, and at the end of words:
   thin becomes /fin/; *Cathy* becomes /kæfi:/; *both* becomes /bouf/
2 They often use /v/ to replace the -*th* sound we hear in *then* in the middle and at the end of words:
   together becomes /təgɛvə/; *bathe* becomes /baɪv/
3 They use /d/ instead of the -*th* sound we hear in *then* at the beginning of words like *the*, *these*, and *then*.

Some consonants, strangely enough, are turned into vowels or diphthongs:

1 Speakers from London and the surrounding area change /l/ into a vowel when it occurs in the following places:
   * at the end of a word and after a vowel: *Paul* becomes /pou/;
   * before a consonant when it is part of the same syllable: *milk* becomes /miʊk/;
   * when /l/ is a syllable in itself in words like *table*: /tæɪbʊ/.
2 When /l/ follows the vowel /ɔ:/ it may be dropped altogether: thus *Paul's* may become /pɔ:z/ and sound exactly like *pause*.

Trudgill and Hughes note that:

> The vowels which represent /l/ can alter the quality of the vowels preceding them in such a way as to make homophones of pairs like: *pool/pull; doll/dole; peal/pill.*

This tendency, like turning diphthongs and triphthongs into monophthongs, seems to be spreading – evidence of the rising tide of 'estuary English' that is sweeping the southern half of the country.

Activity | Find the three phonetic symbols that, put together, will give the sound of 'well' in the accent of the London area.

▓ *Exceptions to the general trend*

There are two exceptions to this practice of dropping consonants:

1 Non-RP users in Birmingham, Manchester, and Liverpool not only pronounce /ŋ/ at the end of words; they add an extra /g/ for good measure: *singer* becomes /sɪŋgə/, *thing* becomes /θɪŋg/.
2 Speakers of both RP and regional dialects are in the habit of adding *intrusive* /r/ in places where no /r/ was ever used. The source of *intrusive* /r/ seems to have been the dropping of /r/ before a consonant in words like *carport* and the retention of /r/ before a vowel, in compounds like *car-engine*, where it is known as a *linking* /r/. If /r/ is pronounced before a vowel in places like this, the unconscious reasoning seems to run, it should be inserted before all vowels. We therefore find examples like *draw up* /drɔːr ʌp/, which used never to have an /r/, side by side with *soar up* /sɔːr ʌp/, where /r/ is customary.

Activity

1 a Listen to one of the Australian soaps and discuss the way in which the characters' vowel sounds differ from those of RP.
   b Now do the same for the consonants.

2 a Record a British pop/rock star
   ❈ speaking in his/her ordinary voice,
   ❈ singing.
   b Note and record any differences in pronunciation between the spoken and the sung register.

3 a Record ten television advertisements.
   b Assess the accent used in each (RP? Regional? American? Imitation American?); discuss the relationship between accent and product (remember that RP carries with it overtones of high status and authority).

4 a Record an American actor/actress or politician.
   b Find out which part of America they come from.
   c Note and record the differences between their vowel and consonant sounds and those of English English.
   d Discuss any differences of vocabulary and/or grammar that you recognize.

5 a Make a recording of someone who uses the dialect and accent of your locality.
   b Make a phonetic transcript of your recording.
   c Using the evidence of your recording, describe how
   ❈ the vowel sounds
   ❈ the consonants
   used by your speakers differ from those of Received Pronunciation.

Black English

Over one per cent of the British population today is of British West Indian or, as many now prefer to call it, Afro-Caribbean descent. Most of them speak some form of the dialect known as British Black English.

Key words

> *Creole*: creoles begin as *pidgins* – artificial languages specially invented to allow peoples who do not know each other's language to talk to each other. At first only good for passing simple information, they blossom eventually into *creoles* – fully developed languages capable of expressing anything their users want to say; in some cases, they replace the original language spoken by one of the peoples concerned and become mother-tongues.
>
> Creoles from different parts of the world share many common features – a fact that has lead to two different theories about their origins:
>
> 1 they all spring ultimately from one fifteenth-century Portuguese pidgin used in Africa, Asia, and the Americas;
>
> 2 they all arose out of the same innate human tendency to pare language down to its essentials when communication has to be quick and simple. (See the account of how children handle prepositions, and the remarks on telegrams in *The Vexed Question of Grammar*, page 94.)
>
> *Patois*: a synonym for *creole*.

As earlier chapters of this book have shown, very few people in this country speak completely pure Received Pronunciation and Standard English, or use exclusively dialect forms of grammar and regional accents. The majority use some form of modified RP and SE, diverging upwards or downwards as the situation demands. Exactly the same is true of people of Afro-Caribbean descent. *Black English*, like any other dialect, is a continuum, with full creole at one end, RP at the other, and modified forms of each in the middle. Most British Blacks born in this country since the 1970s, for instance, use only certain elements of creole or patois, and then only in informal contexts. And the same is true of pronunciation. Afro-Caribbeans might pronounce SE *town* (/taʊn/) for example as *tong* and *brown* as *brong* among friends, but would use a pronunciation closer to RP in most formal situations.

Like the rest of the British nation, therefore, Afro-Caribbeans have several varieties of accent and dialect from which to choose:

1 RP and Standard English, used by the more educated, like barrister and MP Paul Boateng or newcaster Moira Stewart;
2 Standard English spoken with the accent of the regions in which they happen to live;

3 Modified Jamaican creole, spoken by young Blacks when they feel in high spirits, or angry, or aggressive, or for any of the following reasons:
   * to establish a group identity/racial solidarity (Rasta or 'Dread-talk' is an extreme form of this);
   * to reject white (or black) outsiders;
   * to show contempt for people who think black culture inferior;

4 Full Jamaican creole, spoken largely by older members of the Afro-Caribbean community.

Far from being able to speak only creole, then, many young Blacks can use all these dialects, changing their register to suit context and audience. It therefore makes much more sense to talk of Jamaican creole (JC) and Black English (BE) rather than lump both together under the common label West Indian English.

The extreme end of the continuum: Jamaican creole

Jamaican creole (often called *patois*) is a language in its own right, with a full range of grammatical features and its own *lexis* (vocabulary) and *phonology* (system of pronunciation). (Afro-Caribbean immigrants did come from other islands of the West Indies, but the majority were from Jamaica, and so Jamaican creole has come to dominate the very similar dialects of Barbados, Guyana, St Vincent, and so on.)

Spoken largely by the older generation, full JC is difficult for English people to understand. Try your hand at the following example. (You will find you can recognize many of the words if you say them aloud, quickly. Black English is largely an oral language, and when it is written down, it is spelt as it is pronounced.)

We go luk aan di difran wie hou di langwij we wi taak mos impaatan fi di blak pikni-dem iina skuul.

Literal translation

We (are) go(ing to) look at the different ways how the language that we talk (is) most important for the black children in school.

Standard English translation

We shall consider various aspects of language as they pertain to the education of West Indian children.

Creole, age, and gender

You might expect that West Indian immigrants to this country would bring up their children to speak creole like them, at least in the home. In fact, many Afro-Caribbean parents speak creole to their children but refuse to allow their children to use it to them in return, because:
   a they think it unseemly for children to speak in such a familiar way to their parents;
   b older West Indians are conscious of the undesirable associations that cling to creole: slavery, poverty, lack of education, and so on.

Edwards quotes typical reactions to this parental attitude:

> 'Dem a stop me and say, "We bring you over here fi h'educate you, a
> learn fi speak better", and all this kind of thing. Well, me used to listen to
> dem, but after dem gone, me used to speak the same.'
>
> 'Every couple of months Mum will go, "Look at Mrs Grant or
> somebody's children down the road, they speak lovely Henglish. A what
> wrong with unu?" . . . Then we go, "How now brown cow, the rain in
> Spain falls mainly on the plain." So she goes, "A what you a do? Lef' me
> alone!"'
>
> Viv Edwards, *The West Indian Language Issue in British Schools*

Hewitt mentions another factor that operates against the learning of creole:

> Really dense creole is used strictly for men-talk. The girls, as in other
> British dialects, tend to use Standard English with either a regional or
> modified RP accent.
>
> Roger Hewitt, *White Talk Black Talk*

The middle of the continuum: modified creole

Most young Afro-Caribbeans use a modified form of creole, generally
referred to as patois, among their friends in informal situations. However,
they can diverge upwards towards more ordinary English speech when
necessary, as the following examples from Edwards, *Language in a Black
Community*, show:

1   Don, a young Afro-Caribbean, is talking informally to friends and a black
fieldworker doing research into young black people's use of patois:

> Dem [the questions] alright in a way, right. Dem reasonable. Dem could
> be lickle better, but dem reasonable. Me na bex [angry] wid dem, dem
> alright . . . When white people ready fi write some rubbish bout black
> people, dem can do it, dem can do it, right. So dat's why me say dem
> reasonable. Notn wrong wid dem.

2   Here, the same speaker is talking to black friends about some tickets for a
dance that he has lost:

> Me still naa get in, mi still naa get in because a na fi-dem fault. Dat no
> have notn fi do wid dem.
>   (I still won't get in, I still won't get in because it's not their fault. That
> hasn't got anything to do with them.)

3   Here, Don is again talking to black friends:

> Me say, 'Do it! Flash it!' Dat mean seh im a go beat im.
> (I say, 'Do it! Flash it!' That means he's going to beat him.)

These short extracts contain many patois features:

* the patois pronouns *mi* and *dem*;
* adjectives used as verbs: *dem [are] alright*;
* *fi* before an infinitive;
* *no* in the form of *naa* instead of *is not*;
* the focusing particle *a*;
* the patois possessive *fi-dem* (their);
* the continuative particle *a* to form the present continuous tense: *im a go beat him*;
* *seh* after stative verbs.

4 Talking to white researchers, however, in a formal interview situation, Don's language was much closer to SE:

> I say it come from Africa really. It started from dere true slavery. Dat's di way I see it. It started from there, yeah. But those kids what born over here right, they don't want to admit it. Like Paddy, they don't want to admit it right that our culture started from Africa.

His pronunciation is still very Afro-Caribbean – *tru*, *dere*, *di* rather than *true*, *there*, and *the* – but he inflects his verb endings to show the past tense, uses the SE negative form *don't* instead of *naa*, and puts in linking verbs (copulas like *come*).

Code switching

Many young Blacks, especially girls, do not stick as closely to patois as Don does. They switch easily, often in mid-sentence, between patois words and patois pronunciation, often to show affection or to tease or to jazz things up a bit.

Creole and 'correctness'

The prescriptivist attitude towards both JC and BE speakers is that they use English sloppily, dropping inflexions, and refusing to do as SE users do out of sheer laziness. (They say the same about regional dialect users, too, of course.)

The wrongness of this idea has been pointed out by Loreto Todd in *Modern Englishes, Pidgins and Creoles*. Afro-Caribbeans cannot fairly be accused of dropping inflexions, she points out, because no such inflexions existed in the West African languages that formed the base of their creole. Other grammatical 'errors', such as using the wrong case of the pronoun, may well be due to the same reason.

Creole and slang

Creole has a vivid and immediate quality that makes it very appealing to white children and adolescents. Patois slang like *bad*, *wicked*, and *safe* has found its way into every London school and college. Researching into the use of Black English in Camden schools, Maria Manning found children of many different ethnic backgrounds all using it as slang.

> Barney (aged nine), lip curled in contempt: 'You a *lame* chief, well lame, *serious* lame!'
>
> 'You say that to annoy someone, for instance if they don't score a goal. It's a cuss.'

'EEzee!' and 'rare!' are both terms of praise. The first means relaxed, laid-back, or 'cool', but is pronounced in the same way as the football chant, with both vowels given equal weight. 'Rare!' is an expression of wonder, gasped rather than spoken, and probably coming from DJ's patter at rap parties.

Why should Black English have such a strong influence on the informal speech of these multi-ethnic groups? Manning suggests two reasons:

1 'the spare, emphatic style of Black English' gives it a dynamic, forceful, immediate effect suited to the hard, fast life of city kids;
2 Black English gives them the chance to thumb their noses at Standard English and all the things that go with it: respectability, conformity, passing examinations, and so on.

Black English then, is being used by both white and black children to rebel against a culture that seems to have little to offer them.

Manning:

> All the children I spoke to are white, but Black English speaks to them because they also feel excluded from the mythical 'British culture' enshrined in Standard English.

Activity

1 Ask Afro-Caribbean students in your school or college if they are willing to help you with some research into their own or their family's use of patois. This is a sensitive area, so be tactful and be ready for a refusal.

2 Devise a questionnaire in which you ask them:
   a if they ever use any or all of the following;
   b if so, how often;
   c where they use them (i.e. home or elsewhere);
   d in whose company.

Speakers of light patois will use *d* for *th* and *fi* instead of *to* with the infinitive. Speakers of moderate patois may, in addition to these, also use *fi* to show possession, *mi* for *me*, *im* for *him*, and *dem* after nouns as a plural marker. They may also use *seh* before certain verbs.

The greater the number of non-standard features used after these, the fuller the creole. Non-standard features are listed below.

Differences between Jamaican Creole and Standard English

* no -*s* ending on plural nouns: *3 gal* (3 girls)
* *dem* used to mark plural nouns: *di gal dem* (the girls)
* word order and *fi* used to show possession: *Alvin woman* (Alvin's woman), *fi-mi records* (my records)
* no inflection on pronouns to show cases:
  mi (I, me, and my) *yu* (you, your) *im* (he, him, his, she, her)
  i (it, its) *we* (we, us, our) *unu* (you, your)
  dem (they, them, their)
* no -*s* ending on third person singular of verb: *go* (goes), *taak* (talks)

- no inflection to show tense of verbs: *tel* (tell) is used for the past as well as the present
- -*a* used
  1 to mark the present participle: *a fight* (fighting)
  2 to mark the progressive tense in which actions are continuous: *mi a taak* (I am talking)
- *did*, *don,* and *ben* used to indicate the simple past tense (I have finished work) and the past perfect tense (I had finished work): *I did see her just now* (I saw her just a moment ago), *mi don sliip* (I have finished sleeping), *mi ben waak huom aredi* (I had already walked home)
- *wi* or *go* plus the verb stem used to indicate future tense: *they wi let you know/they go let you know* (they will tell you)
- *fi* used instead of *to* with infinitives: *you ask im how fi cook rice im no know* (if you ask him how to cook rice he doesn't know)
- lack of linking verbs, e.g. *is, seem, become*: *di gal happy* (the girl is happy), *who im?* (who's he?)
- the use of *seh* after verbs like *know, say, talk, hear,* and *be,* in place of *that* in English sentences: *A glad seh im gaan* (I'm glad that he's gone)
- unconventional negatives: use of *noh* before the verb to make it negative: *she decide seh she noh want it any more* (she decided she did not want it any more)
- multiple negation: *she decide seh she no want none no more* (she decided she didn't want any more)
- passives that look like actives: *this can't share* (you can't share this), *that record play a lot* (that record is played a lot)
- actives that look like passives: *he ain't easy to beat up* (he doesn't beat people up easily), *he's easy to annoy* (he annoys other people easily)
- *de* and *deh* used instead of *there*: *it deh* (it's there)

3 Ask your respondents where they learned any patois they may speak.

4 a Make a recording of a speaker with a creole accent.
  b Make a phonetic transcript of part of your recording.
  c Discuss the major differences in pronunciation between creole and RP.

5 Working from your notes, write a report on the use of patois within your locality.

The language of society

● ●

The language of gender

Women make up roughly half the population and over forty per cent of the work-force. They have an appreciable effect on the country's economy, yet their work is given little public recognition and they are often paid less for doing the same jobs as men.

Even women do not show as much respect to women as they do to men in public life. When women students were given two sets of booklets containing the same article, one bearing the name of a male, the other of a female author, they found the writing of John T. McKay superior to that of Joan T. McKay in all areas (Goldberg, 1974, quoted in Spender, *Man Made Language*).

Why is this? One reason may have to do with our use of language.

Gender and grammar

When we look at the world around us we perceive it in two ways:

1 with our physical eyes;
2 through the distorting lens of language – the language of our society.

As they learn to speak, children absorb the values, assumptions, and expectations of the adults who surround them *through the words they are given to learn*. Language therefore shapes our view of reality: there is no such thing as a culture-free view of the world.

It follows that if the language children learn in our society is biased towards men and against women, even girls will grow up to take for granted the superiority of the male over the female sex.

Is there evidence of such an inbuilt linguistic bias? Consider the following facts and make up your own mind:

1 In 1553 the grammarian Wilson ruled that the man should precede the woman in pairs such as *male/female*; *husband/wife*; *brother/sister*; *son/daughter*. It was 'more natural'. (Nobody disagreed with him.)
2 In 1646 the grammarian Joshua Poole ruled that the male should precede the female because this was both more 'natural', and more 'proper', since men were the 'worthier' sex. (Other men seemed happy to agree.)
3 The grammarian John Kirkby ruled that the male gender was 'more comprehensive' than the female, which was therefore to be included in it.
4 Nineteenth century grammarians reinforced the resulting idea of male superiority by condemning the use of the neutral pronoun *they* and *their* in such statements as, 'Anyone can do it if they try'. Their reasoning was that *anyone* and *everyone*, being singular, could not properly be followed by plural pronouns.

The male-as-the-norm syndrome

In any book which deals with human beings in general, the nouns that recur are *men, man,* and *mankind.* The pronoun that inevitably follows these nouns is of course *he.* The result is that women are not linguistically represented. As the American writer, Julia Stanley, puts it, they occupy 'negative semantic space'.

Women are also rendered invisible in the language when the masculine pronoun *he* is used to follow gender-free nouns like *writer, critic, novelist, politician, speaker,* etc.

Writers who are asked why they follow this practice are often bewildered by the question. It seems they had always taken it for granted that *man, mankind, men,* and *he,* automatically included the idea of women in utterances such as, *Men have always worshipped gods,* and *Men fear death as children fear to go in the dark.* And the use of the masculine pronoun after such nouns was simply a matter of convenience, a way of avoiding the long-winded *he or she,* the clumsy *s/he,* or the ungrammatical *they.* (*Man* and *mankind* are both singular collective nouns and so should properly be followed by a singular pronoun.)

I believe these claims are often sincere, having followed words like *writer, novelist,* and *poet* with *he* quite unconsciously myself in the first draft of this book. But the fact that there is no *conscious* bias here is beside the point. The real question at issue is, how far does such writing succeed in:

a making women invisible in large and important areas of life;

b brainwashing younger generations into believing that man is the more important and superior sex?

Anthropologist Elaine Morgan suggests that it might have such effects in the preface to her book on the evolution of man (sorry, the human species), *The Descent of Woman.* Using the masculine noun-pronoun forms *man . . . he* in a book about the human race in general can have unforeseen effects:

> . . . before you are half-way through the first chapter a mental image of this evolving creature begins to form in your mind. It will be a male image and he will be the hero of the story; everything and everyone else in the story will relate to him . . .
>
> A very high proportion of . . . thinking is androcentric (male centred) in the same way as pre-Copernican thinking was geocentric. It's just as hard for man to break the habit of thinking of himself as central to the species as it was to break the habit of thinking of himself as central to the universe. He sees himself quite unconsciously as the main line of evolution with a female satellite revolving around him as the moon revolves around the earth.
>
> The longer I went on reading his own books about himself, the more I longed to find a volume that would begin: 'When the first ancestor of the human race descended from the trees, she had not yet developed the mighty brain that was to distinguish her so sharply from other species'.

Talking point

> 1 How far does the use of *man* at the expense of *human beings* instil and support the idea that men are more important than women?
>
> 2 Male readers of such books presumably form pictures, if not directly of themselves, at least of other men with whom they can associate themselves. What pictures do you suppose women see?

Activity

> 1 Which of the following statements are readily acceptable? Explain why you think so.
>   a Man devotes more than forty hours a week to housework.
>   b Man, being a mammal, breast-feeds his young.
>   c Man is the only animal that commits rape.
>
> 2 Re-write where necessary.
>
> 3 What conclusions do you draw from the above statements, as originally written?
>
> 4 Analyse the following statements taken from books about the development of the human species and draw your own conclusions:
>   a . . . man's vital interests are life, food, access to females, etc. . . . (Erich Fromm)
>   b . . . his back aches, he ruptures easily, his women have difficulty in childbirth . . . (Loren Eisely)

Here is another example of unconscious bias. In his informative book *Advertising*, Frank Jeffkins describes the work of each member of an advertising agency's team. Here is his account of the copy-writer:

> . . . His writing style is unlike any other. He seldom writes complete grammatical sentences, but uses words and punctuation and their typographical presentation like [sic] a painter uses colours and shapes. He can write a one-word one-sentence paragraph that grips the reader's interest and desire. He can virtually mutilate the English language for effect. He can write a thousand words and make every word count. He can sell . . .

These repeated, insistent *he*s fill us with admiration for such outstanding male talent – yet wasn't Fay Weldon one of the best copy-writers of her generation, creator of such brilliant slogans as *Go to work on an egg*? Why does Jeffkins mention only *he*? And what effect might reading this have on young women eager for a career in advertising? Only one member of the team gets the *or she* addition after the *he* – the Account Executive – the inescapable conclusion being that this is the only aspect of advertising at which a woman might succeed. Is this what Jeffkins meant? Or did he remember for one fleeting moment that women, too, exist in the world of work?

Activity

1 a Go to a library and look at books on any of the following topics: anthropology; the origins of man; childbirth or child-rearing; sociology (the chapter on education); sport; hotel management; training to be a chef.
  b Make notes on the gender of the nouns and pronouns used.
  c Explain what Spender means by the following:
  'She' represents a woman but 'he' is mankind. If 'she' enters mankind 'she' loses herself in 'he'.

2 Until recently, girls and women were never mentioned in Maths textbooks. Get hold of as many Maths textbooks as you can and see if
  a girls and women are mentioned,
  b they are given different occupations and/or activities from the boys and men.

3 a Go to the children's section of your library and look at as many story books for each of the different age groups as you can.
  b Record the gender of the chief character(s). (It does not matter whether they are human or animal, since animals are given the same characteristics as human beings.)
  c Record the kind of things the characters are made to do.
  d Read through your notes and assess honestly whether you have any evidence of gender prejudice (male or female characters being made to appear more important and interesting than those of the opposite sex) or role stereotyping (male characters being given exciting and adventurous things to do, and female ones being confined to doing more domestic things or following timidly behind).
  e Write your research up in report form, adding your conclusions as to the possible effects of such stories on the boys and girls who read them.

Is all this talk of female invisibility merely the nit-picking of embittered feminists? Two pieces of evidence suggest that it is not:

1 Men themselves have recognized the consequences of leaving women out of the language used to describe all the most important areas of public life:

> . . . that our language employs the words *man* and *mankind* as terms for the whole human race demonstrates that male dominance, the *idea* of masculine superiority, is programmed, institutional, and rooted at the deepest level of our historical experience.
>
> Richard Gilman, *Life* magazine

2 Men are themselves bitterly hurt and distressed when they are made invisible by language in this way. Spender relates how in the 1960s, when most primary schoolteachers were female, articles referring to them habitually followed the gender-free noun *primary schoolteacher* with the

feminine pronoun *she*. One of the few males in the profession wrote a letter to protest:

> The interests of neither the women, nor of the men, in our profession, are served by grammatical usage which conjures up an anachronistic image of the nineteenth century schoolmarm . . .

He preferred the male pronoun to be used instead, on the 'objective' and 'correct' grounds that the women would be understood to be included in *he*. Women would still be in the majority within the profession, but it was 'neither incorrect nor improper to exclude them linguistically'.

(Miller & Swift, *Words and Women: New Language in New Times*)

Talking point

Men consider it improper to refer to individuals within mixed groups as *she*, but not as *he*. Why do you suppose this is?

Activity

1 a Assemble a group containing both males and females.
   b Give the members of the group an extract from a textbook (e.g. on nursing) that uses the feminine pronoun *she* throughout.
   c Ask the group to replace *she* with *he* throughout.
   d Record any comments.
   e Now give them an extract that uses *he* throughout and ask them to replace all the *he*s with *she*s.
   f Record any comments.
   g Write up:
      ◦ the responses of the members of the group,
      ◦ your own reactions to the experiment.
2 a Assemble an unsuspecting all-male group and get them to discuss the topic 'What I think about women'. Record the discussion.
   b Now do the same thing with an all-female group on the topic 'What I think about men'. Record the discussion.
   c Analyse the way in which the two sexes talk about each other to see how well it accords with the material you read in this section.
3 Report the conclusions you have formed on male and female attitudes towards gender and language as a result of these experiments. You can do this in the form of an article for your school or college magazine or a woman's magazine, or a letter to the editor of a daily newspaper.

Gender, titles, and naming

Marriage

Just as the use of masculine nouns and pronouns helps to render women invisible in public life, so, it is claimed, the practice of giving up their own name and taking on their husbands' robs women of a public identity of their own. In so far as they have an identity, it is one shared with their husbands. The individual Gertrude Coppard, for instance, becomes Mrs Walter Morel, part of that new creation, 'the Morels'. ('Have you heard the Morels have got a son?/lost their eldest boy?') In *Man Made Language*, Spender points out that the only real names belong to men, since these are handed down from father to son. Without a male heir, a family dies out.

Talking point

> 1 How far does changing her name make it difficult for a woman to preserve an identity for herself outside the home?
>
> 2 Why do famous actresses, singers, dancers, etc. choose to keep their maiden names?
>
> 3 How would a visitor returning to the town where she grew up set about tracing her old school-friends? What might make it difficult?
>
> 4 How far do you think the practice of giving up their names on marriage reinforces the idea that women are the property of their husbands?
>
> 5 In *Sons and Lovers* Gertrude Morel's ambitions, aspirations, and social status were limited by her husband's job and attitude towards her. How far is this still true of the average woman today? Does her access to the wider life of society still depend upon her husband?
>
> 6 Why is it important that women should reveal their marital status (calling themselves 'Mrs', wearing a ring on the left hand third finger), but not men?

▓ Work

Women who enter the professions are not always given the same gender-free title as their male counterparts: *doctor, lawyer, solicitor, constable*. The appropriate noun is used, but prefaced by *lady* or *woman*. In the same way, women are not given job titles such as *waiter, steward*, or *drum major*. The diminutive *-ette* or *-ess* is added, signalling, it is claimed, that they are somehow 'not the real thing' in not being male.

Talking point

> Does it diminish the dignity and importance of a woman who writes poetry to call her a poetess? Or to call a woman who acts an actress? Explain your point of view.

▓ Social life and personal relationships

Ask any group of women – including those happily married to, or living happily with, men – and they will agree unanimously on one point: many men patronize, insult, and control women by calling them offensive names.

Patronizing terms include *dear, love,* and *pet.* They are patronizing when used by a man to a girl or woman he does not know simply because they imply that

    a it is his right as a man to speak to them like this, and

    b any right-minded female will welcome it.

The test for patronage is easy: would he use the same terms to a man he didn't know? Calling grown women *girls* is another patronizing ploy used to make women feel inferior. When it was used against women at the 1983 Labour Party Conference (male socialists aren't all democratic enough to treat women fairly), they retaliated by referring to Comrade Chairboy and the boys. Not very witty, admittedly, but the best they could do at the time.

Talking point

> **1** If a man calls a woman *dear, pet,* or *love,* is he necessarily patronizing her, or simply being friendly?
>
> **2** Women on City & Guilds Catering Courses have been known to complain because their college lecturers address them as 'dear' and the male students as 'chef'. Is their complaint justified? Explain your answer.

The **insulting** and **controlling** aspects of male language can be dealt with together, since the insults are the means of control. Julia Stanley has shown not only that there are more words available to describe men than women, but also that more of these words show men in a favourable light. In the large vocabulary of words used to describe men, only twenty-six words implying sexual promiscuity were found, and of these many – such as *stallion* and *stud* – were felt to be complimentary. It is simply not possible to call a man the equivalent of *slut.* In the much smaller list of words used to describe women, by contrast, 220 terms signalling sexual promiscuity were found. All were of a degrading nature. (Some degree of confusion in male thinking is shown by the fact that a girl is damned if she shows too much interest in sex and damned if she does not show enough: derogatory words like *tight bitch* then come into play.)

In her book on sexuality and adolescent girls, *Losing Out,* Sue Lees argues that men control female sexual behaviour by the use of such derogatory terms – in particular, the word *slag.* This is used, not necessarily of girls who actually sleep with boys they love before marriage, but of girls who want to make the running in sexual relationships; who actively pursue boys and show their interest in them; who treat boys, in fact, as boys treat girls. These it seems are the real *slags,* whether they actually do it or not. Nice girls wait for boys to make the first move.

Since the male equivalent of *slag* is *stud,* and *stud* is a term that confers prestige, the language men use to discuss sexuality seems biased rather heavily in their favour.

Talking point

> 1 Which of the following once equal pairs of words now have negative or unpleasant associations?
>
> spinster/bachelor   baronet/dame   master/mistress
> king/queen   old master/old mistress old man/old woman
>
> 2 Can you call a group of girls 'you guys'?
>   Can you call a group of boys 'you girls'?
>   Can you call a girl a 'bachelor'?
>   Can you call a boy a 'spinster' or an 'old maid'?
>
> 3 Which is the possibly ambiguous statement here:
>   he's a professional; she's a professional?
>
> 4 Consult at least five other people of either sex and list as many derogatory words as you can find to describe
>   **a** women,   **b** men.
>
> 5 Now do the same for words that describe the conversation or talk of
>   **a** women,   **b** men.

Activity

> 1 Write an essay, newspaper or magazine article, or script for a TV or radio show on the topic of Gender and Language. Jazz up the title as you wish.
>
> 2 Argue the case for or against reforming the practices described in the first section, *Gender and Grammar*.

The language of advertising

The language used in advertising is designed to:

1 grab and hold our attention;
2 stamp a message on our minds;
3 create images that will forge a link between our emotions and the products on offer.

Colloquial language in advertising

In his *Confessions of an Advertising Man* David Ogilvy advises would-be copy-writers to write their copy in the kind of colloquial language used by their customers in everyday conversation. Pretentious words such as *obsolete* go over the heads of many people. (When surveyed, forty-three per cent had no idea of what it meant.) Every word – and particularly those in the headline or slogan introducing the ad – must *impact* the readers'/viewers' minds (note the neologism replacing that 'boring' old phrase *make an impact upon*), and make them want to buy, and Ogilvy tells would-be copy-writers exactly how to go about it.

There is a tried and tested vocabulary for the selling of food and domestic items, the most effective and therefore most frequently used examples of which are given below.

Adjectives

new	good	crisp	better	fresh

natural (especially when linked to *goodness*)

fine	free	wonderful	best	clean	safe
easy	extra	special	rich	big	sure
great	delicious	amazing	fantastic	sensational	real

Verbs

buy	give	taste	go	look	feel
start	take	make	use	choose	come

(According to Ogilvy, the two most powerful adjectives you can use to attract attention in a header are *free* and *new*.)

For extra effect, copywriters sometimes use compound adjectives such as *fast-foaming, fresh-roasted*. As well as adding force, these save space by compressing meaning.

Copywriters also use the journalists' technique of treating nouns as adjectives, giving us compounds such as *jelly-addict, man-appeal, coffee-pot-fresh, one-action cleaner*.

Other attention-grabbing words and phrases are:

How to	Suddenly	Now	Announcing
Introducing	It's here	Just arrived	Important development
Improvement	Amazing	Sensational	Remarkable
Revolutionary	Startling	Miracle	Magic
Offer	Quick	Easy	Wanted
Challenge	Advice to	The truth about	Compare
Bargain	Hurry	Last chance	

'All shopworn cliches', Ogilvy remarks, 'but they work. That's why they're shopworn clichés.'

As well as sensational language, advertisements have other features in common with the tabloid newspapers:

* they use short sentences;
* they have a tendency to tell their readers what to think or do;
* they adopt a chatty, friendly, 'neighbourly' tone.

Activity

1 Check the accuracy of the above statements by looking at as many ads as possible and noting:

   a the kind of adjectives used in ads for different products, e.g. toothpastes, deodorants, detergents, soaps, disinfectants, frozen foods;

   b the frequency of their occurrence.

Can you draw any conclusions from your notes?

2 Do the same check on verbs. Are most of the verbs used monosyllabic? If so, why? Which are used most often? Why?

3 Check the length of sentences in your ads and assess the tone they adopt towards their readers/viewers.

The use of patterned sound

Pick up a Penguin, A P-P-P-Penguin

The alliteration and assonance displayed in this Penguin ad is one more thing copy-writers share with reporters who write for tabloid newspapers (these like to run captions such as *Brothers of Blood* under photographs of IRA terrorists). Advertisers often use repetition and patterned sound to catch our attention and make their sales patter stick in our heads:

Drinka Pinta Milka Day
Great Little Rooster Booster
Milk has Gotta Lotta Bottle
Nice Cold, Ice Cold Milk
We Knew How Before You-Know-Who
The Freezer-Pleezers
Beanz Meanz Heinz
Mint, choc, Mint, choc, Mint, choc, Mint, choc, Mint, choc, Mint, choc, Mint, choc . . . (imitating the ticking of a clock).

There is real inventiveness in these slogans. No wonder some TV ads are more fun than the programmes they interrupt. Sometimes alliteration and assonance are used less obviously, in a way that (given the difference in subject matter) is closer to poetry. Note the soothing effect got by the repeated *s, m, f,* and *l* sounds in the examples below:

. . . an automatic applicator gently smooths on soft creme or high-shine colour, for a smooth silky finish that lasts . . .
. . . colours that look lastingly tempting. Longer.

The use of metaphor

Copy-writers occasionally use metaphor to create the kind of emotional associations they want to implant in our minds. Examples of these are *Fire and Ice* and *Cherries in the Snow* for individual lipstick shades; *a taste of Paradise* for the coconut 'Bounty' bar.

Perhaps the most successful metaphors in recent years have been used in campaigns for Palmolive soap and Esso petrol:

Palmolive brings back that schoolgirl complexion
where schoolgirl complexion = new skin = Palmolive soap
(much more exciting than Palmolive makes skin new again).

Put a tiger in your tank
where tiger = strength = Esso petrol

Metaphor demands imagination on the part of the ordinary consumer, however, and is usually replaced by easier, visual, images. These are used to build a bridge in the consumers' minds between the product and the highly desirable person, object, or situation that buying it will lead them to:

Product	Visual image	Heart's desire
a coconut bar	a south-sea island	holiday paradise
a fabric conditioner	smiling husband and children	happy family life
a liqueur	glamorous party scene	social success
a scented body spray	young man buying flowers for girl he's just met	sexual success

There is a *metonymic* relationship between product and image here. (See the section entitled *Metaphor and Metonymy*, page 207.)

The use of puns

David Ogilvy advises against puns on the grounds that anything too clever in an advertisement distracts attention to itself and away from the product. And in fact, puns are comparatively rare. A toothpaste ad that declares it to be 'minty tasty' may be striving after the Joycean style of pun by word blending (minty-mighty?), but it doesn't really come off. Ads have to appeal to our lower drives and desires rather than to our intellectual centres.

Using language to mislead

In advanced technological societies, items such as soaps, shampoos, and washing powders are made to much the same formulae. One is pretty much the same as another. This puts the advertisers in a double bind: they must find what in the trade is known as a USP ('Unique Selling Point'), yet they have nothing solid and factual to base their USP on. They cannot come straight out with the claim that their product will beat anything else on the market, and so they have to resort to indirect means that get the idea across without laying their clients open to charges of libel. One technique used is known in the trade as *expectation*. A slogan like *You can't get better than a Kwik-fit fitter* leads us to expect that, if you can't get better than a Kwik-fit fitter, Kwik-fit fitters must be the best. Why else would you bother to say it, to people who are wanting new tyres or exhausts? When you look at it carefully, however, all the slogan actually asserts is that Kwik-fit fitters are as good as any others around. The consumers have been misled, at no risk to the manufacturers.

Activity

> Read the advertisements below and explain:
> a what they *expect*;
> b what they actually *assert*.
>
> X is the light moisturizing cream. It's not greasy or sticky.
> X's additive-free chips.

The ads cited above both make negative claims, but the same *principle of expectation* applies when the assertion made on the behalf of the product is a positive one. If the copy-writer emphasizes the solubility of a certain brand of painkiller, for example, the expectation he or she creates is that all or most other brands are *in*soluble – which may well not be true.

Using language back to front

Here is one final example of the advertiser's deliberate misuse of language in order to mislead.

David Ogilvy has pointed out the danger of using negative words in advertisements. Faced with a slogan like, *Our salt contains no arsenic*, consumers will see the 'arsenic' and overlook the 'no' – exactly the opposite of what was intended. This may be due to the tendency of inexperienced readers to concentrate on content rather than structure words (see *The Vexed Question of Grammar*, pages 66 and 96). Similarly, when a qualifying adverb such as *deceptively* is placed next to an adjective in a phrase like *deceptively intelligent*, inexperienced readers ignore *deceptively* and register only *intelligent*. The phrase is taken to mean 'intelligent' rather than 'stupid', or 'not very bright'. Recognizing this danger, copy-writers have come up with advertisements like the ones below:

Loewenbrau – deceptively strong beer
Deceptively strong = deceiving us into thinking it strong = weak.

This deceptively spacious three-bedroomed terrace
Deceptively spacious = deceiving us into thinking it spacious = small

If they were to use the word correctly and write, *Loewenbrau – deceptively weak beer*, or *This deceptively small three-bedroomed terrace*, consumers would not interpret these statements to mean:

deceptively weak = deceiving us into thinking it weak = strong;
deceptively small = deceiving us into thinking it small = large.

They would see only the turn-off words *weak* and *small*, and refuse to buy. (Would words like *deceptively* need to be used at all if the beer were really strong and the house genuinely spacious?) Remember, truth is irrelevant in advertising. As Oscar Wilde remarked on a different subject, 'In matters of great importance, style, not sincerity, is the vital thing'.

The language of law

Every aspect of our lives is governed by law, expressed in the form of legal documents. We need to be able to read them, since it is through such documents that obligations are imposed and rights conferred upon us, yet it is neither easy nor pleasant to do. The reason is two-fold:

1 The writers of legal documents use legal jargon, made up of
   a technical terms such as *tort* and *lien*;
   b archaic words and phrases such as *jeopardy* and *curtilage*.
2 They write in 'bad' – that is, clumsy and obscure – English. Indeed it would be true to say that the drafters of legal documents break every rule in the English style book in constructing their sentences. Their major faults are listed below. (Examples are taken from Anderson, *The Written Word*.)

1   **The awkward placing of subordinate clauses and phrases.** These are often piled up at the beginning of a sentence:

> If, after the confirmation of an order made by a local authority under the last preceding section, the owner or occupier of, or any person interested in, any private dwelling which is or will be within a smoke control area as a result of the order, not being a new dwelling, incurs expenditure on adaptations in or in connection with the dwelling to avoid contravention of the last preceding section . . .

The result is that the unfortunate readers have several things to remember before they arrive at the main statement. The main statement itself is then all too often interrupted by further subordinate clauses and phrases:

> . . . the local authority shall repay to him seven-tenths of that expenditure and may, if they think fit, also repay to him the whole or any part of the remainder of that expenditure . . .

Activity

> Re-write the above extracts, placing the main statement first. The qualifying restrictions and conditions can then be added in the form of separate points, listed by numbers (i, ii, iii, etc.) or letters (a, b, c, etc.).

Key word

> To *qualify* a statement: to impose restricting or limiting circumstances on it, e.g.:
> Any gaming shall be lawful if, but only if, it is conducted in accordance with the following conditions: . . .

Notice that the arrangement of the sentences here is complicated by a further technique: the insertion of one or more subordinate clauses and phrases inside another. In lines 1-5, for example, the subordinate clause introduced by *If* is first interrupted by the lengthy phrase beginning *after the confirmation*, then by the adjectival clause beginning *which is*, then by the two further phrases, *as a result of* and *not being*. This practice breaks up the flow of the sense and makes it difficult to grasp the relationship of:
  ※ each subordinate clause to the other subordinate clauses;
  ※ each subordinate clause to the main clause.

What is the cause of this poor arrangement of clauses and phrases? The answer lies in the need to eliminate ambiguity.

When a legal draftsman writes down the provisions of an Act or bill or contract, he or she must try to anticipate every condition or qualification that might be attached to them and write these in, to prevent later lawyers and/or judges finding loopholes due to ambiguous phrasing. In the above extract, the writer is so anxious to avoid loopholes that he or she begins with one qualifying clause – *If . . .* – then interrupts it immediately with another one qualifying the first: *after the confirmation of an order made by a local authority under the last preceding section . . .*

For the same reason, the writer cannot leave the subject of the *If* clause – *the owner or occupier of any private dwelling* – unqualified, but has to add *or any person interested in*, to cover any set of circumstances to which the act might apply. The dwelling itself is then qualified by a further subordinate clause – *which is or will be within a smoke control area* – which is itself promptly qualified by the phrases *as a result of the order* and *not being a new dwelling*. Only after this can the initial *If* clause that began the sentence be completed: *incurs expenditure on adaptations in or in connection with the dwelling . . .* Sentences written like this may avoid ambiguity, but they are jerky, wooden-sounding, and very difficult to read.

Activity

> List all the qualifying clauses and phrases in the extract below, indicating what each is qualifying. (The first one, for instance – *Subject to the provisions of this section* – qualifies the clause *a child shall not . . .*)
>
> 32.– (1) Subject to the provisions of this section a child shall not, except under and in accordance with the provisions of a licence granted and in force thereunder, take part in any entertainment in connection with which any charge, whether for admission or not, is made to any of the audience; and every person who causes or procures a child, or being his parent or guardian allows him, to take part in an entertainment in contravention of this section, shall, on conviction by a court of summary jurisdiction, be liable to a fine not exceeding five pounds, or, in the case of second or subsequent offence, not exceeding twenty pounds.

Talking point

> Why did the writer use both *second* and *subsequent* in the last two lines?

2   **The use of repetition** to excess, again in the attempt to avoid ambiguity. If two parties are involved in a contract, there must be no loose pronouns to cause confusion. Better to repeat a noun like *Hirer* ad nauseam, for example, where necessary with a *said* or *aforesaid* in front of it, than to leave readers in doubt as to the identity of a *he*. For example:

> Should the Hirer fail to pay in full any instalment within fourteen days after the same shall have become payable or should the Hirer die or be made bankrupt or should the goods be seized under any distress of the Hirer for rent or other obligation or the Hirer do or suffer anything . . .

Replace the second *Hirer* here with *he* and doubt as to the antecedent of the pronoun (the antecedent is the preceding noun to which a pronoun refers) would provide lawyers with a loophole. (The outcome of a case has depended before this upon the antecedent of a *heretofore*.)

Note: one of the things that makes legal language so impersonal and abstract is its preference for neuter words like *hirer* and *party*, which express function rather than gender. When a personal pronoun has to be used, as in the case of *child*, the masculine *he* is used consistently throughout.

Talking point

> Why does the writer of the above use the inelegant expression *the same* in lines 1–2?

3 These two writing faults – the use of subordinate clauses, and of repetition – add up to a third: **the use of sentences that are far too long**.

4 Minor faults are:

a **the tendency to use verbs in the passive** rather than the active voice, making for wooden-sounding, awkward, impersonal constructions. (In the example below, the passive constructions are in italics.)

> In the event of a breach of any of the conditions specified in the last foregoing subsection during the period during which *they are required by that subsection to be observed* with respect to a dwelling, or in the event of *the voluntary alienation of a dwelling* by the owner thereof during the said period, the following provisions shall have effect: . . .

The following version using the active voice is easier to read:

> In the event of a breach of any of the conditions specified in the last foregoing subsection during the period during which that subsection requires them to be observed with respect to a dwelling, or in the event of the owner of a dwelling voluntarily transferring the dwelling to another during the said period, the following provisions shall have effect: . . .

b **the tendency to use words in sets of three**, where often merely the last one in the set would suffice. The following examples are all taken from a lease agreement of 26 August 1842 concerning property in London, quoted by David Levine in *The State of the Language*):

> rest, residue, and remainder;
> heirs, successors, and assigns;
> covenants, conditions, and agreements;
> leave, surrender, and yield up;
> enter and come into and upon;
> carry on or permit or suffer to be carried on;
> retain, repossess, and enjoy.

Is it the job of those who draft legal documents, then, to make them as watertight as possible? Well, up to a point.

Levine refers to a kind of 'artful vagueness' employed by some law-makers. For example, the employment of phrases like 'reasonable restrictions on the time, place, and manner' (of performing some action) allow legal writers to give general guidance while reserving the right to become more specific about what is unreasonable later on, in the light of experience. And lawyers drawing up a contract in the best interests of their clients will sometimes take care not to be too precise: if the client is, say, a heating engineer, lawyers will draft a document contracting her or him to supply equipment *in working order*. Not, you will note, *in good working order*, for that might adversely affect the client's interests. Just *working order*, so that if it gives out any heat at all, however inadequate, the client is covered and cannot be sued for breach of contract.

Should we criticize legal writing then, and demand its urgent reform, or are there arguments to be made in its defence?

The use of jargon in legal documents is usually justified on the grounds of convenience and brevity: lawyers know exactly what they mean by their technical terms; spelling them out so that laymen could understand them would consume large amounts of time, energy, and space. The definition of *tort*, for example, takes up twelve words in the *Concise Oxford Dictionary*, and still gives us only the most general and therefore vague notion of what it means: hundreds of books have been written on tort, and the rulings made by judges in any given case are always open to interpretation by other legal experts in other cases at other times. For this reason, even lawyers may not know how to interpret a given legal term in a particular context unless they are familiar with every case in which it has been used: the same term may have been differently construed in the different cases in which it has occurred. The jargon term *equal protection of the law*, for example, means one thing when applied to a particular set of people in a particular State of America, and another when applied to another set of people in a different one.

If jargon is as difficult to interpret as this, even for lawyers, should it be replaced by more ordinary, simple language? Experience shows that this is more dangerous. The ordinary man or woman might write 'I leave all my goods and possessions to (so-and-so)' and think that all eventualities are covered. The legal mind works very differently from this.

Talking point | What loopholes could a lawyer find in the last statement of the paragraph above?

The following illustrates the dangers of such simplicity. Use of the apparently straightforward word *simultaneously* led to complications in a recent British court case. Before embarking on a cruise a middle-aged couple made a will leaving all their money and property to their various children in the event of their simultaneous death. Unfortunately, they were drowned at sea and the will was contested in court. The judge's legal mind pondered the word *simultaneously* and ruled that it could not be held to apply to the case of death by drowning. Only if death were caused by an explosive device such as a bomb could the two be said to have died simultaneously, i.e. in the same instant of time. The will was therefore overturned. A ruling like this may lead you to conclude with Sam Weller that 'the Law is an ass', but it does illustrate rather well the characteristic working of the legal mind.

The person who drafts a legal document must try to imagine every possible combination of circumstances to which the words may be applied, and to think of every possible way in which they might be misinterpreted. If loopholes can be found, lawyers will find them, even if it seems to contravene the findings of common sense and natural justice. Tax lawyers and tax law drafters for instance are engaged in 'a continuous game of linguistic cat and mouse'. There is little we can do about jargon, it would appear, except hire a legal expert to employ it on our behalf and hope we've picked a good one.

What about the bad writing legal experts are guilty of?

Writing that is 'bad' in the literary sense is usually justified on the grounds of expediency: those who write legal documents *must* write inelegantly, they claim, in order to make their meaning precise and unambiguous.

Not even lawyers accept this claim. Wydick has demonstrated convincingly that legal writing can be both unambiguous and well, if not elegantly, written, and the English Society for Plain English has led the way by helping to draft documents that are both legally watertight and accessible to ordinary readers.

(See also pages 89 to 98 in the section, *The Vexed Question of Grammar.*)

The role of language in literature

Sentence structure, meaning, and style

In the work of good writers the structure of a sentence is an integral part of its meaning; it underpins and emphasizes what is being said. Consider for example this sentence from *David Copperfield* describing the death of Barkis:

> And, it being low water, he went out with the tide.

The rise of the voice towards the comma and its falling away from it afterwards reflect both the rise and fall of the tides and Barkis's movement towards death, creating at the same time a mood of gentle melancholy. Reverse the order of the clauses and you ruin the effect:

> He went out with the tide, it being low water.

As writers re-create experience (real or imagined) they reach instinctively for the particular words and structures that will bring it to life. Thus in the following extract Dickens, having chosen the steam engine as his symbol for the destructive greed of an increasingly mechanized society, calls up its sounds and rhythms in his head and recreates them in the structures of his sentences. Read carefully and you will hear in the first sentence exactly where the train settles down to run smoothly on a level gradient, and in the second, the actual moment when it goes through the points, changing rhythm before settling down again to a new, rapid, even pace:

> Away, with a shriek, and a roar, and a rattle, from the town, burrowing among the dwellings of men and making the streets hum, flashing out into the meadows for a moment, mining in through the damp earth, booming on in darkness and heavy air, bursting out again into the sunny day so bright and wide; away, with a shriek, and a roar, and a rattle, through the fields, through the woods, through the corn, through the hay, through the chalk, through the mould, through the clay, through the rock, among objects close at hand and almost in the grasp, ever flying from the traveller, and a deceitful distance ever moving slowly within him: like as in the track of the remorseless monster, Death!
>
> Through the hollow, on the height, by the heath, by the orchard, by the park, by the garden, over the canal, across the river, where the sheep are feeding, where the mill is going, where the barge is floating, where the dead are lying, where the factory is smoking, where the stream is running, where the village clusters, where the great cathedral

> rises, where the bleak moor lies, and the wild breeze smooths or ruffles it at its inconstant will; away, with a shriek, and a roar, and a rattle, and no trace to leave behind but dust and vapour: like as in the track of the remorseless monster, Death!
>
> Charles Dickens, *Dombey and Son*

In all good writing, even of a non-fictional kind, the structure of sentences underpins and intensifies their meaning. In this extract from a piece of journalism, for example, the dreary length of the concrete walkways on a council estate and the time it takes to reach the haven of your own front door are reflected in the deliberate piling up of subordinate clauses and phrases before the main statement:

> In through the concrete passage with its close-set black iron railings, past the battered grey lift which seldom works, up two flights of concrete stairs which smell of urine and drink, past graffiti saying, 'Where can we go for a hit, honey?' and along a concrete walkway, partly blocked by the remains of a brown moquette armchair, you'll find number 86.

The different kinds of effects that writers can achieve through the use of different kinds of sentence structures are illustrated below.

The simple sentence

It is possible to write well using mainly simple and compound sentences. Hemingway, for example, did so. In his opinion, the lengthy complex sentences and ornate diction of writers such as Henry James distracted attention from what was being said, focusing it instead on the writer's style. Hemingway chose to write in simple sentences, using few adverbs or adjectives, so that the truth of a situation could speak for itself. These characteristic features of his style can be seen in the extract below from *A Farewell to Arms*:

> I sat down on the chair in front of the table where there were nurse's reports hung on clips at the side and looked out of the window. I could see nothing but the dark and the rain falling across the lights from the window. So that was it. The baby was dead. That was why the doctor looked so tired. But why had they acted the way they had in the room with him? They supposed he would come round and start breathing probably. I had no religion but I knew he ought to have been baptized. But what if he never breathed at all? He hadn't. He had never been alive. Except in Catherine. I'd felt him kick there often enough. But I hadn't for a week. Maybe he was choked all the time. Poor little kid. I wished the hell I'd been choked like that. No I didn't. Still there would not be all this dying to go through. Now Catherine would die. That was what you did. You died. You did not know what it was about. You never had time to learn. They threw you in and told you the rules and the first time they

> caught you off base they killed you. Or they killed you gratuitously like
> Aymo. Or gave you the syphilis like Rinaldi. But they killed you in the
> end. You could count on that. Stay around and they would kill you.

The varied rhythm and intonation here are created through the skilful
alternation of
  a sentence lengths, and
  b questions and statements.

The same apparently simple technique puts us inside the character's mind
as he asks his anguished questions and comes to equally painful
conclusions: *But what if he never breathed at all? He hadn't. He had never
been alive. Except in Catherine. I'd felt him kick there often enough. But I
hadn't for a week. Maybe he was choked all the time. Poor little kid.* The
short, often abrupt sentences suit both the context (the situation the
character finds himself in) and the prevailing mood of bewildered grief.

Ian Fleming, on the other hand, chose the simple/compound sentence
style for its ability to create tension and move a story along at speed –
something else that lengthy complex sentences full of dependent clauses
cannot do. In the extract from his *Dr No* that follows, seventy-nine of the
eighty-nine sentences are simple, four compound, and only six complex;
yet Fleming varies their structure so well that they never become
monotonous or dull.

Activity

Read the passage to see how well Fleming manages this style, then
carry out the activities suggested below.
(007 has been woken in the night by something crawling up his leg. His
instincts tell him it is a tropical centipede.)

The centipede had reached his knee. It was starting up his thigh.
Whatever happened he mustn't move, mustn't even tremble. Bond's
whole consciousness had drained down to the two rows of softly
creeping feet. Now they had reached his flank. God, it was turning
5 down towards his groin! Bond set his teeth. Supposing it liked the
warmth there! Supposing it tried to crawl into the crevices! Could he
stand it? Supposing it chose that place to bite? Bond could feel it
questing among the first hairs. It tickled. The skin on Bond's belly
fluttered. There was nothing he could do to control it. But now the
10 thing was turning up and along his stomach. Its feet were gripping
tighter to prevent it falling. Now it was at his heart. If it bit there,
surely it would kill him. The centipede trampled steadily on through the
thin hairs on Bond's right breast up to his collar bone. It stopped. What
15 was it doing? Bond could feel the blunt head questing slowly to and
fro. What was it looking for? Was there room between his skin and the
sheet for it to get through? Dare he lift the sheet an inch to help it?
20 No. Never! The animal was at the base of his jugular. Perhaps it was
intrigued by the heavy pulse there. Christ, if only he could control the
pumping of his blood. Damn you! Bond tried to communicate with the

centipede. It's nothing. It's not dangerous, that pulse. It means you no harm. Get on out into the fresh air!

25 As if the beast had heard, it moved on up the column of the neck and into the stubble on Bond's chin. Now it was at the corner of his mouth, tickling madly. On it went, up along the nose. Now he could feel its whole weight and length. Softly Bond closed his eyes. Two by two the
30 pairs of feet, moving alternately, tramped across his right eyelid. When it got off his eye, should he take a chance and shake it off – rely on its feet slipping in his sweat? No, for God's sake! The grip of the feet was endless. He might shake one lot off, but not the rest.

35 With incredible deliberation the huge insect rambled across Bond's forehead. It stopped below the hair. What the hell was it doing now? Bond could feel it nuzzling at his skin. It was drinking! Drinking the beads of salt sweat. Bond was sure of it. For minutes it hardly moved.
40 Bond felt weak with the tension. He could feel the sweat pouring off the rest of his body on to the sheet. In a second his limbs would start to tremble. He could feel it coming on. He would start to shake with an ague of fear. Could he control it, could he? Bond lay and waited, the
45 breath coming softly through his open, snarling mouth . . .

The centipede stirred. Slowly it walked out of his hair on to the pillow. Bond waited a second. Now he could hear the rows of feet picking softly at the cotton. It was a tiny scraping noise like soft fingernails.

50 With a crash that shook the room Bond's body jack-knifed out of bed and on to the floor.

At once Bond was on his feet and at the door. He turned on the light. He found he was shaking uncontrollably. He staggered to the bed.
55 There it was crawling out of sight over the edge of the pillow. Bond's first instinct was to twitch the pillow on the floor. He controlled himself, waiting for his nerves to quieten. Then softly, deliberately, he picked up the pillow by one corner and walked into the middle of the
60 room and dropped it. The centipede came out from under the pillow. It started to snake quickly away across the matting. Now Bond was uninterested. He looked round for something to kill it with. Slowly he went and picked up a shoe and came back. The danger was past. His
65 mind was wondering now how the centipede had got into his bed. He lifted the shoe and slowly, almost carelessly, smashed it down. He heard the crack of the hard carapace.

Bond lifted the shoe.

70 The centipede was whipping from side to side in its agony – five inches of grey-brown, shiny death. Bond hit it again. It burst open, yellowly.

Bond dropped the shoe and ran for the bathroom and was violently sick.

1 How does Fleming manage to vary the pace and movement of his writing here, while working almost exclusively with simple sentences? (Are they all statements, for instance? Does the subject always come at the beginning of the sentence, or at the same place in the sentence? What other parts of speech does he use to begin sentences? Are there any phrases? If so, how do they help to keep things moving?)

2 There are three compound sentences in the paragraph beginning at line 43 (*At once Bond was on his feet and at the door*) and a further compound sentence closes the extract. Do they all move at the same speed, in the same rhythm? How does he manage to vary their movement to suit the physical actions they describe?

3 Fleming uses very little punctuation other than full stops. Why do you suppose he placed a comma after *It burst . . .* in line 71?

4 How far do you consider Fleming's style a simple one?

The simple sentence style can of course be over-done by less skilful writers. One literary critic wrote this gentle parody to call Gerald Seymour to task for doing so:

He writes like old *Daily Express* leaders.
He likes short sentences.
Often he uses one sentence paragraphs.
When his man is in bed with a girl, some of the sentences become longer, sometimes even a bit soppy. But not very soppy.
He has written an exciting book.

Even writers like Hemingway and Fleming however were forced to use complex sentences at times, simply because they offered a wider range of stylistic effects. These will be illustrated below.

The complex sentence

Traditional textbooks tell us that there are three distinct varieties of complex sentence:

* the **periodic**, in which the independent main clause comes last and is preceded by dependent clauses and phrases;
* the **balanced**, which is made up of two independent main clauses that are closely similar in structure;
* the **loose**, in which the independent main clause comes first and is followed by dependent clauses and phrases.

It is true that sentences answering to these descriptions can be found in English writing. Here are three:

Periodic

That learning belongs not to the female character, and that the female mind is not capable of a degree of improvement equal to that of the other sex, are narrow and unphilosophical prejudices.

Balanced

All days march towards death; only the last one reaches it.

Loose

I was born in the year 1632, in the city of York, of a good family, though not of that country, my father being a foreigner of Bremen, who settled first at Hull; he got a good estate by merchandise, and leaving off his trade, lived afterward at York, from whence he had married my mother, whose relations were named Robinson, a very good family in that country, and from whom I was called Robinson Kreutznaer; but by the usual corruption of words in England, we are now called, nay, we call ourselves, and write our name, Crusoe.

Talking point

> Why is the loose sentence a good structure to use to depict a man telling a story in this rambling kind of way?

To say that a writer has used a balanced, loose, or periodic sentence to express an idea, however, is not very useful. What really matters is to see *why* the writer has constructed his sentence in that particular way. In other words, to understand how the structure of a sentence helps in conveying its meaning.

▓ *The uses of the periodic sentence*

Periodic sentences can emphasize ideas of length or weight or abundance, as in the example below. The abundant minor clauses are used to intensify an impression of luxuriance and ease and beauty, and therefore to bring out more strongly the hint of menace lurking at the end:

> Even in May, when the lilacs frothed into purple, paved the lawns with shadows, steeped the air with scent; when soft leaves lipped one another consolingly, when blackbirds sang, fell in their effortless way from the green height to the green depth, and sang again – still, something that haunted the place set the heart fluttering.
>
> Mary Webb, *Gone to Earth*

They can intensify the idea of delay before achievement:

> A last swell of snow, the wind gusting hard, threatening to blow us from our perch, and we were on the South Summit.

They may perhaps be used to spring a surprise if a piece of startling information is saved for the sentence end; but perhaps their main purpose is to build up the importance of a subject by giving a long list of all the qualities it has before actually mentioning it by name:

> [At the beginning, to French-Norman blood was added Scots-Irish blood.] And when you add to these the Indian strain supplying the mystery, and the Jewish strain supplying spectacular showmanship, and you overlay all this with his circumstances, social conditioning, and religious upbringing . . . you have the enigma that was Elvis.

▓ *The uses of the balanced sentence*

Balanced sentences are also of rather limited use, though very effective in creating effects of contrast:

> Children begin by loving their parents; after a time they judge them; rarely, if ever, do they forgive them.

> The country is so lovely; the man-made England is so vile.

In balanced sentences such as these the nouns, the adjectives, and the verbs all match each other in form and contrast with each other in ideas. Such sentences have an air of incontrovertible authority, of giving the last word to be said on a subject. This is achieved partly by the symmetrical balance and neatness of the structure, partly by the reflective pause introduced by the intermediate semi-colon, and partly by the falling intonation in the final clause.

The last example is typical of balanced sentences with contrasting ideas, the structure of the second clause being a mirror image of the structure of the first:

Subject noun	Verb	Adjective
The country	is	so lovely;
the man-made England	is	so vile.

Because the two clauses are so similar in construction and so close together, the contrast between their ideas reveals itself more strikingly.

▓ *The uses of the loose sentence*

The loose sentence has an enormously wide range, from the bland through the lively to the pleasantly balanced and the rhythmically beautiful. Consider this fast-moving passage from James Agee's *A Death in the Family*:

> They walked downtown in the light of mother-of-pearl, to the Majestic, and found their way to seats by the light of the screen, in the exhilarating smell of stale tobacco, rank sweat, and dirty drawers, while the piano played fast music and galloping horses raised a grandiose flag of dust.

The opening sentence of Jane Austen's *Pride and Prejudice* is more dignified and controlled:

> It is a truth universally acknowledged that a single man in possession of a fortune must be in need of a wife.

Turn this into a periodic sentence and its elegant balance and rhythm would be lost:

> That a single man in possession of a large fortune must be in need of a wife is a truth universally acknowledged.

So would the air of clinching finality that comes from the falling intonation on 'must be in need of a wife.' In one of the most famous examples of the loose sentence in English, Gibbon creates a mood of gentle melancholy and nostalgia – for his own, as well as Rome's, vanished past:

> It was at Rome, on the 15th of October 1764, as I sat musing amidst the ruins of the Capitol, while the bare-foot friars were singing Vespers in the Temple of Jupiter, that the idea of writing the decline and fall of the city first started to my mind.

Read sensitively, this sentence moves downwards in a series of descending steps, clause by clause, to a final falling intonation on *first started to my mind*. Rearrange the clauses in any other way and the graceful rhythm and falling intonation would be lost:

> It was at Rome, on the 15th of October 1764, that the idea of writing the decline and fall of the city first started to my mind, as I sat musing amidst the ruins of the Capitol, while the bare-foot friars were singing Vespers in the Temple of Jupiter.

The following sentence by Conrad is different again. It also has superb rhythm and sensuous appeal, but this time what is evoked is physical – the last moments of a sinking ship:

> The scuppers of the brig gurgled softly all together when the waters rising against her sides subsided sleepily with a slow wash, as if playing about an immovable rock.

It makes us feel in its rise and fall the rise and fall of the waves; it echoes in the softness of its repeated *s* sounds (*subsided sleepily with a slow wash*) what Auden called the 'swaying sound of the sea'.

Between these two extremes there are all kinds of loose sentences that make no special appeal yet please us with their elegance and clarity.

Evelyn Waugh is a master of the loose sentence, using it to create a series of visual images that unroll in the mind like scenes from a film:

> It is thus I like to remember Sebastian, as he was that summer, when we wandered alone together through that enchanted palace; Sebastian in his wheelchair spinning down the box-edged walks of the kitchen gardens in search of alpine strawberries and warm figs, propelling himself through the succession of hothouses, from scent to scent and climate to climate, to cut the muscat grapes and choose orchids for our button-holes; Sebastian hobbling with a pantomime of difficulty to the old nurseries, sitting beside me on the threadbare, flowered carpet with the toy-cupboard empty about us and Nanny Hawkins stitching

> complacently in the corner, saying 'You're one as bad as the other; a
> pair of children the two of you . . . '
>   The autumnal mood possessed us both as though the riotous
> exuberance of June had died with the gillyflowers, whose scent at my
> windows now yielded to the damp leaves, smouldering in a corner of the
> quad.
>
> Evelyn Waugh, *Brideshead Revisited*

Henry James is another frequent user of this form, piling clause upon
clause until his sentence is as long as most writers' paragraphs:

> It was the hour at which ladies should come out for an airing and roll
> past a hedge of pedestrians, holding their parasols askance. Here,
> however, Eugenia observed no indications of this custom, the absence of
> which was more anomalous as there was a charming avenue of
> remarkably graceful arching elms in the most convenient contiguity to a
> large, cheerful street, in which, evidently, among the more prosperous
> members of the bourgeoisie, a great deal of pedestrianism went
> forward.
>
> Henry James, *The Europeans*

Social manners were what interested James – the good or bad behaviour of
people constrained by the conventions of polite society – and both his
sentence structure and his old-fashioned and formal diction (choice of
words and phrases) are suited to his subject. A phrase like 'a great deal of
pedestrianism went forward' is stilted to the point of being comical to
readers of the present time (Hemingway would have written 'people were
walking' – if he'd bothered to mention it at all), and the long, rolling,
carefully controlled clauses help to create a general air of remoteness from
the chaos and crises of ordinary life.

The working together of sentences in prose

Whatever they are like individually, however, the sentences we read do
not exist separately, in a vacuum. They are designed to work with other
sentences that precede and follow them, like notes and phrases in a piece
of music. In good writing, short clauses and phrases balance longer ones
that alternate in turn with others of medium length. In the same way,
clauses or phrases with rising intonations are 'answered' by others with
intonations that fall. Sometimes paragraphs of such sentences
complement one another, working towards the same end; sometimes they
work to the opposite effect, creating strong contrasts of mood and
atmosphere. Consider the following extracts, the end of chapter 4 and the
beginning of chapter 5 of James Joyce's novel *A Portrait of the Artist as a
Young Man*. In A Joyce is re-creating the 'epiphany' (moment of
revelation) in which he recognized his vocation of creative artist. (The
character, the same in A and B, is Stephen Daedalus – Joyce's portrait of
himself as a young man):

A

He closed his eyes in the languor of sleep. His eyelids trembled as if they felt the vast cyclic movement of the earth and her watchers, trembled as if they felt the strange light of some new world. His soul was swooning into some new world, fantastic, dim, uncertain as under sea, traversed by cloudy shapes and beings. A world, a glimmer, or a flower? Glimmering and trembling, trembling and unfolding, a breaking light, an opening flower, it spread in endless succession to itself, breaking in full crimson and unfolding and fading to palest rose, leaf by leaf and wave of light by wave of light, flooding all the heavens with its soft flushes, every flush deeper than the others.

Evening had fallen when he woke and the sand and arid grasses of his bed glowed no longer. He rose slowly and, recalling the rapture of his sleep, sighed at its joy. He climbed to the crest of the sandhill and gazed about him. Evening had fallen. A rim of the young moon cleft the pale waste of skyline, the rim of a silver hoop embedded in grey sand; and the tide was flowing in fast to the land with a low whisper of her waves, islanding a few last figures in distant pools.

B

He drained his third cup of watery tea to the dregs and set to chewing the crusts of fried bread that were scattered near him, staring into the dark pool of the jar. The yellow dripping had been scooped out like a bog-hole, and the pool under it brought back to his memory the dark turf-coloured water of the bath in Clongowes. The box of pawn tickets at his elbow had just been rifled and he took up idly one after another in his greasy fingers the blue and white dockets, scrawled and sanded and creased and bearing the name of the pledger as Daly or MacEvoy.

Other things than sentence structure are at work here to give passage A its power:

    a the sound effects, for example: the feeling of space got by the long -*a* sound in *vast* (line 2);

    b the falling intonations on the endings of the participles: *glimmering, trembling, unfolding, breaking*, etc.;

    c the powerful sexual connotations of many of the words: *trembling, unfolding, opening, breaking in full crimson and unfolding and fading to palest rose, flooding all the heavens with its soft flushes.* (Why does Joyce use the metaphor of sexual orgasm to convey Stephen's state of spiritual rapture?)

Nevertheless, the majority of clauses and phrases in A work towards creating a sense of spiritual exaltation, just as those in B combine to create the opposite mood and atmosphere. For example, in the fifth sentence of A, beginning *Glimmering and trembling . . .*, a sense of expansion, of lifting and soaring, is got by the placing of several phrases before the main clause:

it spread . . .
an opening flower,
a breaking light,
trembling and unfolding,
Glimmering and trembling,

Notice how the voice rises on the commas at the end of each phrase, carrying us up onto the plateau of the main clause – *it spread in endless succession to itself, breaking in full crimson* – before allowing us to fall again, level by level, on a second series of phrases, back to the world of external reality:

and fading
to palest rose,
leaf by leaf
and wave of light by wave of light,
flooding all the heavens
with its soft flushes,
every flush
deeper than
the others.

In contrast, the flatness of the compound sentences in B, together with the sordid objects they describe, confront us with a world that is gross in its sheer physicality.

▧ *A note on intonation*

Falling intonations are very common in English, simply because of its characteristic stress patterns. Nouns, verbs, adjectives, and adverbs of two syllables always carry the main stress on the first syllable, followed by a lighter stress (or 'off-beat') on the second. The voice drops as a consequence on the off-beat, resulting in a falling intonation. Test this for yourself by pronouncing the following words taken from the first Joyce extract above:

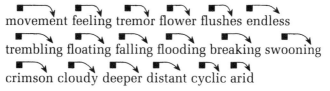

movement feeling tremor flower flushes endless

trembling floating falling flooding breaking swooning

crimson cloudy deeper distant cyclic arid

Despite their inbuilt tendency to fall, however, rising intonations can still be created with words like these when

a they are followed by a comma: e.g. . . . *her watchers,*
b they are closely linked with the word or phrase that follows:

e.g. *endless succession, movement of the earth.*

Monosyllabic words like those in the second Joyce extract –

tea dregs crust bread pool jar bog-hole bath box pawn scrawled creased

– on the other hand have no inbuilt rise and fall, and taken together tend to create an air of flat monotony.

Activity

> Look at the imagery of the two passages and discuss what it contributes to the overall meaning. What is suggested by the new moon, for instance, and the swiftly in-flowing tide? How do the images of the dripping-bowl and the stagnant water of school bath and bog-hole contrast with these?

Sentence structure and the passage of time

Sentence structure, like vocabulary, changes from age to age. The rhythms of the first Elizabeth and her successor James I's reigns are no longer possible in ours, as the following versions of parts of St Paul's first *Letter to the Corinthians*, chapter 13, should show. The first is from the Authorized Version of the Bible, printed in the seventeenth century; the second from the *New English Bible*, first published in 1961.

Activity

> Read these differing versions, then discuss the critical points raised below.
>
> **A 1** Though I speak with the tongues of men and of angels, and have not charity, I am become as sounding brass or a tinkling cymbal.
> **2** And though I have the gift of prophecy, and understand all mysteries, and all knowledge; and though I have all faith, so that I could remove mountains, and have not charity, I am nothing.
> **3** And though I bestow all my goods to feed the poor, and though I give my body to be burned, and have not charity, it profiteth me nothing.
>
> **B 1–3** I may speak in tongues of men or of angels, but if I am without love I am a sounding gong or a clanging cymbal. I may have the gift of prophecy, and know every hidden truth; I may have faith strong enough to move mountains; but if I have no love, I am nothing. I may dole out all I possess, or even give my body to be burnt, but if I have no love, I am none the better.
>
> **1** In verses 1 to 3 of the Authorized Version the writers use a periodic sentence. What is the effect of this structure, and what happens to the tone and rhythm of the modern version when the structure is changed?
> **2** Which version do you find the easier to understand?
> **3** Which version seems to you to be the most beautiful in literary terms?

As a final illustration of how sentence structure is related to style, you are invited to do a little literary detective work before reading two passages of descriptive writing. A is taken from a piece of descriptive prose called *Flowery Tuscany* by D. H. Lawrence, B from a piece on Cornwall, entitled *The Spirit of Place*, by the poet Edward Thomas. Lawrence's theme is life: the sudden, rapidly burgeoning life of flowers in sunny Mediterranean countries, and beyond that, the life-force itself that runs through everything alike – flowers, animals, and human beings. Thomas's theme is death, ruin, and decay: death as represented by the ruined churches and ancient burial mounds (barrows) of the high Cornish moors; decay in the abandoning of the tin mines and the selling out of the farmers to a more commercial way of life.

Activity

1 Bearing in mind that:

※ good writers communicate as much through the structure and rhythm of their sentences as through the meaning of the words themselves,

※ Lawrence's theme is life and Thomas's decay and death,
   which of the following features would you expect to find in the Lawrence passage, which in the Thomas? (It might be a good idea to divide a page in half and list each feature under the appropriate writer's name.)

   a short, assertive, one-clause sentences
   b longer, more leisurely sentences, with lengthy phrases and dependent clauses (to create the impression of stagnation and decay over long periods of time)
   c the use of rather conventional verbs and adjectives
   d the use of strong, vivid, active verbs (to suggest energetic activity)
   e the use of normal word-order, with the subject preceding the verb
   f the inversion of the usual word order from time to time, with subject and adjective coming before the verb
   g strings of rapid simple sentences joined by commas and dashes (to get the effect of rapid movement or growth)
   h conventional punctuation and a frequent use of heavy semi-colons
   i sentences with varied intonation and rhythm (to reflect different qualities of movement, whether plant or animal)
   j a general sameness of rhythm and structure
   k the use of falling intonations (to suggest melancholy, parting, decay, and death)
   l sentences in which phrases and dependent clauses are piled one on top of the other (to create an atmosphere of excitement or rising emotion)
   m sentences that hold back their main statement until the end (to create the impression of dramatic arrival after long delay)
   n short, incisive simple sentences (to suggest brevity and speed)
   o unconventionally constructed sentences, crammed full of phrases and adjectives, unchecked by punctuation (to describe a landscape overwhelmingly rich in growth)
   p sentences beginning with 'And' or 'But', that give an urgent feel to the writing.

2 When you have finished your detective work, give the two passages a careful preliminary reading.

3 Now read them again, carrying out the tasks below:

   a Look for at least *one* example of each of the structures you forecast would be present in each writer.

   b Make notes for your own use on the effects each writer is getting with these structures.

   c Write an account of the style of either Lawrence or Thomas, bringing out the writer's particular strengths.

A Flowery Tuscany

And still there is a difference. There are several kinds of wild crocus in this region of Tuscany: being little spiky mauve ones, and spiky little creamy ones, that grow among the pine trees of the bare slopes. But the beautiful ones are those of a meadow in the corner of the woods, the low hollow meadow below the steep shadowy pine-slopes, the secretive grassy dip where the water seeps through the turf all winter, where the stream runs between thick bushes, where the nightingale sings his mightiest in May, and where the wild thyme is rosy and full of bees, in summer.

Here the lavender crocuses are most at home – here sticking out of the deep grass, in a hollow like a cup, a bowl of grass, come the lilac-coloured crocuses, like an innumerable encampment. You may see them at twilight, with all the buds shut, in the mysterious stillness of the grassy underworld, palely glimmering like myriad folded tents. So the Apaches still camp, and close their tepees, in the hollows of the great hills of the West, at night.

But in the morning it is quite different. Then the sun shines strong on the horizontal green cloud-puffs of the pines, the sky is clear and full of life, the water runs hastily, still browned by the last juice of crushed olives. And there the earth's bowl of crocuses is amazing. You cannot believe that the flowers are really still. They are open with such delight, and their pistil-thrust is so red-orange, and they are so many, all reaching out wide and marvellous, that it suggests a perfect ecstasy of radiant, thronging movement, lit-up violet and orange, and surging in some invisible rhythm of concerted, delightful movement. You cannot believe they do not move, and make some sort of crytalline sound of delight. If you sit still and watch, you begin to move with them, like moving with the stars, and you feel the sound of their radiance. All the little cells of the flowers must be leaping with flowery life and utterance.

D.H. Lawrence

B The spirit of place

Of all the rocky land, of the sapphire sea white with quiet foam, the barrows are masters. The breaking away of the rock has brought them nearer to the sea as it has annihilated some and cut off the cliff-ways in mid-career. They stand in the unenclosed waste and are removed from all human uses and from most wayfaring. Thus they share the sublimity of beacons and are about to show that tombs also have their deaths.

Linnet and stonechat and pipit seem to attend upon them, with pretty voices and motions and a certain ghastliness, as of shadows, given to their cheerful and sudden flittings by the solemn neighbourhood. But most of their hold upon the spirit they owe to their powerful suggestion that here upon the high sea border was once lived a bold proud life, like that of Beowulf, whose words, when he was dying from the wounds of his last victory, were: 'Bid the warriors raise a funeral mound to flash with fire on a promontory above the sea, that it may stand high and be a memorial by which my people shall remember me, and seafarers driving their tall ships through the mist of the sea shall say: "Beowulf's Mound."'

In Cornwall, as in Wales, these monuments are the more impressive, because the earth, wasting with them and showing her bones, takes their part. There are days when the age of the Downs, strewn with tumuli and the remnants of camp and village, is incredible; or rather they seem in the course of long time to have grown smooth and soft and kind, and to be, like a rounded languid cloud, an expression of Earth's summer bliss of afternoon. But granite and slate and sandstone jut out, and in whatsoever weather speak rather of the cold, drear, hard, windy dawn. Nothing can soften the lines of Trendreen or Brown Willy or Carn Galver against the sky. The small stone-hedged ploughlands amidst brake and gorse do but accentuate the wildness of the land from which they have been won. The deserted mines are frozen cries of despair as if they had perished in conflict with the waste; and in a few years their chimneys standing amidst rotted woodwork, the falling masonry, the engine rusty, huge and still (the abode of rabbits, and all overgrown with bedstraw, the stern thistle and wizard henbane) are in keeping with the miles of barren land, littered with rough silvered stones among feather and furze, whose many barrows are deep in fern and bramble and foxglove. The cotton grass raises its pure nodding white. The old roads dive among still more furze and bracken and bramble and foxglove, and on every side the land grows no such crop as that of grey stones. Even in the midst of occasional cornfield or weedless pasture a long grey upright stone speaks of the past. In many places men have set up these stones, roughly squaring some of them, in the form of a circle or in groups of circles – and over them beats the buzzard in slow hesitating and swerving flight.

Edward Thomas

Literary techniques

Irony

Key word

> *Irony:* the technique of implying precisely the opposite of what is being said, often in a sarcastic tone (from Greek *eironeia*, simulated ignorance; *eiron*, dissembler).

The word *irony* has three main meanings. It denotes:

1 the technique of implying the opposite of what is actually said, e.g. the common use of 'Charming!' as a response to something unpleasant. It is especially effective when the writer pretends to admire and respect someone's behaviour or ideas in order to ridicule them or reveal their vices, e.g. Chaucer's apparently guileless comments on the Wife of Bath:

> She was a worthy woman al her lyve.
> Husbondes at chirche doore she hadde hadde fyve

where he leaves the tension between the two statements to do the work of casting doubt on her reputation for 'worthiness' or noble behaviour.

2 some incongruity between what we expect or intend to happen and what actually does occur, or a situation showing such incongruity: e.g. a man who never does anything for his children decides to build a cage for their pet hamster, finishes it to great applause then steps back on to the animal and kills it.

3 a situation in the theatre in which the audience understands the implications of what is going on better than most of the characters, e.g. Hamlet's calling Polonius a fishmonger: Polonius takes this coded remark as evidence that the prince is mad; the audience understands Hamlet to mean that Polonius is
   a a pimp,
   b a fisher for secrets.

For our purposes here, the first definition of irony is the important one and we shall concentrate on it.

Dictionaries often confuse irony with sarcasm, or at least make the meanings of the two words overlap to such an extent that it is difficult to tell one from the other. There are similarities between the two, it is true, but there are also differences.

Similarities and differences between sarcasm and irony

1 Both intend to insult, hurt, and ridicule their victims;
2 Both may be uttered or written in a 'sarcastic' tone of voice that makes this intention clear; **but**
3 Irony always works indirectly through pretence, whereas sarcasm (from Greek *sarkazein*, to tear flesh) attacks openly and goes straight for the throat.

Points 1 to 3 can be illustrated on a trivial level.

Scenario: wife and husband wash up and he breaks something:
Sarcasm: 'It's ham-fisted idiots like you that keep John Lewis's profits up. Have you got shares?'
Irony: 'What a deft, light-fingered touch you have, my love. Ever thought of working in a china shop?'

4 Sarcasm works on a lower intellectual level than irony. 'This is stupid. I hate it!' is the gist of its message. It appeals to the emotions rather than to the brain, leaving us with negative feelings of anger, dislike and contempt. Irony, in contrast, forces us to think. 'Look at this', the ironist says with tongue in cheek. 'See how good, how fine, how unselfish, how intelligent this is! Don't you love it?' And, because the ideas or behaviour have been exaggerated just enough to bring out their true quality, we realize that
   a we do not love it at all;
   b we know exactly why we dislike it.

Listening to simulated advocacy or support of things that are bad has clarified our ideas about what is good. We have been pushed into making a moral choice.

Talking point

1 Decide which of the two passages below is an example of irony, which of sarcasm:

A . . . The visitor to London is wonderfully looked after by the benign empire of Sir Charles Forte and need never be out of sight of his modern hotels . . . If he drives out of London he runs still less risk of doing without the uniform standards of Forte. He can stop at a Post House hotel, or at a Little Chef café, in the confidence that the food will always be the same . . . There will be the same kind of steaks – never too tender – the same prawn cocktails, with plenty of lettuce, and the same honest English-style pizzas. And Sir Charles's great system of Portion Control – the secret of so much of his financial success – will ensure that he doesn't eat too much. In at least thirty towns the only hotel is a Forte hotel, which removes any tiresome business of having to choose. What a marvellous change after travelling through France, with all those eccentric little family hotels, where you never know what sort of food will be served, and where it changes from one region to the next!
Anthony Sampson

B . . . Of all the callosities produced in Thatcher's Britain, a majority of our Press has become the most callous . . . Now we are colonized by journalistic muggers with cabbage ears and blocked noses who beat at their typewriters with leaden coshes. Under those indiscriminate blows the keys meld into mere slugs of metal within which there is no decipherable meaning other than hostility. The muggers do not forge words but blunt instruments with which to render those who read insensible, if not permanently brain-damaged. When you actually handle the newspapers for which they commit their acts of aggression, holding them away from you as you might an old sock, you realize that, indeed, time has a warp. Fresh from the presses each issue may be, but it already smells of its near future, the contents of dustbins and the wrapping of fish.

Jill Tweedie

2 Which passage leaves you with a clearer idea of the good qualities that are to be preferred to the ones described?

▇ *Irony and style*

Irony has different moods for different purposes. When a writer is amused at some minor stupidity, the front he puts on is not a very serious one. The sentence structure is relaxed, the vocabulary is informal, the tone is playful – rhetorical questions may even be asked in a friendly, conversational manner. When writers use irony to attack vice or injustice, however, the style changes to suit the seriousness of the mood. If the technique is to work, we must be lured into believing that the writer means every word of the case that is put forward. Only if we think it is serious will we feel moral indignation and choose to oppose it. The writer, in other words, must pretend to be in love with evil in order to shock us out of indifference and make us choose good. If the tone is too 'knowing', the attitude too relaxed, and the register not quite appropriate, the reader will know and the game will be up.

Activity

Read extracts A to C, then write responses to the following questions:
1 Explain what each writer is attacking.
2 Describe the tone or emotional atmosphere of each passage.
3 Choose
  a the least effective,
  b the most effective
of these passages of irony. Discuss the qualities of each that led you to make your choice.

A Dear thingy . . .

A new and perhaps insurmountable problem now crops up in writing to a commercial firm. The standard form used to be 'Dear Sirs,' on the chauvinist assumption (usually correct) that all those in charge would be men. But if that assumption is invalid (or is deemed on liberationist grounds to be invalid) how should the letter begin? 'Dear Sirs or Madams' is obviously inadequate because there might be several sirs and only one madam or several madams and only one sir. Moreover, it might prove that the madams, if any, were senior to the sirs, in which case 'Dear Madams or Sirs' would be more accurate, though still begging the question of the number of sirs and madams involved. In an extreme case, the top person might be a madam, her immediate deputies sirs, and the third rank another set of madams, so that the appropriate form would have to be 'Dear Madam, Sirs, and other Madams'. Such a form could not be used however unless the hierarchy of the firm were known in intimate detail and it is precisely in cases where the hierarchy is not known that the person wishing to engage in correspondence is at a loss. 'Dear Sirs, including Madams' would raise again the sensitive issue of whether the term 'man' includes both sexes, and if the letter came into the hands of one who felt deeply on this question the reply could well be taken up with a procedural rebuke instead of dealing with the subject of the correspondence. Most letter writers would bridle at the form 'Dear Persons', for to address a member of either sex simply as 'Person' is manifestly less polite than to use the appropriate title (if only one knew what it was). After rejecting frivolous alternatives we have concluded that the correct way of starting a letter to a group of people whose sexual composition is not known is 'Dear Sir or Sirs, Madam or Madams; Madam or Madams, Sir or Sirs'. This can, however, be nothing more than an interim solution, and a highly objectionable one at that, because it puts the sirs before the madams in the opening words, thus perpetuating the assumption of seniority of man over woman which it sets out to avoid. A logician might have to have recourse to the form 'Dear Member or Members of the class of persons designated, if male, by the title Sir and if female by the title Madam.'

But it is doubtful whether the average managing director, let alone his or her secretary, when he or she types the letter, is ready for that yet.

Third leader, *The Guardian*, 16 September 1980

B Jason Prong meets the objectives

Having read *English from 5 to 16*, I wondered how one of my fifth year pupils, Jason Prong, measured up to expectations.

Jason's clenched, tattooed fists demonstrate his mastery of both the abstract noun and antithesis: 'love' on his right knuckles, 'hate' on his left.

On his demin jacket messages show his liking of brevity: he uses both a subject and a predicate in 'Sid Lives', while in his local bus shelter he has scrawled his favourite metaphor: 'Carole is a cow'. The alliteration appeals to him, you see.

When he roams the playground, free after a restless morning trapped at a small desk in a dusty classroom, where he has grappled with a faded blue worksheet which obliged him to fill in gaps in a close procedure exercise, he demonstrates his ability to 'give instructions or orders to someone else'. 'Tell Jonesy that I'm off school, or I'll knack yer.' In influencing a weaker member of his class he has 'chosen an appropriate register'.

He is also 'sensitive to the language limitations of others', kneeing the unfortunate boy in the groin in case he did not understand the verbal threat.

Jason uses 'the resources of the voice expressively'. He leads a raucous chorus of 'Here we go, Here we go, Here we go' as the fifth formers charge into the desk-filled hall for the CSE mockery exams.

When Jason goes to St James's Park he demonstrates 'a range of uses of English'. In the queue outside the ground he 'uses language to speculate' on the outcome of the match: 'Do you think we'll hammer them like we did last year?' He then makes a 'polite request' to the police officer above him. 'Can yer get yer horse's hoof off me Dr Martin's, I've only just bought them?' To the gateman he gives precise information: 'Two please, and that's a fiver I've given you.' Once inside the ground he shows 'a control of emphasis, pause and repetition'. He begins with the effectively repetitious:

'Haway the Lads
Haway the Lads',

while his emphasis in:

'We hate Nottingham Forest,
We hate Liverpool too
We hate Man United
But Newcastle we love you'

is impeccable, bringing out the subtle assonance in 'Not', 'For' and 'Pool', 'too'. It is also apparent that his 'accent is intelligible' to the 28,000 listeners in the crowd. Moreover, he is 'sensitive to the non-verbal accompaniments of speech', hoisting 'V' signs and making threatening gestures to the opposition supporters caged in the Leazes End.

When he returns to school on Monday, Jason will 'describe clearly the experiences he has undergone'.

'After the match we chased these Chelsea supporters to the Central Station. There was this kid who fell down in a back lane and about twenty people kicked him in . . .'

As far as reading is concerned, I was surprised to learn that he had 'read whole books of some length requiring some persistence'. He is into both fiction and non-fiction. He has read *Skinhead*, *I Stamp on Your Face*, *Nazi War Crimes* and *A History of Motorbikes*. Nor can you pull the wool over his eyes when it comes to distinguishing between 'explicit and implicit meanings'. He much prefers the explicit sexual details of *Rape of the Dusky Virgin* to the implied sexuality of the Mills and Boon book he flicked through in Carole's house while waiting for her to dry her hair.

Writing is not his favourite pastime, but he still meets most of the HMI's objectives. He 'explains processes clearly' in his weekly journal. He tells you precisely how to gut a rabbit or a pigeon and how to break into a house silently. He also writes 'accurate descriptions of people', being particularly observant about the headmaster's less savoury mannerisms. He does not often 'write imaginatively in verse', but there was one poem about Jews being gassed in a concentration camp, which, though frighteningly insensitive, showed 'awareness of structure and stylistic effects'.

Unfortunately, Jason's success is not total. I tried to help him 'experience literature and drama of high quality not limited to the twentieth century, including Shakespeare'. He did manage to make it to the Theatre Royal to see the matinee performance of *Romeo and Juliet* by the Royal Shakespeare Company. Perhaps it was the attraction of an afternoon out of school that drove him to it. Nevertheless he went. His attention began to wander after thirty lines and he began spitting on some poor souls in the stalls below. He was escorted somewhat noisily from the theatre and spent the afternoon doing some Christmas shoplifting in Northumberland Street.

So Jason Prong has met many of the HMI's demanding objectives. Unfortunately he is leaving school at Easter and refuses to have anything to do with profiles.

John Price

C Are cans constitutionally iffy? Once put, the question is not the sort to be ignored. It is not, to be sure, a poser that occupies us in the normal way of business. It does not weigh heavily as we shave in the mornings. It does not get in the way of the breakfast toast. The Common Market and that squeak in the car demand answers that seem for the moment more insistent. But this is just because our minds are muddied by the dross of material things. Then once in a while there comes a question that hammers at the ramparts of intellectual man. Are *cans* constitutionally iffy? There is one. It is quoted from the philosophical papers of the late Professor Austin reviewed this week on another page.

Second leader, *The Times Education Supplement*, 15 December 1961

Metaphor and metonymy

Key words

> Metaphor: 'Application of name or descriptive term to an object to which it is not literally applicable'. (*Concise Oxford Dictionary*)

The word derives from Greek *meta* 'change', and *phero* 'I bear', and has come to mean a change or transfer of significance from one object to another. A ship, for example, is literally a vessel that sails on the sea; a desert can be thought of as a 'sea' of sand: the camel that travels across this metaphorical ocean as the ship sails across the real one can therefore be called a ship of the desert.

Essentially, metaphor depends upon similarity. However dissimilar the two components of the metaphor may be in other ways (is a ship anything like a camel?), they share some particular property that throws light on the thing being described.

Talking point

> Discuss the metaphor in the preceding sentence.

Metaphors do not belong exclusively to poets and writers. Ordinary conversation is riddled with them:

> I see, light dawns, I've got the picture (I understand);
>
> he broke down (likening the mind to a machine), her heart melted;
>
> it left me with a nasty taste in my mouth, he tried to feed me the usual routine but I wouldn't swallow it, it gave food for thought, students shouldn't be spoonfed, she needs some work she can really get her teeth into;
>
> this is a seminal book (it has given birth to many others);
>
> you've painted yourself into a corner, your back's up against the wall, you're on the skids/going to the dogs/down the drain/the tubes;
>
> I'm going to disappear in a minute.

In the sentence that introduced this list, 'riddle' itself is a metaphor (from *to pierce or perforate with holes*).

The fact that we use metaphor spontaneously and naturally like this shows us the way in which we mentally organize the world by looking for correspondences and patterns in our experience. In fact, extending the meaning of words by using them metaphorically may be one of the ways in which language developed more sophisticated, abstract concepts: the Arab word for 'justice', for example, apparently derives from another word denoting the even distribution of weight on either side of a camel's back; the Hebrew word for 'sin' derives from a word meaning 'to miss the target'. It is easy to see how the metaphysical meaning might grow naturally out of the physical by metaphorical extension. (See also the extract from Randolph Quirk's *The Use of English* in the section *The Origins of English Vocabulary,* page 29.)

All good metaphors seem fresh and vivid when they first enter the language, but their shelf-life is short and they soon pass their sell-by date.

Talking point	Discuss the expression of the ideas in the previous sentence.

The more obvious the similarity drawn by the metaphor, the more enthusiastically it will be taken up and used, and the more quickly in consequence it will grow stale and die. Dead metaphors linger on, unrecognizable as images any more, in the guise either of ordinary nouns (*river mouth* for instance), or of clichés (*the iron fist in the velvet glove, the dead hand of the law*). Most of the ones quoted above would also qualify as clichés now, in that they spring into our minds ready-made for use whether we want them to or not.

The greater the leap the imagination has to make between the two things brought together in the metaphor, that stronger that metaphor's chance of out-living its time. It will not grow stale through over-use. It will continue to surprise and amuse and interest because it engages the imaginative power of the mind. For metaphor at its best, therefore, we have to turn to literature.

▓ *Metaphor in literature*

Metaphor is used in exactly the same way in literature as in common speech: to bring out some point of similarity between things otherwise unlike. The purpose is twofold:

1 to reveal as exactly as possible what the thing described is like;
2 to please readers with originality, wit, and strength of style.

The difference between the literary and common use of metaphor lies in the degree of dissimilarity between the two objects involved.

Marvell's vegetable love in *To His Coy Mistress*, and Donne's paired lovers, seen as the twin legs of a pair of compasses in *A Valediction, Forbidding Mourning* work so well precisely because the thread of thought connecting them is so tenuous. We have to stretch our minds to follow where the poet's imagination leads. We are surprised and amused and delighted by his audacity and wit.

Consider for example the metaphor in the following verse:

> . . . wind wielded
> Blade-light, luminous black and emerald,
> Flexing like the lens of a mad eye.

Properties that belong to one thing – the sharpness and gleam of a knife blade, say – remind the poet of something similar in another – the quality of the light on a stormy day, perhaps, when light flashes out from behind wind-driven clouds – and the two are brought together in the metaphor *blade-light*.

Metaphors are more condensed and allusive than similes, as these lines show. Both are based on similarity, but while similes signal that a comparison is being made by using *as* and *like*, metaphors give us the thing direct and leave us to work out the connections for ourselves. In this respect, the metaphor is a stronger, more concentrated version of the simile. A simile would say that the light was as clear and sharp as the blade of a knife; the metaphor calls it *blade-light*.

Metaphors of a similarly condensed nature are found in the first verse of the poem from which the blade metaphor was taken – *Wind*, by Ted Hughes:

> This house has been far out at sea all night,
> The woods crashing through darkness, the booming hills,
> Winds stampeding the fields under the window
> Floundering black astride and blinding wet . . .

The first turns landscape into seascape: the house and woods are vessels helplessly adrift, the hills, booming waves. The second turns the fields into panic-stricken cattle stampeded by the wind, itself a rider on some cosmic range. But we have to work to see the qualities that these disparate things have in common. Metaphor often demands closer reading and more imaginative input than the simile.

Talking point

> Discuss the quality of the metaphors in the following lines:
>
> **A** Cows are going home in the lane there, looping the hedges
>   with their warm wreaths of breath –
>   A dark river of blood, many boulders,
>   Balancing unspilled milk.
>
> **B** There is the laburnum, its blond colonnades,
>   And the petticoats of the cherry.
>
> **C** Over us the planes build
>   The shifting rafters
>   Of that new world
>   We have sworn by.
>
> **D** . . . the departed lodger, innocence.

Sometimes poets work out the similarity between two apparently dissimilar things in greater detail, carrying the comparison on through several verses or even throughout the whole poem. Hughes uses extended metaphor in this way in *Thought-Fox*:

> I imagine this midnight moment's forest:
> Something else is alive
> Beside the clock's loneliness
> And this blank page where my fingers move.
>
> Through the window I see no star:
> Something more near
> Though deeper within darkness
> Is entering the loneliness:
>
> Cold, delicately as the dark snow,
> A fox's nose touches twig, leaf;
> Two eyes serve a movement, that now
> And again now, and now, and now
>
> Sets neat prints into the snow
> Between trees, and warily a lame
> Shadow lags by stump and in hollow
> Of a body that is bold to come
>
> Across clearings, an eye,
> A widening deepening greenness,
> Brilliantly, concentratedly,
> Coming about its own business
>
> Till, with a sudden sharp hot stink of fox
> It enters the dark hole of the head.
> The window is starless still; the clock ticks,
> The page is printed.

▦ *Metonymy*

Key word

> *Metonymy:* 'Substitution of the name of an attribute or adjunct for that of the thing meant' (*Concise Oxford Dictionary*)
> e.g. *bottle* for *alcohol*;
> From Greek *meta* indicating 'change', and *onoma*, 'name'.
> Metaphor is based on similarity, metonymy on contiguity (from Latin *contingere*, to touch).

Metaphor makes imaginative leaps to connect things that are physically dissimilar. Metonymy uses the name of one physical thing – the Crown or the White House, say – to refer to another entity of which it is a part, or to which it is closely related – the Queen or the President. Like metaphor, metonymy is also part of everyday speech. 'Do you like Shakespeare?' we say (meaning his plays). 'She's in insurance' (meaning the profession). 'The steak is ready for table number four'; 'I'd love a jar' (glass of beer); 'Hollywood is finished'; 'I can always recognize a Bonnard' (meaning the style of the painter); 'Would you take the Chair at the next meeting?'

Metonymy overlaps with *synecdoche* – a term derived from the Greek 'understand along with'. This is the technique of using the name of the part for the whole – 'She's not just a pretty face'; 'Who's the suit?' (formally dressed man); 'That's a nice set of wheels' (car); 'Don't stick your nose in here'. Alternatively, it can use the name of the whole to signify the part(s): 'England did well to beat New Zealand' (for the cricket or rugby teams); 'The Croatians are short of bread as well as weapons' (where *bread* equals food in general). It is often difficult to sort out whether metonymy or synecdoche is being used in expressions like 'Hollywood is finished' and 'Wall Street closed early today': is Hollywood the part here, being used to refer to the film industry as a whole – directors, actors, technicians, etc. – in which case it's synecdoche, or is it a case of one attribute or entity – the physical region called Hollywood – being used to refer to another – the film industry – that is related to it (metonymy)? The sensible solution would seem to be to subsume synecdoche under the umbrella of metonymy and not to worry about the difference.

Talking point

> Discuss which of the following are metaphors, which examples of metonymy:
>
> | | |
> |---|---|
> | The Smoke
The Great Wen | terms used to describe the city of London in the eighteenth century (a wen was a kind of cyst) |
> | smokes
coffin-nails
cancer-sticks
the pernicious weed | terms used to describe cigarettes |

Activity

> 1 Read the following extract from *Nice Work*, by David Lodge. (Robyn Penrose, a lecturer at Rummidge University, is talking to Vic Wilcox, Managing Director of J. Pringle and Sons Casting and General Engineering. She has been assigned to 'shadow' him as the University's contribution to Industry Year.)

'One of the fundamental tools of semiotics is the distinction between metaphor and metonymy. D'you want me to explain it to you?'

'It'll pass the time,' he said.

'Metaphor is a figure of speech based on similarity, whereas metonymy is based on contiguity. In metaphor you substitute something *like* the thing you mean for the thing itself, whereas in metonymy you substitute some attribute or cause or effect of the thing for the thing itself.'

'I don't understand a word you're saying.'

'Well, take one of your moulds. The bottom bit is called the drag because it's dragged across the floor and the top bit is called the cope because it covers the bottom bit.'

'I told *you* that.'

'Yes, I know. What you didn't tell me was that "drag" is a metonymy and "cope" is a metaphor.'

Vic grunted. 'What difference does it make?'

'It's just a question of understanding how language works. I thought you were interested in how things work.'

'I don't see what it's got to do with cigarettes.'

'In the case of the Silk Cut poster, the picture signifies the female body metaphorically: the slit in the silk is *like* a vagina –'

Vic flinched at the word. 'So you say.'

'All holes, hollow spaces, fissures and folds represent the female genitals.'

'Prove it.'

'Freud proved it, by his successful analysis of dreams,' said Robyn. 'But the Marlboro ads don't use any metaphors. That's probably why you smoke them, actually.'

'What d'you mean?' he said suspiciously.

'You don't have any sympathy with the metaphorical way of looking at things. A cigarette is a cigarette as far as you are concerned.'

'Right.'

'The Marlboro ad doesn't disturb that naive faith in the stability of the signified. It establishes a metonymic connection – completely spurious of course, but realistically plausible – between smoking that particular brand and the healthy, heroic, outdoor life of the cowboy. Buy the cigarette and you buy the life-style, or the fantasy of living it.'

'Rubbish!' said Wilcox. 'I hate the country and the open air. I'm scared to go into a field with a cow in it.'

'Well then, maybe it's the solitariness of the cowboy in the ads that appeals to you. Self-reliant, independent, very macho.'

'I've never heard such a lot of balls in all my life,' said Vic Wilcox, which was strong language coming from him.

'Balls – now that's an interesting expression . . .' Robyn mused.

'Oh no!' he groaned.

'When you say a man "has balls", approvingly, it's a metonymy, whereas if you say something is a "lot of balls", or "a balls-up", it's a sort of metaphor. The metonymy attributes value to the testicles whereas the metaphor uses them to degrade something else.'

'I can't take any more of this,' said Vic. 'D'you mind if I smoke? Just a plain, ordinary cigarette?'

'If I can have Radio Three on,' said Robyn.

2 How does this discussion of metaphor and metonymy bring out the difference between
  a Robyn and Vic's characteristic ways of thinking,
  b the essential nature of the different kinds of work they do?

▣oregrounding

Key word

> *Foregrounding:* the technique of deviating from the norm in which a piece is written in order to draw attention to the properties and/or functions of language itself.

Writers use foregrounding when they deviate from:

1 the style in which the rest of the work is written;
2 the style in which the work as a whole is expected to be written.

To illustrate the first of these uses, here is an extract from Stella Gibbons's satirical novel, *Cold Comfort Farm*. The writer highlights the over-blown use of language in the romantic novels of Hugh Walpole and Mary Webb by switching from a conventional style into the kind of writing known as 'purple prose'. (She draws her readers' attention to these passages of 'fine' writing by introducing them with one, two, or three asterisks, after the style of a restaurant guide):

> 'Hullo', said Flora, getting her blow in first. 'I feel sure you must be Reuben. I'm Flora Poste, your cousin, you know. How do you do? I'm so glad to see somebody has come in for some tea. Do sit down. Do you take milk? (No sugar . . . of course . . . or do you? I do, but most of my friends don't.)'
>
> *** The man's big body, etched menacingly against the bleak light that stabbed in from the low windows, did not move. His thoughts swirled like a beck in spate behind the sodden grey furrows of his face. A woman . . . Blast! Blast! Come to wrest away from him the land whose love fermented in his veins, like slow yeast. She-woman. Young, soft-coloured, insolent. His gaze was suddenly edged by a fleshy taint. Break her. Break. Keep and hold and hold fast the land. The land, the iron furrows of frosted earth under the rain-lust, the fecund spears of rain, the swelling, slow burst of seed-sheaths, the slow smell of cows and cry of cows, the trampling bride-path of the bull in his hour. All his, his . . .
>
> 'Will you have some bread and butter?' asked Flora, handing him his cup of tea. 'Oh, never mind your boots. Adam can sweep the mud up afterwards. Do come in.'

On the whole, however, writers foreground language to reveal their characters' personalities, motivations, attitudes, or aspirations. *Sons and Lovers*, for instance, is written largely in conventional English against which passages of dialect stand out. Dialect is used to signal Paul's close physical relationship with Clara:

'Nay, never thee bother! But tha shouldna worrit!'

The reserve that exists always between himself and Miriam is conveyed by the more formal register he uses to talk to her:

'I am glad I came back to you. I feel so simple with you – as if there is nothing to hide. We will be happy?'

In *Lady Chatterley's Lover*, by contrast, Lawrence uses dialect to get just the opposite effect: one of alienation rather than intimacy. Mellors deliberately draws himself back from Connie, keeping the upper hand in their relationship by speaking a language that she does not know:

> 'I mean as 'appen Ah can find anuther pleece as'll du for rearin the pheasants. If yer want ter be 'ere, yo'll non want me messin' abaht a' th' time.'
> She looked at him, getting his meaning through the fog of the dialect. 'Why don't you speak ordinary English?' she said coldly.
> 'Me! I thowt it wor ordinary.'

Sometimes the normal positions of conventional English and dialect are reversed, however, and Standard English is seen as the deviation. Where traditional novels use formal Standard English for the narrative and foreground dialect, in *The Color Purple* Alice Walker writes largely in dialect and foregrounds Standard English. Thus Celie, whose letters form the main body of the book, writes as the people around her speak – in the dialect of Georgia, in a colloquial, often crude, always pithy and elliptical style:

> . . . God ain't a he or a she, but a It.
> But what do it look like? I ast.
> Don't look like nothing, she say. It ain't a picture show. It ain't something you can look at apart from anything else, including yourself. I believe God is everything, say Shug. Everything that is or ever was or ever will be. And when you can feel that, and be happy to feel that, you've found It.

The letters she receives from her educated sister Nettie contrast so strongly with this vivid colloquial style that it is almost an effort to read them. The ideas in the following extract parallel those of Shug above; the expression is very different:

> God is different to us now, after all these years in Africa. More spirit than
> ever before, and more internal. Most people think he has to look like
> something or someone – a roofleaf or Christ – but we don't. And not
> being tied to what God looks like, frees us.

Conventional English pronunciation is foregrounded in the speech of
Henrietta. Everyone around her says 'yeah' for 'yes' and refuses to use the
-*s* inflection on plural nouns – 'He got problem', not problems. Henrietta
however says 'Yesssss' and 'Prob-limbszzzz' – 'like somebody on the
radio'.

Poetry itself may be taken as an example of foregrounding. It calls
attention to the rhythms and intonations of ordinary speech by
heightening them and arranging them in a recurring pattern. But the poet
can foreground other elements within this original foregrounding. Here is
Chaucer's Franklin calling attention to his (and Chaucer's) use of
circumlocutio – the poetic technique of describing something in a
roundabout way, using elaborate imagery – by explaining to his listeners
what the imagery means:

> Til that the brighte sonne loste his hewe;
> For th'orisonte hath refte the sonne his lyght, –
> This is as muche to seye as it was nyght!

'Look at the technique I'm using to express this idea!' the foregrounding
implies. 'Aren't I clever? Perhaps I'd better explain what it means, in case
you aren't bright enough to see it'. The apparently artless last line here is
full of irony at the Franklin's expense. He has revealed himself to be well
enough read to be able to use poetic techniques, but also conceited enough
to want to boast about it.

The second use of foregrounding can be illustrated by some of the more
experimental novels written in the twentieth century. The traditional
novel presents us with a more or less coherent world described in
conventional educated English. With this fact in mind, consider the
opening of Russell Hoban's novel, *Riddley Walker*. Instead of the 'proper
English' we expect of a novel, we find in the author's own words 'a broken
up and worn down vernacular of it':

> On my naming day when I come 12 I gone front spear and kilt a wyld
> boar he parbly ben the las wyld pig on the Bundel Downs any how there
> hadn't ben none for a long time befor him nor I ain't looking to see none
> agen. He dint make the groun shake nor nothing like that when he come
> on to my spear he wernt all that big plus he lookit poorly. He done the
> reqwyrt he ternt and stood and clattert his teef and made his rush and
> there we wer then. Him on 1 end of the spear kicking his life out and me
> on the other end watching him dy. I said, 'Your tern now my tern later.'
> The other spears gone in then and he wer dead and the steam coming
> up off him in the rain and we all yelt, 'Offert!'

> The woal thing felt jus that littl bit stupid. Us running that boar thru that las littl scrump of woodling with the forms all roun. Cows mooing sheap baaing cocks crowing and us foraging our las boar in a thin grey girzel on the day I come a man.

Talking point

> What properties or aspects of language are foregrounded here? (Remember that this time the work as a whole may be seen as a deviation from traditional norms.)

Hoban's purpose in *Riddley Walker* may have been to show that language is the source of all our ideas and knowledge of the world, and that, because their language is now debased (presumably after a nuclear holocaust), the people of Riddley's generation have reverted to near savagery.

Modern poetry also foregrounds language use, often mixing very different registers within a single poem to make its points.

Activity

> 1 a Read T.S. Eliot's poem *The Hollow Men*.
>   b Describe the four different kinds of register used in Section V.
>   c Suggest what Eliot may have been trying to say through them about the nature or quality of human life.
>
> 2 Do the same for Philip Larkin's poem *Vers de Société*.
>
> 3 Any aspect of language, written or spoken, can be foregrounded in the ways described above. Read the first and last pages of Joyce's *Finnegan's Wake* and see if you can discover at least three aspects of conventional language being foregrounded there.

The difference between prose and verse

The difference between prose and verse (also called poetry) centres on one main feature: regularity of stress. Stresses in prose fall in an irregular fashion; stresses in verse are determined in advance. At bottom, verse is an artificial heightening or exaggeration of the stress patterns of ordinary speech.

We saw earlier that English speakers like to space out the stresses in their statements, leaving one or two unstressed syllables or off-beats between them. We even unconsciously adjust our stresses to get this desired effect, pronouncing *thirteen* with the stress on the second syllable when it stands alone – she's thirteen – but on the first in phrases like thirteen elephants – just to avoid two heavy stresses in a row. We should not be surprised, then, to find that English verse of every kind works on the principle of alternating light and heavy stresses. (Heavy stresses are marked ´ in the examples that follow.) In

Jáck and Jíll went úp the híll

for example, English readers will usually stress the words as marked above, even though in ordinary conversation a structure word like *up* would never be given so much emphasis. A stress on *went* instead of *up* would bring two main stresses uncomfortably close together; a stress on *up* spaces them out more widely, as we prefer. The technical word for this is *isochronous* (equally spaced) stress.

Regular stresses like this are very appealing to the ear, and once a pattern has been set up, we want it to go on. So much so, that if the next line doesn't have exactly the number of stresses we expect to hear, we mentally supply the one that's missing. Consider Jack and Jill again. The next line has only three main stresses, as marked –

To fétch a páil of wáter [ ]

– and so we add another beat at the end of the line – one that is heard only within our heads. (Attridge calls these *unrealized beats*.) (*Stress* and *beat* are used synonymously in this account.)

Activity

> 1 Write out the first verse of *Mary Had a Little Lamb*.
> 2 Mark the stressed syllables with an oblique line above the first vowel.
> 3 Indicate any unrealized beats at the end of lines with the symbol [ ].

Why we are so fond of alternating stresses and off-beats in this way, nobody knows. But this is the pattern in which most of our popular verse is written, from ballads and solemn hymns through nursery rhymes to advertising jingles.

You'll néver pút a bétter bít of bútter ón your knífe.

Certainly it is very old, as can be shown by this extract from *Piers Plowman*. Written somewhere between 1360 and 1400, it has four main stresses to the line, separated by one to three unstressed syllables.

I was wéry forwándred	and wént me to réste
Vnder a bróde bánke	bi a bórnes síde,
And as I láy and léned	and lóked in the wáteres,
I slómbred in a slépyng	it swéyued so mérye.

The change from stress to metre occurred when poets began to arrange their lines into regular groups of two or (less often) three syllables, with the main stress falling on the same syllable in the group each time.

Key word

> *Metre*: the regular arrangement of stresses within lines of verse.

These groups of syllables are called metrical *feet* – a strange term left over from the study of Latin poetry. Just use it as a shorthand term for a group of two or three syllables and try not to let it bother you.

The four-stress line combined with metre to give us several different verse forms. In one of the oldest and most traditional forms of English poetry it appears in stanzas in which two lines of four stresses alternate with two lines of three, the three-stress lines ending with an unrealized beat. (Unrealized beats are indicated by the symbol [ ].)

Wi' lightsome heart I pu'd a rose,
Frae aff its thorny tree;
And my fause luver staw the rose,   (staw = stole)
But left the thorn wi' me.

This is ballad or common metre.

More rarely, this stanza of alternating three- and four-stress lines is transformed into the metre known as the *fourteener*. The four-stress line and the three-stress line are run together to make up one of fourteen syllables – seven stresses and seven off-beats:

No image carved with cunning hand, no cloth of purple dye . . .

The heavy pause between the first four stresses and the last three give the game away, however, and we can easily recognize the 4.3 structure with the unrealized beat at the end of the line.

In many hymns we find the four-stress line in the form known as long metre or long measure – stanzas of four lines of four stresses:

The day Thou gavest, Lord, is ended,
The darkness falls at Thy behest,
To Thee our morning hymns ascended,
Thy praise shall sanctify our rest.

Tovey has shown (*Rhythm*, *The Encyclopaedia Britannica*, 11th edition) that at the heart of all these variations on the 4 × 4 line lies a hierarchy of pairs: a pair of beats (off-beat and stress), a pair of this pair (the half-line), and a pair of half-lines (the full four-stress line).

Poets with something serious to say have to be careful with the 4 × 4 line. The shorter it is, the more likely it is to strike us as funny. If it also has a lot of one-syllable words that create a thumping rhythm, and rhymes so obvious as to be banal, the effect is bound to make us laugh. Consider the following anonymous offering, for example:

The primal termite looked on wood,
Tasted it and found it good,
And that is why your Auntie May
Fell through the parlour floor today.

Activity

1 Read *The Germ* by Ogden Nash, in *The Rattle Bag*, edited by Seamus Heaney and Ted Hughes. Write a paragraph on how well the form of the poem suits its subject matter.

2 Read Blake's poem *Never Seek to Tell thy Love*.
  a Blake is seeking to express a general truth about sexual love. What makes the traditional 4 x 4 stanza suitable for his purpose here?
  b There are unrealized beats at the ends of lines 6, 8, and 12. Can you see any particular effects these unrealized beats help the poet to achieve?

In all the examples of verse so far you should notice a very regular foot made up of an off-beat followed by a stress. The conventional way of marking this is to use an × followed by an oblique line: ×‑. For example:

The primal termite looked on wood . . .

This is known as the iambic foot.

The iambic foot

There are several different kinds of metrical foot, but the most popular, because the closest to the stress patterns and rhythms of ordinary English speech, is the iambic.

Key words

> *Iambic foot*: a pair of beats of which the first is an off-beat, the second a stress: this arrangement of stresses is marked ×‑.
>
> *Iambic metre*: lines of verse divided into iambic feet.
> |Was this| the face| that launched| a thous|and ships|

Iambic verse, like other kinds of metre, can have different numbers of feet to the line. The examples we have seen so far have had only three or four feet, but there are also lines of six, seven, and eight feet. Each kind has a Greek or Latin name: trimeter (three feet), tetrameter (four feet), pentameter (five feet), hexameter or alexandrine (six feet), heptameter (seven feet), and octometer (eight feet).

The most commonly used metre in English verse, however, is iambic pentameter. *Penta* means five, *meter* means measure, so *iambic pentameter* is a measure or line of poetry in which there are five feet each containing an off-beat followed by a stress. To put it another way, it is a line containing ten syllables, only five of which are stressed. Much of the greatest English poetry is written in this metre. It is the metre Chaucer used for *The Canterbury Tales*, Shakespeare for his sonnets and plays, Milton for his *Paradise Lost* and *Paradise Regained*, Wordsworth for his *Prelude* and Dryden and Pope for their heroic couplets.

Sometimes iambic pentameter rhymes, sometimes it does not. When it does not, as in Milton's *Paradise Lost*, it is called *blank verse*.

Activity

> 1 Look at the verse below to assess what metre it is written in.
>
> 2 Write out the verse, then divide the lines into feet by placing vertical lines between each foot. (Remember that a foot marking will sometimes cut through the middle of a word.)
>
> 3 Two light stresses follow one another in an irregular foot somewhere in this verse. Where do they occur?
>
> 4 Mark the light and heavy stresses by putting the appropriate × and ‑ symbols above the words.
>
> I wandered lonely as a cloud
> That floats on high o'er vales and hills,
> When all at once I saw a crowd,
> A host of golden daffodils . . .
>
> What two Latin words would you use here to describe the metre?

Other kinds of metre

There are other types of foot than the iamb, some of which are listed below:

the **trochee**: (a stress followed by an off-beat) ´×: líttle; gétting

the **spondee**: (two stresses) ´´: stánd stáble

the **anapaest**: (two off-beats followed by a stress) ××´:
the Assyr|ian came down|

the **dactyl**: (a stress followed by two off-beats) ´××: merrily,
Lift her up| tenderly

The anapaest and the dactyl are less common than the iamb, trochee, and spondee. This is probably because they are further from the rhythms of ordinary speech than are other kinds of feet, and sound more artificial. Read Thomas Hood's *The Bridge of Sighs*, and Byron's *The Destruction of Semnacherib*, however, to see how well the difficult triple measures of dactyls and anapaests can be used.

Though comparatively little verse is written in trochees and spondees, these feet do occur often as variations within basically iambic metres, simply because the meaning of the poem dictates this kind of stress.

■ *Summary*

Most English metres are made up of a particular kind of foot repeated a fixed number of times. The kind of metre is defined by
a the type of foot,
b the number of feet to a line.

Variation within regularity

Consecutive lines of absolutely regular iambic feet are very hard to find, for several reasons:

1 The little structure words that English is so full of prevent it. Because words like *of*, *as*, *a*, *the*, *up*, and *in* are normally unstressed, they combine with content words to form perfect iambic feet: the moon, for example. When they combine with each other, in pairings like *to a*, *in the*, *by my*, they form irregular feet of two light stresses (××). (People sometimes mistake these irregular pairs of stresses for a regular Latin foot called the *pyrrhic*.)

2 Meaning often demands that stresses should fall irregularly. Consider for example the opening lines of this Shakespearean sonnet:

Shall I	compare	thee to	a summ	er's day?
Thou art	more love	ly and	more temp	erate.
Rough winds	do shake	the dar	ling buds	of May,
And summ	er's lease	hath all	too short	a date.

It is obviously written in iambic metre – that is, there are more iambic feet than feet of any other kind – and yet it is obviously irregular in several places to suit the sense. Note for instance the reversed foot at the beginning of line 2, where a trochee (⁄×) replaces the expected iamb, and the two light stresses on *to a* in line 1. (Syllables on which the stress may also be irregular are indicated with a question mark.)

Talking point

> 1 Say the first line of the poem aloud. Do you think *Shall* should be stressed slightly more heavily than *I*? Or *I* slightly more heavily than *Shall*? What difference would it make to the meaning? Should *Shall* and *I* be equally stressed? What alternative kinds of feet are possible here?
>
> 2 Should the two *mores* be given a heavy stress to emphasize the triumph of human over natural beauty? What kind of foot would result?
> Would it make sense to give an equal stress to *Rough* and *winds*? What kind of foot would that create?

Different readers will give different answers to these questions. The points to grasp about metre are these:

1 English metre is flexible; it accommodates meaning easily by allowing slight variations in the metrical pattern.

2 The metre a poem is written in is determined by the predominant foot. If there are more iambs than trochees, it is iambic, and so on.

3 Much of the pleasure of listening to English poetry comes from hearing the irregular rhythms of natural speech played off against the regular stress pattern of the metre. As Attridge puts it in *The Rhythms of English Poetry*:

> . . . what we are aware of in reading a metrical line is an onward movement which at times approaches a marked regularity and at times departs from it, constantly arousing and thwarting rhythmic expectations.

Activity

> 1 Read Thomas Gray's poem, *Elegy Written in a Country Church-yard*.
>
> Now fades the glimmering landscape on the sight,
> And all the air a solemn stillness holds,
> Save where the beetle wheels his droning flight,
> And drowsy tinklings lull the distant folds . . .
>
> Write a short paragraph on the above verse, indicating
> a the basic foot;
> b any deviations from that foot;
> c the particular kind of metre it is written in.
>
> 2 a Examine any soliloquy of Hamlet's for variations in the iambic metre;
> b Speculate on the reasons for these variations. What is Shakespeare showing through them about Hamlet's thoughts and feelings?

The difference between poetry and prose

In theory, the difference between poetry and prose is simple: poetry is everything that is written in metre; prose is everything that is not. In practice, things are not quite so simple as this, for the following reasons:

1 Poetry moves close to prose in the hands of many modern writers who use the form called *free verse*.
2 Prose often moves close to poetry when writers are emotionally involved with their subjects. (See the death of the crossing-sweeper, Jo, in Charles Dickens' novel *Bleak House*, for instance.)
3 Prose also deals at times with things of deep emotional, spiritual, and intellectual significance, in a style that has elements of poetic beauty.

▓ *Poetry that approaches prose*

Free verse (or *vers libre*) is called 'free' because it is not bound by any set pattern of stresses. It was devised by poets trying to throw off the pervasive influence of metre, and the iambic foot in particular. If they were to say anything new, they felt, they had to have a new form to say it in. Metre was worn out: they would do without it.

At first sight, free verse looks like prose chopped up into shorter lines. When handled well, however, it is more regular in its rhythms than is ordinary prose.

The earliest examples of free verse are probably to be found in the Bible. For example:

> At that time, saith the Lord, they shall bring out the bones of the kings of Judah, and the bones of his princes, and the bones of the priests, and the bones of the prophets, and the bones of the inhabitants of Jerusalem, out of their graves. And they shall spread them before the sun, and the moon, and all the host of heaven, whom they have loved, and whom they have served, and after whom they have walked, and whom they have sought, and whom they have worshipped: they shall not be gathered, nor be buried; they shall be for dung upon the face of the earth.
>
> The Book of Jeremiah, from the Authorized Version of the Bible

Compare this with the extract from the poetry of Walt Whitman below:

> When I heard the learn'd astronomer,
> When the proofs, the figures, were ranged in columns before me,
> When I was shown the charts and diagrams, to add, divide, and measure
>   them,
> When I sitting heard the astronomer where he lectured with much
>   applause in the lecture room,
> How soon unaccountably I became tired and sick . . .

The regularity of free verse like this comes from different things. Sometimes lines like those above can be arranged into small rhythmic groups of similar proportion: for instance,

> whom they have loved, and whom they have served,
> and whom they have sought, and whom they have worshipped . . .

Sometimes the impression of regularity will come from the rhythmic groups' having much the same number of syllables and/or stresses, and therefore much the same duration:

> When I heard the learn'd astronomer,
> When I was shown the charts and diagrams,
> When I sitting heard the astronomer . . .

Sometimes it will come from the repetition, with variations, of significant phrases or image patterns, or sequences of rising and falling intonations, as in the Whitman below:

> I celebrate myself;
> And what I assume you shall assume;
> For every atom belonging to me, as good belongs to you
>
> I loaf and invite my soul;
> I lean and loaf at my ease, observing a blade of summer grass.
>
> Walt Whitman, *Song of Myself*

Activity | Read D. H. Lawrence's poem *Snake* and discuss whether you think it is poetry or heightened prose.

▓ *Prose that approaches verse*

If poetry approaches the condition of prose in examples like these, prose often approaches the condition of poetry. The following extracts, A from Walter Pater's account of the Mona Lisa, B from D. H. Lawrence's *The White Peacock* have qualities commonly associated with poetry: heightened language; imagery; sound patterning; rhythms that are akin to poetry rather than to prose.

A | She is older than the rocks among which she sits; like the vampire, she has been dead many times, and learned the secrets of the grave; and has been a diver in deep seas, and keeps their fallen day about her; and trafficked for strange webs with Eastern merchants: and, as Leda, was the mother of Helen of Troy, and, as Saint Anne, the mother of Mary; and all this has been to her but as the sound of lyres and flutes, and lives only in the delicacy with which it has moulded the changing lineaments, and tinged the eyelids and the hands.

B | Till the heralds come – till the heralds wave like shadows in the bright air, crying, lamenting, fretting forever. Rising and falling and circling round and round, the slow-waving peewits cry and complain, and lift their broad wings in sorrow. They stoop suddenly to the ground, the lapwings, then in another throb of anguish and protest, they swing up again, offering a glistening white breast to the sunlight, to deny it in black shadow, then a glisten of green, and all the time crying and crying in despair.

There is very little difference between prose like this and what is called free verse.

Activity | Arrange either of the above passages into the form of free verse. Keep the same punctuation, but break the lines where it seems best to you. You are free to make them all much the same length if you wish, as in metrical poetry (this will bring out any similarity of stress), or you can make some lines significantly longer than others to suit the rhythm. It's entirely up to you.

Some free verse abandons altogether such things as imagery, repetition, sound patterning, and so on.

Consider the poem by Leonard Cohen below, lined first as prose, then as he wrote it first, in free verse:

I almost went to bed without remembering the four white violets I put in the button-hole of your green sweater and how I kissed you then and you kissed me shy, as though I'd never been your lover.

I almost went to bed
without remembering
the four white violets
I put in the button-hole
of your green sweater

and how I kissed you then
and you kissed me
shy, as though I'd
never been your lover.

Talking point | Do you consider the above piece to be closer to poetry or prose?

▮ntegrating speech rhythms into poetry

However far it may move away from it, poetry is based on colloquial speech. The poet listens to its stresses, heightens them, and organizes them into rhythmic patterns. The more regular and predictable these rhythmic patterns become, the closer they come to being metre.

When, through the passage of time and social change, metrical rhythms begin to sound too artificial to convey living speech, poets have to look for other ways of achieving their effects. Eliot discovered this problem when he began to write plays and dramatic monologues in verse. How, he wondered, could one character ask another to do something as ordinary as closing a door in traditional metrical lines?

Stress or accentual poetry

Poets such as Eliot have solved the problem by throwing away strict metrical patterns – the division of lines of verse into regular feet – and reverting to an older system of stress: the four-beat line discussed at the beginning of this section. The result is *stress* or *accentual poetry*.

Like the older poetry it is patterned on, stress poetry creates its rhythms purely by the number of strong stresses in each line: usually four.

The writers who use this four-stress line treat it as a base, often moving away from, but always returning to, the basic four-beat pattern. The number of stresses in a line can rise to as many as eight on occasions, but seldom falls below three or rises above six. (The number of off-beats between the stresses doesn't much matter and varies widely from line to line.)

Some writers of stress poetry also follow the medieval tradition of using alliteration, seen in the *Piers Plowman* extract quoted above. Consonants used in the first half of the line are picked up and used again in the second, as demonstrated in the extract below from Gerard Manley Hopkins's *As Kingfishers Catch Fire, Dragonflies Draw Flame*:

> I say more: the just man justices;
> Keeps grace; that keeps all his goings graces;
> Acts in God's eye what in God's eye he is –
> Christ. For Christ plays in ten thousand places,
> Lovely in limbs, and lovely in eyes not his
> To the Father through the features of men's faces.

Eliot uses alliteration more sparingly, but he has succeeded in making the basic four-stress line flexible enough to cope with the expression of complex emotion, and the rhythms of contemporary speech and music, as you will discover if you carry out the activities suggested below.

Activity

1 For Eliot's skill in using a line of four main stresses, read lines 117 to 124 of Eliot's *Fragment of an Agon* ('These fellows . . . continue his story').

   a Mark where the stresses fall in these lines.
   b Look for two shorter lines with an unrealized beat at the end.
   c Explain how his handling of stress in these seven lines helps Eliot to get the effect of people talking in different ways.
   d Read the first thirty lines of the same poem. Can you find anywhere in these lines the same kind of rhythms you find in jazz?

2 For Eliot's mastery in handling lines of varying numbers of stresses, read the first twenty lines of *Little Gidding* in his *Four Quartets*:

Midwinter spring in its own season
Sempiternal though sodden towards sundown . . .

3 For examples of accentual poetry using four-stress lines with varying numbers of unstressed syllables, see Auden's *1st September, 1939*, and Yeats's *Why Should Not Old Men be Mad*?

Summary

It may be useful to think of poetry and prose as the opposite ends of a continuum, rather than two quite separate and clearly defined forms. At the two extremes, they are easy to distinguish. In the middle they move close together and are much more difficult to tell apart. Each may deal with things of deep emotional or spiritual significance; each may be beautiful in language, sound and rhythm. The only criterion we can use to distinguish them then is regularity. The rhythms of prose are looser, freer, and less regular because its emotions are less controlled. The poet imposes metre upon emotion, intensifying it by putting it under restraint. Prose that disciplined itself by taking on these restraints would become poetry, just as poetry that relaxed them would become prose.

Practical writing skills

· ·

Essay writing

There are three main essay types:
* the argumentative or controversial
* the discursive
* the imaginative/creative.

Interpreting the title

Ponder the key word or words. If you decide to write an imaginative response to a title like 'The River', or 'Mountains', the key word will be defined indirectly by the behaviour of the character or characters in the story. If you choose to write a controversial or discursive response to a title such as 'Prejudice has no place in a civilized society', on the other hand, you will have to define each of the key words in your opening paragraph and indicate how you intend to treat them in the main body of your essay.

Remember, *you* are writing the essay. The treatment you decide to give it is entirely up to you.

Talking point

> Interpret and define the key words in the following titles:
>
> 'There are no great causes left to fight for in society today.' How far do you agree?
>
> What do you take to be the function of the Arts in our society?
>
> Dreams

How to find ideas for your essays

Before you can think about structuring essays you have to have something to structure. In other words, you need ideas.

How do you get them? It depends to a certain extent upon the essay set. Some essays ask for such specialized knowledge that relatively few candidates can answer them: examples are 'Soul', or 'Write about specific paintings, or pieces of sculpture or pieces of music which have challenged you'. If neither soul music nor religion moves you and you know nothing about painting, sculpture, or music you can't write a thousand words on these subjects. In the same way, you can't use a formula to dredge up characters and plot for a creative or imaginative essay. Your mind can either work in this mode or not, and there's probably not much you can do about it. Plenty of essay titles lend themselves to either an argumentative or a discursive treatment, however, and a method of finding ideas for these is given below.

Structured brainstorming

This method asks you to search your mind for ideas in a systematic way by using an acronym (a word formed from the initial letters of a group of other words) as a mnemonic (an aid to memory).

Suppose your mnemonic is the acronym PHRASEEMS. All you have to do is write it vertically down a page, then ask yourself if you can find any ideas for your essay topic by looking at it from the points of view indicated by the individual letters. Thus:

P for political
H for historical
R for religious
A for artistic/aesthetic (aesthetics deals with the question of what is beautiful. Include literature here.)
S for social
E for economic
E for ecological/environmental
M for moral/ethical
S for scientific/technological. (Include medical science here).

You may want to add other letters to the list – another P for psychology or philosophy, or an E for education, for instance – but I hope you see the idea.

Let's look at how it works with an actual title. (The 'Yes' or 'No' after each letter indicates whether you can find anything to say or not.)

Title: Has technology been a blessing or a curse to the human race?

P? Yes. Societies that possess advanced technology have military and economic power.

H? Yes. Development of tech from the wheel on. Plus a lot to say about the explosion of tech from Indust. Rev. to present day.

R? Yes. Tech focus on material things and materialism can lead us to neglect the spiritual and emotional aspects of our being/nature.

A? Yes, e.g. Auden's sonnet on the first Moon-landing, making the point that the first chipping of a bone by our Stone-age ancestors made this moment inevitable; Arthur C. Clarke's sci/fi novel, '2001'.

S? Yes. Much to say on the impact of tech on society, e.g. change from rural to urban communities during Ind. Rev.; impact of tech/inventions on quality of our life and relationships, e.g. car, plane, frozen food, microwave; organ transplants, joint replacements, hormone replacement therapy, etc.; impact of machinery on craftsmanship; effect of robots/machines on jobs.

E? Yes. Enormous cost of tech e.g. Defence, Transport, Communications, etc.

E? Yes. Impact of tech on environment: radiation, acid rain, etc.

M? Yes. If not already covered under R. But remember that you don't have to belong to a religious sect in order to have ethical principles. You need not mention religion with a capital R at all.

As you run through the mnemonic looking for points you will find them lining themselves up on the side of blessing or curse (or on both sides), and your choice of what structure to use will be made much easier.

Activity

> 1 Using the mnemonic suggested above (or one of your own), find ideas for essays entitled
>
>   a 'How far do you agree that science and technology have created more problems than they have solved?'
>   b 'What do *you* expect of a good newspaper?' or 'How important is the role of newspapers in a democratic society?'
>
> 2 Since the above are rather difficult topics which you may have to do a little research on, try the mnemonic method on these less demanding titles:
>
>   'Discuss the case for banning the private motor-car.'
>   'What, in your opinion, are the qualities of a civilized society?'

How to structure your essays

Once you have assembled your ideas you can begin to think about the structure you need for your essay.

How to structure the argumentative/controversial essay

Key words

> *Thesis:* a case or argument put forward for consideration by the writer of an essay or other piece of writing.
>
> *Antithesis:* a case or argument put forward in opposition to the thesis.
>
> *Synthesis:* a case or argument that combines points made in both the the thesis and antithesis.

When you want to write an essay of this type, choose a structure from what I call the *thesis group*:

   a Introduction – thesis – conclusion.
   b Introduction – thesis – antithesis – conclusion.
   c Introduction – thesis – antithesis – synthesis – conclusion.

Structure (a) could be used, for instance, in response to the one-word title 'Ambition', if you wanted to present arguments only in favour of ambition: that it is an entirely good human attribute, the driving force behind progress, and so the main cause of our present sophisticated and luxurious lifestyle. You would therefore:

1 begin by defining ambition as you see it – 'the desire to better yourself by achieving something which will win you praise and respect and/or financial reward', perhaps;

2 put forward your thesis in support of this (that without ambition the life of individuals and society would stagnate; that nothing noteworthy would be achieved in any field – academic, scientific, artistic, literary, musical,

sporting – and man would never have progressed beyond the level of hunter-gatherer);

3 draw your conclusions: that ambition should be held up as a virtue and encouraged in children from an early age by whatever means you can think of. (Most children love to compete.)

If your essay title asked you to discuss ambition from both angles before coming down on one side or the other, structure (b) would be the obvious choice.

In this case it's usually best to put the arguments you *don't* agree with first, straight after your introduction. You can then demolish them and leave your readers with the argument you *do* believe in ringing in their ears:

1 Define ambition and remark that it is a controversial topic, with arguments for and against its being a good attribute.
2 Discuss the arguments that people put forward either for or against (depending upon which you disagree with).
3 Show how mistaken these arguments are.
4 Put forward the arguments you *do* believe in.
5 Draw your conclusions.

You might also choose structure (b) if you are asked to discuss whether ambition is a good or a bad attribute and you wish to look fairly at both sides of the question, leaving your readers to judge for themselves. (This is always a good structure to adopt if you know you have trouble in getting to a thousand words. Obviously you'll cover far more ground if you give both sides of the question.)

You might choose structure (c) however if you think that ambition is a two-edged sword capable of good *and* evil. In this case, you would:

1 begin by defining ambition as above, but remark that it is an attribute that can lend itself to good or to evil uses.
2 put forward your thesis in support of its being good (as in (a) above);
3 put forward your antithesis (or counter-argument) in evidence of its being an undesirable attribute;
4 put forward your synthesis: that ambition does much to further human happiness if the goals aimed at benefit other people as well as oneself; is bad if its goals lead to the exploitation of other people out of ruthless self-interest.
5 draw your conclusion that while ambition should be fostered as good, children should be warned of its dangers while young, by whatever means you can think of. (There are many examples of the destructive effect of ruthless ambition on the lives of ordinary people in our own age: Hitler, Stalin, and Saddam Hussein to name only three.)

How to structure the discursive essay

Some essay titles lend themselves to a less tightly structured, more conversational and rambling approach. What I call the 'panoramic structure' is ideal for such subjects. (A panorama is an unbroken view around a whole landscape.)

The idea is to look at the essay topic from as many different viewpoints as possible, so that you see the thing as a whole. Subjects such as 'Ambition' or 'Prejudice' can be looked at in this way, as the diagrams below reveal:

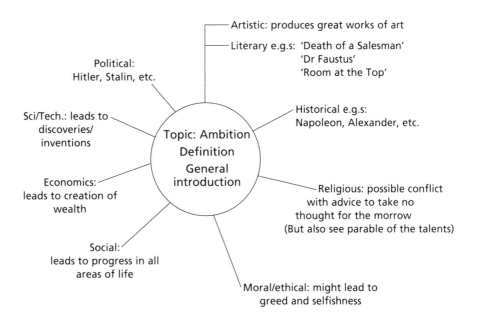

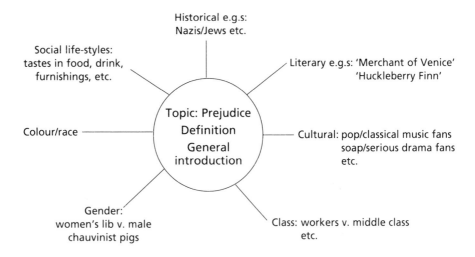

Use your mnemonic to find points, then look at what you've got and think how you might arrange them. Although the order can be fairly arbitrary – it doesn't matter whether you put class prejudice before gender prejudice or vice versa, for instance – there are two guidelines you should follow:

1 Either deal with less important points first and work up to serious ones later, or reverse the procedure, discussing the serious ones first than tailing off into minor ones towards the end; don't, for instance, hop from gender prejudice to food prejudice; your readers will think you have no sense of relative values.

2 Group any reasonably similar points together and deal with them in consecutive paragraphs: don't, for instance, hop from colour prejudice to religious prejudice to racial prejudice; colour and race have a logical connection because both are innate (programmed into a person's genes), whilst religious faith can be a matter of choice.

When you have arranged your points in order, follow the guidelines below:

1 Define your terms: for example, 'Prejudice is a dislike of a person or thing formed in advance of any knowledge of it. It is not the same as dislike, which is based on experience.'

2 Write a general introduction to the topic (see the note on writing introductions below).

3 Use your mnemonic plus any ideas of your own to give you different angles from which to attack the subject. (Would E for education and M for mass media be useful additions to your list?)

4 Write your conclusion, which in the case of 'Ambition' and 'Prejudice' may well be that these things are endemic in human nature and impossible totally to eradicate – whether we would like to or not.

Titles such as 'What qualities are most important to you when choosing a partner?' can be treated in the same way. In fact, a multi-angled approach is particularly important with topics like the last two if you are to reach the necessary target of one thousand words. Concentrate on only colour or class prejudice and you may find that you quickly run out of material or become very repetitive; interpret 'a partner' exclusively in the sexual sense and the same thing will happen.

A note on how to write introductions

The introduction to an essay should tell its readers what it will broadly be about.

It should therefore talk about the topic in general, not specific terms. It would be repetitive (though business-like) to mention in the introduction all the things you are going to deal with in the body of your essay – like this:

Prejudice is a dislike of someone or something in advance of any experience or knowledge. It can take the following forms: colour or

racial prejudice; class prejudice; gender prejudice; culture prejudice –
even prejudice against certain kinds of food. I shall deal with each of
these in turn.

First, colour or racial prejudice . . .

Instead, give a broader lead-in to the topic by briefly mentioning such
things as the following:

* its causes or origins
* the part it plays in our lives
* what kind of circles it is found in
* whether it is common, necessary or desirable
* whether its consequences are good or bad
  – things of a *general* kind.

For example:

Prejudice is a dislike of someone or something in advance of any
experience or knowledge of it. Psychological research seems to suggest
that it has its roots in fear; anything unfamiliar to us is a potential
threat and we react to it with hostility. Certainly prejudice is
widespread in our society. It affects our attitudes towards almost
everything that we know little about, and hardly anyone is free from
its taint.

Activity

Draw a diagram showing your panoramic approach to any of the
following titles:

'Happiness'
'What kinds of censorship exist in our society where there is, officially,
no censorship?'
'Drugs'
'Snobbery'

Guidelines for handling your essay well

Once you have written down the points you want to make and chosen a
structure, your essay will practically write itself. Just follow the simple
guidelines given below.

Here, for example, are some points you might jot down if you were
asked to argue the case for or against the return of capital punishment:

Points

P Most ordinary people want it; it's MPs who say no.
H All civilized societies have had the death penalty for murder and many
   still do.
R The Bible says 'an eye for an eye and a tooth for a tooth'.
A No.
S Killing murderers makes people feel safer, victims' families feel better.
E Cheaper to kill them than to keep in prison.

E   No.

M   It is only right and fair that murderers should be killed for killing.

S   No.

▓ *Express your points in categorizing phrases*

These points can then be expressed in a more sophisticated way with the help of categorizing nouns and appropriate adjectives. For example:

P   'Most ordinary people want it' = *public opinion*; 'only a handful of MPs' = *political influence, a political elite*;

H   'All civilized societies have had the death penalty' = *precedents* (Precedents have been set/Precedents exist for the death penalty/Precedents for capital punishment can be found in, etc.).

R   'The Bible says' = *A religious argument* can be made in support of capital punishment; 'an eye for an eye and a tooth for a tooth' = *retributive justice*;

S   'Killing murderers makes people feel safer', etc. = *social happiness/the well-being* of people in *society*;

E   'Cheaper to kill them than to keep in prison' = *an economic case/argument* can be put forward/*economic considerations* suggest that/looked at from the *economic angle*;

M   'It is only right and fair that murderers should be killed for killing' = there is a strong *moral case/argument*; capital punishment is necessary to uphold *morality* and *justice*.

▓ *Expand your categorizing phrases into topic sentences*

Key word | *Topic sentence:* the sentence that most fully sums up the topic discussed in any given paragraph.

Once you have found your categorizing phrases, incorporate them into the topic sentences that introduce each paragraph. The reader of your essay will then be able to see at a glance what aspect of the subject you are discussing in any particular paragraph. For example:

P   There is no doubt that if a referendum were to be held on the question tomorrow, public opinion would demand a return to capital punishment; it is only the influence of a political elite that prevents ordinary people from having their way.

H   There are historical and legal precedents for capital punishment: all civilized societies have imposed the death penalty for murder, and many still do.

R   Religious doctrine/teachings/authority support the reintroduction of capital punishment: the Bible sanctions the killing of those who break the second commandment by ruling that we should take 'an eye for an eye and a tooth for a tooth'.

S   The happiness and well-being of society would be promoted by the return of the death penalty: the execution of murderers makes people in general feel more secure, and comforts the families of the victims.

E Since it costs roughly £400 a week to keep convicted murderers in prison, there is an obvious economic case for bringing back the death penalty: hanging a man is far less of a burden on the tax-payer than locking him away for twenty to thirty years.

M One of the strongest arguments for the return of capital punishment is based on ideas of morality and justice: the vast majority of people – even those with no specific religious faith – feel that it is only right and just to execute a man who has taken someone else's life.

Link your paragraphs to the title and to each other

Your writing will sound disjointed and abrupt unless you use linking phrases to make one paragraph flow easily into the next.

The most obvious, but least satisfactory way to link is by using formulae like 'Firstly . . . Secondly . . . Thirdly . . . Fourthly . . . Fifthly . . . Finally'; or 'One good argument against . . . is . . . Another convincing argument is . . . A further good point to mention is . . . Still another argument is . . .' etc.

A more satisfactory way is to:

1 group similar points together, showing the connections between them by using links such as 'in the same way', then,

2 counter these points with others that give the opposite point of view, showing contrast by using linking words and phrases like 'however'.

Look at how this could be done with the topic sentences on capital punishment above. E stands out from the rest as a purely practical argument, M, R, and S can be grouped roughly together on the grounds of religion and morality, while H points out that there are historical and legal precedents for capital punishment.

Since the financial argument should carry less weight than the other ones it is a good ploy to introduce it first:

On the purely practical level it might be argued that the burden on the tax-payer would be eased by the reintroduction of capital punishment.
(*Elaboration and illustration of this topic sentence.*)

In the same way, others might claim that the money presently spent on keeping convicted murderers alive would be better spent in compensating their victims' families.
(*Elaboration and illustration of this topic sentence.*)

You can then make a contrast with it in your second paragraph. For example:

There are, **however**, stronger arguments in favour of **executing convicted murderers** based on moral grounds . . .
(*Elaboration and illustration of this topic sentence.*)

Or

Opponents of **capital punishment, on the other hand,** might object to talking about money when a man's life is at stake . . .
(*Elaboration and illustration of this topic sentence.*)

Useful linking words and phrases

Showing similarity

in the same way,	this is/could be supported by . . .
in addition to this,	evidence to support this can be found in . . .
moreover,	an illustration of this is . . .
considerations of this kind,	such things as these . . .

Showing contrast

on the other hand,	against this it could be argued that . . .
conversely	it might be objected that . . .
looking at it from the opposite point of view . . .	

Neutral

on balance,	it could be argued/pointed out that . . .
as a consequence of this,	nevertheless . . .
such things as these,	on the whole . . .

▓ *Put the meat on the bones*

How do you expand the points given in the sample essay schemes above into an essay of seven hundred to a thousand words? There are two main techniques.

Immediately you have written the topic sentence containing your point:

1 **Elaborate** on it by explaining more fully what you mean, in greater detail, e.g.:

Topic sentence ——— On the purely practical level it might be argued that the burden on the tax-payer would be eased by the reintroduction of capital punishment. *It*
Illustration ——— *costs a minimum of £400 to keep a man in prison for a week; many people feel that this money would be better off in their own pockets, rather than spent on providing free meals and colour television for a prisoner who has done nothing to deserve such generosity. If it has to be spent at all, it would be better spent on compensating the family of the victim than on rewarding the perpetrator of the crime.*

Topic sentence ——— There are, however, stronger arguments in favour of executing convicted murderers, based on moral grounds. *Everyone knows, even if*
Illustration ——— *they oppose capital punishment, that murder is evil, and the only way to deal with evil in a civilized society is to stamp it out at the source. If out of mistaken kindness we do not punish it severely enough, the evil will spread until it contaminates all areas of society. The whole point about evil, after all, is that it lacks conscience. It does not – it cannot – recognize the constraints that civilized men and women put upon their behaviour. With the best will in the world evil people cannot be taught to be good, and we can exterminate their evil only by exterminating them.*

(Paragraphs referring to biblical support and legal and historical precedents could follow this one).

Topic sentence ———

Illustration ———

> Opponents of capital punishment, on the other hand, might object to talking about money when a man's life is at stake. *If the cost to society is to be the crucial factor in deciding whether an individual lives or dies, how long before our attention turns to those who, while they may not actively harm society, provide it with no useful service? The mentally and/or physically handicapped, the senile, the drug-addicts who are a drain on the resources of our already over-stretched economy – how much better off we should be without them in every way.*

2 **Illustrate** what you are talking about in one or more of the following ways, by:

    a giving examples from your own and other people's experience (e.g. refer to a recent notorious murderer such as Ian Brady who was reportedly cruel from childhood);

    b using contrasting material (e.g. remark that there were fewer terrorist bombs and less mugging of elderly people when the death penalty was in place);

    c using images (e.g. a metaphor like *stunted seedlings will never grow into healthy plants*, to show that inherent evil cannot be eradicated);

    d referring to what happens in other societies (e.g. the treatment of murderers in Middle Eastern countries and in some American states);

    e talking about attitudes to capital punishment in the past;

    f telling anecdotes about famous people (e.g. the case of Ruth Ellis);

    g referring to literature (e.g. Hamlet's reluctance to execute Claudius resulted in the death of himself and seven other innocent people).

Activity

> Write your own essay on capital punishment, presenting both sides of the case.

▧ *Finally, a word about writing conclusions*

Never use either of the two following formulae:

1 Therefore, because of what I've said above/in the body of my essay, that's what I think about (for example) capital punishment.
2 Therefore, because of all the following reasons (quick recap on all the points made in the essay) I think that capital punishment should be re-introduced as quickly as possible.

Quick and superficial gabbles like this don't cut much ice with examiners, who are looking for a more stylish rounding off. Try instead to give a final, general overview of the present situation in regard to your topic, then suggest what may happen to it in the future.

For example:

Nothing stirs popular feeling more than a brutal murder, as the tabloids know. 'Sex fiend slays 11 year old' scream the headlines, and once again the cry goes up for the return of the ultimate penalty. In spite of public opinion, however, a majority of Cabinet ministers and MPs continues to reject demands to restore the death penalty, and as long as the Government of the day rules that they should be allowed to vote according to their individual conscience on this issue, rather than on party lines, then, however you or I may feel about it, there is little prospect of hanging being reintroduced.

How to structure the imaginative/creative essay

Sometimes you are given a one-word title that you can respond to creatively if you wish: 'Winning', for instance, or 'Ambition'.

Sometimes you are given a more specific brief: 'Write a fairy story on the subject of growing up'; or 'Write a story involving a family, a foreigner, a boat, a horse and sunflowers'.

Whatever the title, what this really boils down to is 'Write a short story.'

Fortunately, some clear guidelines can be offered for this.

To start with, you need an idea.

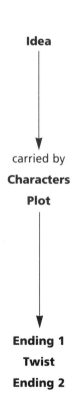

Idea

carried by

Characters

Plot

Ending 1

Twist

Ending 2

If you were writing on 'Growing Up' for example, ask yourself what you would want to convey about it to other people. That it's a hard and painful process? That facing loss or rejection teaches us how to do it? That having to take responsibility for something or someone forces us to do it whether we want to or not? That hardly anybody ever does grow up completely, and that most of us still behave like children at times?

Once you've got your idea, you have to create characters and a central event (the plot) that will bring it to life for other people. Whether the central event or situation causes the characters to behave as they do, or whether the characters create the event or situation by what they do doesn't really matter. The point is that they get the writer's idea across by demonstrating it in action.

Thus, your idea might be that marriage entered into for the sake of convenience and respectability is worse than no marriage at all; you would demonstrate this by creating the character of a lonely woman who turns down a loveless proposal in favour of occasional meetings with her married lover (the plot of *Hotel du Lac*).

There is one further thing to note. Many good short stories have what is called a 'twist' in the tail: a sudden reversal of fortune or an unexpected change of attitude on the part of one of the characters. In a way, therefore, the story has two endings: one, the one we expect because of everything that has happened up to that point; the second, one we didn't expect at all, that gives the story a greater depth of meaning.

Thus, in Angus Wilson's story, 'Mother's Sense of Fun', we watch a man battle to free himself from his domineering mother's clutches, and we share his joy at her sudden death. And then we are suddenly ambushed, like him, by the revelation that he can't cope in the big wide world without her to tell him what to do: 'She had had the last word in the matter as usual. "My poor boy will be lonely," she had said. She was dead right.' (Note the macabre pun.)

Talking point

> All the points I have made about the structure of short stories are beautifully illustrated in the one written by Somerset Maugham below – probably the shortest narrative in English literature, but brilliantly handled. Test your understanding by reading it and answering the following simple question: what idea is Somerset Maugham trying to convey to us in this story? To put it another way, what is its theme?
>
> Death speaks
>
> There was a merchant in Baghdad who sent his servant to market to buy provisions and in a little while the servant came back, white and trembling, and said, Master, just now when I was in the market-place I was jostled by a woman in the crowd and when I turned I saw it was Death that jostled me. She looked at me and made a threatening gesture; now, lend me your horse, and I will ride away from this city and avoid Death. I will go to Samarra and there Death will not find me. The merchant lent him his horse, and the servant mounted it, and he dug his spurs in its flanks and as fast as the horse could gallop he went. Then the merchant went down to the market-place and he saw me standing in the crowd and he came to me and said, Why did you make a threatening gesture to my servant when you saw him this morning? That was not a threatening gesture, I said, it was only a start of surprise. I was astonished to see him in Baghdad, for I had an appointment with him tonight in Samarra.

▓ *Help in creating story-lines*

It has been claimed that there are only eight basic story-lines in fiction, and that everything written is based on these. In case you have trouble in thinking up plots, these eight story-lines are outlined below by Rory Johnson (*The Guardian*, 9 September 1991). Like the 'phraseem' mnemonic, they may shape your thinking.

1 **Cinderella** – or unrecognized virtue at last recognized. It's the same story as the Tortoise and the Hare. Cinderella doesn't have to be a girl, nor does it even have to be a love story.
2 **Achilles** – the Fatal Flaw that is the groundwork for all classical tragedy.
3 **Faust** – the Debt that Must be Paid, the fate that catches up with all of us sooner or later.
4 **Tristan** – that standard triangular plot of two women and one man, or two men and one woman.
5 **Circe** – the Spider and the Fly, e.g. *Othello*.
6 **Romeo and Juliet** – Boy meets Girl, Boy loses Girl, Boy either finds or does not find Girl – it doesn't matter which.
7 **Orpheus** – the Gift Taken Away.
8 **The Hero Who Cannot be Kept Down**.

These plots can be presented in many different forms – tragedy, comedy, farce, whodunnit – and they can be inverted, but they still form the basis of all good writing. The fault with many contemporary plays is simply that they do not have a strong enough plot.

A further plot contributed by another *Guardian* reader is **David and Goliath** – the individual against the repressive/corrupt powers of the state or community, or their rival claims, as in Ibsen's *An Enemy of the People*, or *Antigone*.

Scriptwriter Stan Hayward on the other hand claims that

> there are only about seven themes in fiction, and they include Love, Money, Power, Revenge, Survival, Glory, and Self-Awareness. It is the quest for these that makes a story. Most stories have more than one theme and it is the superimposition of themes, with the arising conflicts, that makes a story interesting.

Activity

1 The cult movie *Casablanca* is one of the world's most enduringly popular films. Why? One explanation is that it contains almost all the themes listed above – Cinderella, Achilles, Faust, Tristan, Circe, Romeo and Juliet, Orpheus, The Hero Who Cannot be Kept Down, plus one more – the Eternal Traveller or Exile who can never return home – so that there is something in it for everyone.

Watch a videotape of the film and see if you agree that this is the secret of its appeal.

2 Consider each of the literary texts you are currently studying in the light of the above themes.

Talking point

Discuss any recent films, TV plays and/or episodes from soap operas you may have seen, from the point of view of their story-lines. Do they fit the above themes?

The only other thing to remember about the short story is to write to your brief.

If you are asked to include a family, a foreigner, a boat, a horse, and sunflowers in your story, include them all. You need not bring them all on the scene at once: you could be spending a family holiday on a canal boat, for instance, then create an incident involving a foreigner and a horse and some sunflowers.

If you are asked to write a fairy story, write a fairy story – not a science fiction story or an allegory. Fairy stories have stock characters such as handsome princes, wicked stepmothers, beautiful princesses, good and wicked fairies, dwarves, elves, talking birds and animals, giants and ogres. They may be intended to encourage you to think and behave in certain ways – to be brave and risk everything for the sake of your family, for instance, like Jack in *Jack and the Beanstalk* – but their chief intention seems to have been to amuse and shock and entertain on a level simple enough to appeal to children.

Allegories on the other hand are stories with a more obvious interest in teaching us something about ourselves. They work on two levels. On the surface they are tales of physical adventure and hardship – the hero climbs mountains or wades through swamps, or fights dragons or fiendish enemies. On the deeper level they have some sort of moral or spiritual message for us – the swamp for instance might represent the mental and spiritual state of despair or loss of faith that Christians sometimes experience (as in John Bunyan's *The Pilgrim's Progress*). The dragons or fiendish adversaries might represent the forces of evil that attack men's souls and destroy their integrity, as in *Idylls of the King* by Tennyson. On the whole, the world of the allegory is more solemn than that of the fairy story.

Talking point

> Do you think you should use a different tone and style for fairy story and allegory writing?
>
> Which should have the most elevated/the most concrete and down-to-earth vocabulary?
>
> Which should be written largely in simple/compound rather than largely complex sentence structures?
>
> Which should contain jokes and humour?
>
> In which should you write as if you were talking directly to your readers ('Now, Jack's mother saw his handkerchief lying at the foot of the beanstalk and she . . .')?
>
> In which should you keep your distance and write 'seriously'?

Activity

> Write an allegory about the pollution of our environment in which you portray pollution as a monster. (Whether you create a hero to slay the monster is up to you.) (Those of you who have read *The Lord of the Rings* may find inspiration in this.)

Summary-writing skills

Key word

> *Summary:* brief account giving the main points of a text.

To summarize a piece of writing is to give a brief and concise account of its main points, leaving out minor points and irrelevant material. Writing summaries therefore tests your ability:

  a to think logically;
  b to re-express more clearly what has been said – as far as possible in your own words.

Getting rid of irrelevant material

Writers want to interest and entertain you as well as inform and instruct. Above all, they want to make you really understand the full implications of what they are trying to say. That's why they bring in all sorts of information that is peripheral to (only loosely connected with) the main points. This peripheral material may be the liveliest part of the article, but since it's irrelevant to the main points, it has to go. Leave it in and you will muddy the clear line of the argument.

Listed below are some of the different kinds of irrelevant material that writers use to get and keep attention (making life difficult for you in the process):

Material brought in to make a contrast

In order to show us what something is really like, writers often introduce contrasting material:

> We no longer believe, as our ancestors did in the seventeenth and eighteenth centuries, that mad people are figures of fun to be legitimately mocked and scorned . . .

Method of dealing with this

As soon as you read a negative statement such as *This differs from/is not like; We no longer believe that/In the past people believed that*, allow a warning bell to ring in your brain. In a summary you have time only to make *positive* points, to say what something *is* like, or what we *do* do. Allow yourself to be sidetracked into talking about what things are *not* like or what we *don't* do, and

  a you'll run over your allowed word limit, and
  b you'll obscure the clear line of the argument.

Analogies

Writers will sometimes use analogies as well as contrasts, introducing them with such phrases as *This is like . . ., A similar kind of . . .* For example:

> Tragedy gives theatre-goers emotional relief by purging them of the emotions of pity and fear. The apparently coarse and physical game of football can provide *the same kind of* catharsis or emotional purging: powerful emotions of pity and fear build to a pitch of tension that can only be relieved by the scoring or missing of a goal.

Sometimes, however, writers may put the analogy before instead of after the thing they are describing, and to make matters worse, they may not show what they're doing by using introductory words and phrases. In the passage on the interdependence of science and technology, for instance, on page 248, Sir George Thomson wants to make the point that great achievements in science should take their place alongside greatness in the arts and in moral philosophy. Instead of telling us so plainly, however, he begins by mentioning greatness in these other spheres, and brings in scientific ability to understand the world only in his second paragraph:

> The greatness of the human race is indeed many-sided. Thus in the world of art there is a difference between the ability to compose or interpret a great piece of music and that which writes a great novel or paints a great picture. Yet all are evidence of greatness and worthy of the name. Still more is moral greatness. 'There is one glory of the sun and another glory of the moon and another glory of the stars.'
>
> Surely the ability to understand, even to a limited extent, the world around him is one of the powers of which man has good right to be proud.

Method of dealing with this

Simply leave out the analogy.

▓ *Imagery*

Writers often use similes or metaphors to help their readers 'see'. Similes are always introduced by the words *like* or *as*, e.g.

> She looks as pretty as a picture in that dress

whereas metaphors describe a thing directly in terms of something else:

> She's a real picture in that dress.

A writer, for instance, might liken our society to the hierarchical system found inside an ant heap (workers, soldiers, nurses, drones, and a Queen).

Method of dealing with this

Cut out most images. Re-express important ones, like the one about the ant heap, in the form of a simple statement:

> Our society is hierarchical.

▓ *Repetition: double constructions*

Sometimes writers repeat themselves by using double constructions:

> There are two ways in which people can spend money: wisely or foolishly.

Method of dealing with this

Get rid of the unnecessary *There are* construction, put the true subject first, and summarize:

> People can spend money foolishly or well.

▓ *Repetition: repeated statements*

Another kind of repetition involves the use of a negative statement followed almost immediately by a positive one; for example:

> This is not a simple poem; it is a highly complex one.
> Clare never went abroad; he spent all of his life in England.

Method of dealing with this

Look for the most comprehensive statement of the main idea, ignore any repetition, and state the point clearly, once.

This is a complex poem.

Clare spent all of his life in England.

Activity

> Summarize the following by eliminating the double construction:
>
> There are two ways of reading a book. One is to read it sentence by sentence, taking in almost every word; the other is to skim read by taking in whole paragraphs at a time. The first method has the merit of thoroughness, the second of speed.
>
> (You may find it helpful to begin, *You can read*, or *One can read*.)

▨ *Repetition: re-stating the same idea*

Sometimes writers repeat themselves by saying the same thing in several sentences, as in the extract below on Punk:

> While I enjoyed as much as the next person scurrying off to see all those daft bands . . . the attention that the movement attracted was such as to impose a stifling conformity on the music business . . . How laughable that this movement which preached the virtues of individual expression should have been intolerant of any deviation from its own narrowly defined norms. Who knows what talent went unexpressed because of its initial lack of 'punk credibility'?
>
> Whatever the virtues of Punk, it imposed a suffocating lack of variety that was the complete reverse of the situation in 1986.

Clearly a movement that imposes a *stifling conformity* is also one that is *intolerant of any deviation* from its own norms, and as a consequence is guilty of imposing a *suffocating lack of variety*. These phrases all express the same idea, and so qualify as repetition.

Method of dealing with this

Look for the most comprehensive statement of the idea, turn it into your own words as far as possible, and express it as clearly as you can, e.g.

It is ironical that Punk, which began as a drive for individual expression, should eventually stifle originality in other musicians by demanding that they slavishly imitate its style.

▨ *Illustrative material*

To make us understand what they are talking about, writers often give us a number of illustrative examples, as in the passage below:

> In the matter of literary techniques, the 1920s proved to be one of the most fruitful periods in the whole history of English literature. In fiction, the so-called 'stream of consciousness' method was born, matured and moved to its decline within this single decade. In poetry, the revolution [wrought by Pound and Eliot and the later Yeats, by the

new influence of the seventeenth century metaphysicals and of Hopkins], changed the poetic map of the country. As far as technique goes, the period since has been one of consolidation. Nothing so radically new in technique [as Eliot's *Wasteland*] has appeared since, nor have later novelists ventured as far in technical innovation [as Joyce did in *Ulysses* and *Finnegan's Wake* (the latter, though published in 1939, was largely written in and belongs in spirit to the 1920s)]. The sense of excitement which all this experimentation produced, [the battles, the mutual abuse, the innovating exaltation of the little magazines], seems very far away now in the 1950s, and were already lost by the end of the 1930s. A period of consolidation is not exciting, nor is it easy to describe with the literary historian's eye.

Method of dealing with this

The main points here are that the 1920s were a period of exciting technical innovation in poetry and the novel, and that nothing so original was produced in the next two decades. The rest (enclosed in square brackets) is detailed illustration and elaboration of these points and can be left out. As a general rule, it is better to cut illustration ruthlessly than to become bogged down in it. Keep too much illustration and you will have too little room left for main points.

Activity

> Sort out the illustration from the main points in the passage below:
>
> The writers of the Theatre of the Absurd believed that life was a meaningless and chaotic affair. The weird characters and absurd behaviour in their plays are a reflection of this view. *Waiting for Godot* presents us with two tramps on a mudheap, chewing on carrots and passing their time in word games and music-hall routines. *One Way Pendulum* depicts a housewife who spends all her time cooking more food than her family needs just to give the cleaning lady the job of eating it up. Her husband meanwhile is building a DIY Old Bailey kit in the living room, while her son is busy in his bedroom teaching a choir of speak-your-weight weighing machines to sing the Hallelujah Chorus. (People who spend a lot of time watching games shows on television have been known to find these plays offensive.)

However, you cannot always get rid of illustration in this brisk fashion. Sometimes the illustration of a point forms such a large part of a passage that it needs to be included in a generalized form.

Key word

> To *generalize* illustration: to form general categories (of people, things, events, etc.) from detailed examples, e.g. *the mass media* from *Radio, TV, the Press, and Advertising*.

In a piece about the part played by computers in our life today, for instance, a writer might say:

Computers have proved their usefulness in every area of life today: they have revolutionized the administration of large organizations; they are used in schools and colleges by staff and students alike; the new 'virtual reality' programmes allow architects and technical designers to produce three dimensional models of their new projects; authors write plays and novels with their help; businessmen plan sales campaigns and work out their accounts on their spreadsheets; programme schedulers draw up our next year's entertainment on them; aircraft are programmed to fly automatically by them; shops reorder goods automatically through them; medical records are stored on them . . . etc.

If you feel you must include the illustration in some form, cut out the detail but keep the main point by generalizing the illustration. You do this by finding categories into which the specific examples can be filed, as in the examples below:

Specific examples	Categories
the administration of large organizations	administration
schools and colleges	education
architects	architecture
technical designers	technical design
authors	creative writing or literature
businessmen	business
programme schedulers	entertainment
aircraft	transport
medical records	medicine or health care

Rearranging the order a little, 'shops' can be generalized as 'commerce' and moved from the end of the passage to go hand in hand with 'business'.

With a little practice, filing specific items under category headings can become a useful habit.

Activity

> Generalize the illustration below by putting it into three distinct categories:
>
> Some people criticize us students for frittering money away on plays, films, football matches and discos. They say we're always splashing out on new jeans and trainers, and any money we've got left we spend on travelling round Europe. I think they've forgotten they were young once themselves.

▓ *Items of historical or background interest*

Writers often introduce pieces of historical information into their work, to add life and interest.

Discussing the dialect known as the Queen's English, for example, Philip Howard strikes a nicely gossipy note by telling us how it was spoken by Queen Victoria herself:

At the top was the Queen's English (not, as it happens, spoken very well by her Majesty, who retained a faint German accent all her life; she wrote it with naive charm and enthusiasm).

Method of dealing with this

Leave out any items of background or historical interest.

Activity

> Eliminate the items of historical interest in the passage below:
>
> For Samuel Beckett, life was a brief gleam of light surrounded by eternal darkness. As one of his characters remarks:
>
> They give birth astride of a grave, the light glimmers an instant and then it's night once more.
>
> Fourteen centuries earlier a similar view was expressed by an anonymous counsellor of the Anglo-Saxon king Edwin, likening man's brief life to the flight of a sparrow through a banqueting hall:
>
> The sparrow flies swiftly in through one door of the hall, and out through another. While he is inside, he is safe from the winter storms; but after a few minutes of comfort, he vanishes from sight into the darkness whence he came.

▓ *Humour*

Writers sometimes introduce jokes.

Method of dealing with this

Cut them out.

General guidelines for approaching a summary

1 To find the main subject or argument, look first at paragraph one, then at the last two paragraphs. If these mention the same thing you can be reasonably sure you have found the main subject. If they do not, then one of them contains irrelevant material of the kinds listed above.

2 To confirm that you really have found the main topic, skim-read the remaining paragraphs looking for further mention of it. Note any shifts of meaning or changes of emphasis. Writers will often make one of these sudden shifts right in the middle of a piece, as in the passage set for you to work below.

Do this twice if necessary. It will save you from starting off on the wrong foot. To write a good summary you must understand the writer's main drift before you begin.

3 Run through the passage, looking for all the things you have been advised to cut out:
   a material brought in to make a contrast
   b analogies
   c imagery
   d repetition

    e detailed examples of general trends, art forms, movements, etc.

    f items of historical or general background interest

    g humour

It is helpful to rule a line firmly through examples of (a), (b), (c), (d), (f), and (g), and to put square brackets around examples of (e). (This is because you cannot know at this point whether you will need to keep the illustration in a generalized form.)

It is an excellent idea to write your summary on alternate lines. If you should find that you are well under your word limit and have left something out, you can then put an omission mark at the relevant place and slip it in on the blank line above.

4 When you have found your main points and got rid of all the irrelevant material, proceed as follows:

    a Make a list of your main points, looking for any logical connections that can be made between them.

    b Make clear the connections between points with linking words like *this*; *however*; *but if* (as in *But if technology depends upon science, science in its turn needs technology*); *consequently*; *this is because*; *the reason for this is*; *on the other hand*; etc. (Examiners look hard at your ability to make the line of the argument clear in this way.)

Note: you do not have to stick to the same arrangement of facts as the original. It is sometimes possible to begin with a point that comes in the middle or towards the end. Plan first, to see if such a drastic rearrangement will work out, however. It could get you into a lot of trouble.

A sample plan for the technology piece that you will be asked to summarize will be found at the end of the piece. **Do not read the plan until you have read the passage at least twice.**

Working a summary

Now that you have some idea of how to approach a summary, look at the example below and see the techniques in action. (Exam candidates were asked to summarize the passage in 200 words.)

> The greatness of the human race is indeed many-sided. Thus in the world of art there is a difference between the ability to compose or interpret a great piece of music and that which writes a great novel or paints a great picture. Yet all are evidence of greatness and worthy of the name. Still more is moral greatness. 'There is one glory of the sun and another glory of the moon and another glory of the stars.'
>
>   Surely the ability to understand, even to a limited extent, the world around him is one of the powers of which man has good right to be proud. Indeed it seems to be the one that most divides him from the animals. The lark's song, the action of a plover luring an enemy away from her young, the cat who was seen to attack a grizzly in defence of

her kittens – these, if taken at their face value, are notable even by human standards; but I am not aware (though I speak with great diffidence) of any creature which even appears to be trying to discover any general principles. The chance of understanding things of fundamental and permanent importance is what makes the pursuit of science fascinating and worthwhile.

So much for understanding – but what of control? These two aspects of science do not in fact conflict. The best way to make advances in technology, whether on the medical or the engineering side, turns out to be to understand the principles. This is a recent discovery; indeed it has probably only recently come true. It would not have been much use, for example, to man in the Stone Age, or even a few hundred years ago, to try to understand the principles of tanning with no basic knowledge of chemistry to guide him. He did better by trial and error.

This dependence of technology on pure science is now fairly recognized by industry. The more progressive industries maintain research laboratories which both make use of the basic discoveries made in the universities and elsewhere and contribute their own. There are black spots, of course – industries that spend too little on research or organize it badly – but broadly speaking the need is realized and reasonably well met.

The other influence of technology is more subtle but every bit as important. As science advances, concepts tend to become more and more abstract, further from anything that can literally be touched or handled. This being so, is there not a danger that we may lose touch with reality, and end up by supposing that some elaborate piece of mathematics represents reality when in fact it is only a creation of the mind, inspired indeed by physical reality but no more like it than is a modern picture? I think we are safe so long as the people who make these theories are reasonably close to those who use them, not merely in laboratories but in industry.

To me, science without technology is incomplete and inconclusive. Systems of philosophy come and go, some are perhaps true – but who can tell? But when conclusions deduced by mathematical theory, from precise experiments, lead to detailed predictions from which working machines can be designed, machines which without the theory no one would have thought of in a million years, then indeed one knows that one lives in a universe that is rational and that one has found the key to one of its rooms.

Sir George Thomson, *The Listener*

▓ Commentary

Paragraph 1

This is a series of disguised analogies. The writer talks about great human achievements in music, art, literature, and morality so that in the next paragraph he can claim that scientific achievements are every bit as great as these.

Since this is illustrative material, either leave it out or generalize as *greatness in the spheres of the arts and morality*. (It will depend on your word limit).

Paragraph 2

In paragraph 2 the writer goes even further: science is the supreme human achievement. He brings in lower animals to make a contrast, claiming that while they may have the beginnings of art and morality, only man tries to understand the general principles on which the universe is based.

Paragraphs like this clearly show why you should read the whole passage before starting your summary.

Paragraph 3

The logical structure of the writer's argument is clearly signalled in the question that opens paragraph 4: *So much for understanding – but what of control?* It forms a kind of hinge movement in the middle of the piece. It shows us that the subject of the first part of his argument (science that understands) is not going to be the only subject: there is another, equally important one related to this: the technology that controls the world by applying the principles that science discovers. Again, the importance of reading the whole passage thoroughly before beginning is clear.

We could summarize:

Progress in technology depends on a thorough understanding of the general principles discovered by science.

Paragraph 4

The writer offers proof of this: the funding of scientific research by Industry.

Paragraphs 5 and 6

The writer develops his argument: science in its turn depends on technology to provide physical proof that its theories are valid. Only through technology's ability to turn an abstract theory into a working machine can scientists be sure that they have discovered the truth about an aspect of the physical world.

▓ *Sample plan for science/technology passage*

science uniquely great
      BECAUSE increases sum of human knowledge
      BY discovering gen. prins underlying phys. world
      AND BECAUSE BY DOING THIS it makes technology possible
          (evidence: industrial funding of sci. research)
      HOWEVER tech. IN ITS TURN important to science
      BECAUSE offers validation of sci. ideas
      BY MAKING abstract theory concrete fact

Activity

> Using your own words as far as possible, write a summary of the above passage in no more than 200 words.

Activity

> **1** Read the passage on Registers, below, at least twice.
>
> **2** Go through the passage, noting irrelevant material which can be cut as demonstrated above. (In an exam situation, you could strike these through in pencil.)
>
> **3** Make a note of any lengthy passages of illustration that may have to be generalized. (In an exam, you could put square brackets round these.)
>
> **4** Write yourself an organized plan on the model of the one on the science/technology passage given above.
>
> **5** Summarize the passage in no more than 100 words.
>
> **Registers**
>
> Our perception of the English language and how it works has changed radically in the present generation. In the High Victorian world the pristine philologists saw the language in much the same way as they saw Victorian society: as a pyramid. At the top was the Queen's English (not, as it happens, spoken very well by Her Majesty, who retained a faint German accent all her life; she wrote it with naive charm and enthusiasm). The Queen's English was the sort spoken in an Oxford accent by the educated classes in the south-east of England, taught at the great public schools and the old universities, and printed in *The Times* and the books from the main London publishing houses. Lower down the pyramid were lesser kinds of English: some of them perfectly respectable members of the House of Lords of language, such as the dialects and grammars of Scottish and American English; others of them disreputable commoners, unspeakable by the civilized, such as Cockney or Gorbals.
>
> Of course, sensible philologists, such as the great James Murray, recognized that all language is equal, even if some language is more equal than others. But the Queen's English, with correct grammar, and pronounced in received pronunciation, was the standard at the top of the pyramid.
>
> We have come to recognize that such a rigid class system is as silly in language as it is in society. There is not one correct sort of English, and dozens of lesser breeds of English all more or less conforming to the ideal, and having more value the closer they came to the Queen's English, and less value the farther they diverged from it. English is not a pyramid, but a great city with many suburbs and city centres serving many purposes. The same sort of English, whether the Queen's or anybody else's, is not appropriate to all occasions or uses. There is not one standard English, but many overlapping kinds of English with different functions and contexts.

For example we use a quite different kind of English when we are writing a leader in *The Times* from the kind we use when chatting to strangers in the public bar of a pub. If we do not make this distinction, either the editor will receive a great many outraged letters or we shall be left talking to ourselves in the centre of a circle of uneasy mutters. Students of linguistics have recently named these different varieties of English 'registers'.

The *Times* leader and pub chat are registers that are widely different and easy to distinguish. But there are many registers in the Queen's English, and the distinction between some of them is fine. We use different registers to talk to different people: to the Queen, to our solicitor, to a member of the family, to a child. But we use a different register to talk on the telephone from the register we use to talk to the same person face to face.

The two major registers, which take in most of the lesser registers, are written and spoken English. Until recently spoken English was the poor relation. The Queen's English at the top of the pyramid was literary standard English, the grammar and spelling of which were taught at schools and universities across the land. English education was largely carried on by writing and reading. Exams, though they might include a French *dictée*, or a *viva voce* to test whether candidates understood what they had written in their answers, were in writing. When Henry VI founded Eton College in 1440, the tests for the scholars stipulated that they should not only be poor and needy boys of good character, but also that they should have 'a competent knowledge of reading, of the grammar of Donatus and of plain song'. Serious learning was in written English. The spoken word was for recreation.

The emphasis has recently swung from written to spoken English. Schools teach by discussion as well as written tests and essays. Examinations are conducted by multiple-choice questions, in which candidates tick the answer they deem correct, as well as writing answers in prose. The telephone, radio, television, and other new technologies fill the world with the spoken word. Members of Parliament make their speeches *ex tempore* from a few notes, rather than writing them out in stately periods, and learning them by heart. Business of all sorts is conducted by telephone instead of letter. Among the most popular programmes on the radio are phone-ins, in which any member of the public can join in public chat with the presenter. The heroes and sages of the media age are presenters of chat shows, masters of the spoken word, who may well be vacuous blabber-mouths, but who are so fluent that they never commit the unforgivable sin of the new media of the spoken word: drying up. And tape recorders enable academics to record and study spoken English more systematically than ever before.

Philip Howard, *The State of the Language*

How to re-express a piece in your own words

▇ *Images*

Think what the image means in real terms, then re-express it as clearly and precisely as you can. If someone should write, '*Ulysses* is light years away from the work of earlier writers in content and style', think of what the immense length of time represented by *light years* means here – an enormous space – and re-express more simply: '*Ulysses* differs enormously in content and style from the work of earlier novelists.' Simply say that, and throw the image away.

▇ *Illustration containing specific examples*

Generalize specific examples such as *the telephone, radio, and television*, by putting them into categories, in this case *aural media*: see pages 245–246 earlier, for guidelines on how to do this. Preface your category words with the phrase 'Much of the business of' and follow them with the clause 'is carried out orally today' and you will have covered all the points in the last paragraph of the Registers passage (page 252). (A genuine stylist in summary writing however might want to keep the last point separate for the sake of emphasis: ' . . . even academic research into the nature of English itself . . .'

Note: the wrong way to shorten illustration is to keep some specific examples from a list – e.g. the chat-show hosts – and throw out others – e.g. tape-recorders used by academics – at random. This is considered poor technique as there is nothing to suggest that any one of these items is more important than any other. It is known in the trade as 'unbalanced rejection'. Either throw out the lot, or generalize it.

▇ *Emotive language*

Ignore any personal feelings expressed by the writer. For example:

> Some people are crazy enough to believe they can smoke under 20 cigarettes a day without doing themselves any harm

becomes:

> Some people believe light smoking is harmless.

▇ *Rhetorical questions*

To ram home a point, writers sometimes put it in the form of a rhetorical question –

> But was 1976–77 really a golden era in the history of rock?

> Has the Right Honourable gentleman any idea where these policies will lead?

The answers are implied in the questions, and so we rephrase them in the form of statements:

In reality, however, 1976–77 was not a golden era in the history of rock.

The Right Honourable gentleman has no idea where these policies will lead.

Or, if the question was ironical as well as rhetorical,

The Right Honourable gentleman knows perfectly well where these policies will lead.

▓ *Quotations*

Do not quote the speakers' words directly – just extract the points from what they say. For example:

Mr Giles Radice declared, 'We are losing 1,000 scientists a year to the brain drain. Higher education in this country is seriously underfunded and in need of increased resources both for teaching and research.'

becomes either

Mr Radice declared that Britain was suffering a crisis in education

if that is all you have room for, or

Mr Radice claimed that the serious underfunding of higher education in Britain was leading to the loss of scientists to foreign universities.

Similarly,

Have they not left it a little late in the day? Possibly, conceded Professor Wilkinson at Monday's launch but he, for one, was ready for a fight. 'There are some very dangerous ideas about. This is our last chance to defeat them. We are crusaders for education.'

becomes

They (Prof. Wilkinson and his associates) see themselves as crusaders for education, eager for a last-minute battle against dangerous new ideas.

▨ssessment of style

You may be asked to comment on the difference in style between your own version and the original piece of writing.

Answering this is really very simple. All you have to do is look at the list of the things you have thrown out and comment on the plain style and flat tone that results when all these writerly devices (listed on pages 242–247) are missing.

▨irected writing

More recent summaries set by the AEB have asked candidates to summarize the main points of the original, then incorporate them into a new piece of writing for a particular audience.

This means that instead of including every single one of the writer's main points, you may be asked to include only those which are relevant to the job you have to do. If, for instance, you are asked to,

a summarize the main points in an article about the dangers of smoking;

b rewrite it in the form of a piece clearly setting out risks of smoking for thirteen-year-olds,

there would be little point in mentioning the fact that in Norway, a ban on cigarette advertising has caused a fall in smoking among the under 20s. It would be irrelevant to your brief, which is to state the risks, not the safeguards.

A good percentage of the marks for this kind of summary are awarded on the basis of how well you have adapted your tone and style of writing to the needs of your audience. To put it another way, it's a test of your knowledge of register.

Suppose, then, you are presented with a piece of writing on the dangers of smoking, and are asked to set out clearly for thirteen-year-old readers the risks they will run if they decide to smoke.

How do you go about it?

The summarized (relevant) facts are given below, together with a model answer.

Note: the examiners will not expect you to achieve all the different styles of lettering shown in the model answers which appear in this section. Differently sized letters for main and sub-headings will do.

- Smoking causes:
  9 out of 10 deaths from lung cancer and bronchitis;
  at least 20% of deaths from arterial disease (legs get gangrene, are cut off).
- Smoking kills 100,000 people a year.
- Smoking is highly addictive and hard to give up, so better not to start.
- Smoking is rising among the under 20s, falling among adults.
- Most adult smokers want to give up but can't.
- The majority of smokers start before they are 20.
- 80% of teenagers who smoke one or two cigs experimentally go on to become regular smokers.
- Most smokers think there's a greater risk of dying in a traffic accident than from smoking.
- 25 die of smoking for every one killed on the roads.
- Fewer than 20 cigs a day can kill you.
- Risk of lung cancer increases the longer you smoke, declines immediately you stop.
- Passive smoking can increase a non-smoker's chances of getting lung cancer 10–30%.

Punchy headline
Colloquial idiom

Plenty of white space

Forceful opening sentence

Use of 'You' sounds friendly,
personal; avoids talking down

Repetition to add emphasis, force

Capitals for emphasis

Sub-heading to add force and
clarity and create more white
space

Sub-headings also act like Topic
Sentences – tell you what
paragraph will be about

Sub-headings also lure the eye on
to read more

Teenagers think of themselves as
people not teenagers. They would
feel patronized if addressed as
such

Command followed by rhetorical
question to vary sentence
structure, add force and involve
reader in what is being said

Kick those butts

Under 16 and thinking of trying cigarettes?

DON'T!

Smoke, and you'll destroy your lungs.
Smoke, and you'll stop the flow of blood through your arteries.
Your legs will turn green and have to be cut off.

THESE THINGS HAPPEN TO 100,000 SMOKERS
EVERY SINGLE YEAR.

Why you shouldn't take even one puff

Smoking gets you hooked as soon as you start. Try even one or
two cigarettes and the chances are you'll never be able to stop.
One in three adults still smoke – not because they want to, but
because they can't give it up.

SMOKING IS ADDICTIVE – IT'S BETTER NOT TO START
THAN TO TRY TO GIVE UP LATER ON.

Some wrong ideas about smoking

Do you think you're more likely to fall under a bus
than be killed by smoking?

YOU'RE WRONG.

25 people are killed by cigarettes for every one killed on the roads.

Do you think you're safe if you smoke under 20 cigarettes a day?

THINK AGAIN.

A few a day can kill you. Only **none** is safe.

Why people like you are in special danger

Smoking is rising among people of your age, just when many adults
are seeing sense and giving up.

You aren't even safe if you don't smoke yourself – just breathing in
your friends' smoke puts you at risk.

If you and your friends don't smoke, your risks of getting lung
cancer are only 1 in 10.

If the people you go around with smoke, your chances will go up to
4 in 10 – without ever having touched a cigarette yourself.

Think about it. Is it worth being killed by your friends? Tell them the
danger. Get them to stop.

Make sure that **you** don't become one of the hundreds of
thousands of smokers who die in agony every year from breathing
in cigarette smoke.

STOP NOW, BEFORE YOU REALLY GET STARTED.

This kind of layout could be adapted to the writing of an information leaflet or magazine article. A main heading and sub-headings are all you really need. It's largely the register and tone that have to be altered for the different tasks set. If you were asked to write the same kind of leaflet for eighteen-year-old students, for instance, you would keep the same layout but toughen up the tone a bit and include some of the statistics you left out for the thirteen-year-olds. Eighteen-year-olds are cynical enough to demand evidence.

For instance, your opening paragraph might read:

Rhetorical opening question forces reader to respond

> ### Want to die before your time?
> Smoke a few cigarettes a day.
> That does the trick for 100,000 people every single year.
>
> ### Want to die slowly and very painfully?
> SMOKE.
> If lung cancer and bronchitis don't get you
> – and nine out of ten cases are caused by smoking –
> arterial disease will.
> Blood won't be able to flow through your clogged-up
> arteries, gangrene will set in and your legs
> will have to be amputated.

A pamphlet giving advice to ordinary members of the public, on the other hand, should have a more formal style, with a pleasantly conversational tone. Asked to write a pamphlet offering helpful advice to the parents of bilingual children, you might begin:

Personal note struck by use of second person 'You'

> As parents of bilingual children, you may worry about the effects that learning two languages simultaneously may have upon their development. In fact, you have little need for concern . . .

The intimate second person of the pronoun seems more appropriate here than the impersonal third person, used in the version below:

> Parents of bilingual children often worry about the effects that learning two languages simultaneously may have upon their children's development. In fact, there is little cause for them to be concerned . . .

Impersonal third person keeps reader at distance

Sometimes you may be asked to write an article for a newspaper. Again, much the same layout of main headline plus sub-headings can be used, but tone and register will have to be made appropriate to the particular kind of newspaper for which you have been chosen to write.

Broadsheets like *The Times*, *The Telegraph*, *The Guardian*, and *The Independent* have main headlines but no sub-headings. Middle-of-the-road tabloids like *The Daily Mail* and *The Daily Express* have main headings and possibly one sub-heading. Popular tabloids have main headings and between one and three sub-headings, depending on the length of the article.

Sentence structure, vocabulary, and tone all differ to some extent to suit the different kinds of reader, as you will see in the examples given below.

Summary of main points of original

❉ A no. of moderate Tories have founded a pressure group called the Conservative Education Association.

❉ They are Messrs Smith, Merridale, Wilkinson, Hall-Dickerson and Argyropulo.

❉ Normally loyal gov. servants they are aggrieved that their views are being ignored in favour of what they see as the dangerously radical ideas of right-wing extremists.

❉ They are worried about the underfunding of Higher Education, the brain drain of Brit. scientists to foreign universities, and the lack of industrial education and training.

❉ Their policies, outlined in a programme called 'One Last Chance', are:
  • to raise low educational standards by raising low teacher-morale;
  • to keep education in the hands of Local Authorities, all but a small number of which they think do an excellent job;
  • to give precedence to ordinary schools over private schools, grammar schools, and City Colleges of Technology, which they fear will lure teachers away from comprehensives;
  • to strengthen the Technical and Vocational Initiative;
  • to set up a new Dept. of Ed. & Training so that Brit. invests as much in its workforce as its industrial rivals do.

❉ They feel no hostility towards government ministers themselves – they are old colleagues and friends – only towards their policies.

❉ They admit that they have left their stand rather late, but they are ready for a last-minute crusade for education.

▓ *Popular tabloid style*

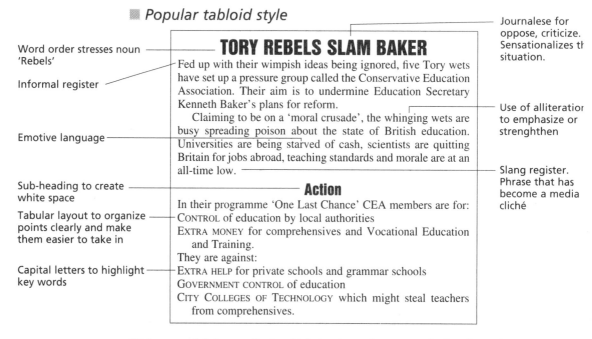

Word order stresses noun 'Rebels'

Informal register

Emotive language

Sub-heading to create white space

Tabular layout to organize points clearly and make them easier to take in

Capital letters to highlight key words

TORY REBELS SLAM BAKER

Fed up with their wimpish ideas being ignored, five Tory wets have set up a pressure group called the Conservative Education Association. Their aim is to undermine Education Secretary Kenneth Baker's plans for reform.

Claiming to be on a 'moral crusade', the whinging wets are busy spreading poison about the state of British education. Universities are being starved of cash, scientists are quitting Britain for jobs abroad, teaching standards and morale are at an all-time low.

Action

In their programme 'One Last Chance' CEA members are for:
CONTROL of education by local authorities
EXTRA MONEY for comprehensives and Vocational Education and Training.
They are against:
EXTRA HELP for private schools and grammar schools
GOVERNMENT CONTROL of education
CITY COLLEGES OF TECHNOLOGY which might steal teachers from comprehensives.

Journalese for oppose, criticize. Sensationalizes the situation.

Use of alliteration to emphasize or strengthen

Slang register. Phrase that has become a media cliché

(Other useful journalistic clichés: *in a desperate bid to/in a last-minute bid to.*)

■ *Up-market tabloid style*

Word order stresses noun 'Tories'

REBEL TORIES DEFY PARTY LINE ON EDUCATION

Confrontational language to create excitement

Exaggerated language to create excitement

Listing method used here to set out points clearly for readers, make them easier to read at a glance

A GROUP OF TORY backbenchers this week committed themselves to a fight against Education Secretary Kenneth Baker's plans for educational reform by founding the Conservative Education Association. Its aim is to spearhead a party revolt against what they see as dangerously radical ideas.

The storm broke when Messrs Smith, Merridale, Wilkinson, Hall-Dickerson and Argyropulo claimed that their moderate views were being ignored in favour of those on the extreme right of the party.

According to the rebels, the government is seriously under-funding higher education, causing a brain-drain of scientists to overseas universities.

In their programme – it is called 'One Last Chance' – they outline the measures they think the Education Secretary should take. They want:

the boosting of education standards by improving low teacher morale;

increasing spending on the ordinary state schools to which most people send their children;

increased funding for the Technological and Vocational Initiative;

the setting up of a new Department of Education and Training to bring Britain's investment in its workforce up to the level of our industrial rivals in other countries.

(Other useful bits of journalese: *pinpoint weak spots*; *voice concern about/that*; *provoked fury among politicians*; *came out fighting against*. Notice the combative, confrontational nature of these clichés; they sensationalize and dramatize perfectly ordinary clashes of ideas until politics is elevated – if that's the right word – to the condition of warfare. Generate spurious excitement and you sell copies.)

■ *Broadsheet style*

Word order emphasizes left wing, 'soft' quality

Ironically exaggerated statement

Lively way of introducing the subject – avoids plain boring statement

Participle to save space, add pace

Formal, educated diction – avoids pejorative terms, e.g. 'loony right'

Tory wets oppose right-wing stance on education

English education is in a dreadful state. Who says so? Not the Opposition, strangely enough, but members of the Government's own party. Dismayed by the Education Secretary's refusal to listen to moderate opinions, erstwhile Tory loyalists Messrs Smith, Merridale, Wilkinson, Hall-Dickerson and Argyropulo have founded the Conservative Education Association, a pressure group designed to oppose what they see as the dangerously radical views of right-wing Tories.

The rebels claim reluctance to offend Government ministers, but point out that the seriousness of the situation leaves them no choice: the under-funding of Higher Education is driving scientists abroad, teacher morale is very low, and educational standards exceedingly poor.

In a lengthy programme entitled 'One Last Chance', CEA members outline the measures they would like implemented: continued local authority control of education; increased resources for state schools …

Note length of sentence – makes no concessions to readers

No bullet points, capital letters or tabular presentation to make things easier for readers

Formal language – cf 'at an all time low'

Activity | Finish off the three articles, including the rest of the facts.

Comprehension

To understand what is expected of you in the comprehension exercise, think of it as summary in reverse.

Summary asks you to concentrate on a writer's main points; it doesn't want to know about

a the writer's personal opinions and attitudes;
b the writer's style.

In contrast, comprehension asks you to concentrate on these very things: the writer's opinions and attitudes, and the style in which he or she expresses them. It does ask questions about the main points being made, of course, but often the main emphasis is not on these and fewer marks are awarded for them than for answers on other questions.

In six recent A level comprehensions, only two questions per passage were asked on the factual content of what the writer was saying. The rest of the questions asked candidates to do some or all of the following:

1　Re-express in your own words definitions and/or statements made by the writer.
2　Explain in your own words the meaning of certain key words and/or phrases.
3　Discuss the writer's approach to a subject.
4　Discuss the writer's attitude towards a subject.
5　Discuss the audience targetted by the writer.
6　Discuss the writer's register in relation to this intended audience.
7　Discuss and evaluate the writer's style.
8　Examine the writer's style for signs of bias.
9　Discuss the use and presentation of any graphical material.

Methods of coping with the nine comprehension tasks

■ *Task 1:* Re-express statements or definitions in your own words

Consider the following extract taken from an article published in *New Society*:

> To begin with definitions: what is poverty in the 1980s? Is poverty (as Professor Peter Townsend argues) purely relative – the poor being defined by the gap between their resources and that of others? Should it, in the subtle version argued by Stewart Lansley and Joanna Mack, be measured by asking people what they think poor people should be able to afford, and accepting as poor those who can't? May there be room for the old-fashioned absolute approach to poverty, as being to do with minimum income required to support life and health – the approach of David Piachaud's 'The Price of a Child'? Or should we just muddle along, in the English empirical spirit, using the state supplementary benefit level as our benchmark?

The question set on this ran:

> What, in your own words, are the **four** definitions which the article suggests to the question 'what is poverty in the 1980s' in lines 18-37?

Method of dealing with this

To demonstrate your grasp of the writer's meaning, get rid of abstract terms like *poverty* and *resources*, and use simple nouns and verbs instead; in other words, get some people in there, doing things. For example, definition 1 – *poverty (as Professor Townsend argues) is purely relative – the poor being defined by the gap between their resources and that of others* – can be re-expressed as:

> Poor people are defined by their having fewer goods and services than the rest of society/most other people.

On the other hand, if the statement you are asked to re-express is already written in clear, simple English, rephrase it with the help of abstract nouns. Thus, a phrase like *asking people what they think* can be turned into the more abstract *consulting public opinion*, and *what poor people should be able to afford* into *what minimum standard of living should be available to the poor.*

Activity

> Using these suggested techniques, re-express definitions 3 and 4 in your own words.
>
> *Definition 3:* The old-fashioned absolute approach to poverty sees it as being to do with the minimum income required to support life and health – the approach of David Piachaud's 'The Price of a Child'.
>
> *Definition 4:* We can just muddle along, in the English empirical spirit, using the state supplementary benefit level as our benchmark.

▓ *Task 2:* Explain key words or phrases

Consider the question,

> Explain what you understand by the differences in meaning between the words 'disillusion' and 'disengagement' as they are used in sentence 2 of the following:
>
> There is no single solution to poverty. To pretend otherwise is to invite a new wave of disillusion and disengagement when the present rediscovery phase is complete.

Method of dealing with this

Again, you are being asked to show that you understand the meaning of abstract phrases. Use the technique of replacing these with simple nouns and verbs as suggested earlier. For example:

> Disillusion describes the state of mind of people who no longer believe in what they have been working for. Disengagement describes

the way in which, as a consequence, they withdraw themselves from their earlier commitment.

Note: when explaining abstract nouns such as *prejudice* and *conscience*, avoid the formula, *Prejudice/conscience is **when** somebody . . .* You are not talking about time but about mental states, and an adverb of time such as *when* is therefore inappropriate.

Difficulties in defining key words

1 Words mean different things in different contexts.
Scrappy for instance may be a term of disapproval in one context and a simple observation of fact in another. Compare for example:

> This work is scrappy in construction; you have failed to integrate it into a coherent whole

with:

> . . . this scrappy and lively and gossipy book . . .

In the first comment, *scrappy* is used disapprovingly: the work is a mess; in the second, it is simply an objective observation: the book is made up of fragments of different kinds – it's a literary *pot pourri*.

2 Words become obsolescent.
They, and consequently the ideas that they express, drop out of use, and when they crop up at a later date they cause confusion. The term 'worldling', for instance, was used by writers in the nineteenth and early twentieth century to describe men or women who were over-fond of the pleasures of this world – food, drink, sex, money, and so on. Students of the Spielberg generation, used to films like *ET* and *Close Encounters of the Third Kind*, misread it as a synonym for 'earthling' and became very confused.

Mistakes can be made in the same kind of way by taking imagery too literally. Talking about his difficulties in reading classical literature, for instance, Richard Church wrote:

> I have had to peer over the railings by standing on Lempriere and Smith's classical dictionaries . . .

Some students took him to mean that he actually stood on dictionaries, instead of simply relying on them for the translation of Latin and Greek words.

3 The special problem of irony.
Writers do not always mean exactly what they say. If a writer tells you, for example, that cheats, liars and scoffers are thoroughly steady and reliable people, do not take him or her at face value. Notice the tension set up between nouns like *cheats* and *liars* and *scoffers*, and the adjectives *steady* and *reliable*. The writer is either contradicting him- or herself, which is unlikely, or is using irony. Read the section on irony, pages 202–207, and be on the look-out for this technique.

Remember that words are fluid and changeable things. The meaning of any word you may be asked to explain is determined by:

a the rest of the words in the sentence;

b the whole context of the passage.

Do not automatically give words the same meaning they had when you met them on a previous occasion.

▓ *Task 3:* Discuss the writer's approach to the subject

As you saw in the section on essay writing, any given topic can be looked at from a number of different viewpoints. A discussion of the censorship of books, plays, films, and television, for example, might be approached from any of the following angles:

* the **aesthetic:** the writer might fear that an artist's work would be damaged by censorship
* the **political:** the writer might fear that censorship of the arts on grounds of 'taste' or 'decency' would lead inevitably to censorship of a political kind
* the **moral:** the writer might fear the corruption of people's minds if total freedom of expression were allowed
* the **social:** the writer might consider the subject from the point of view of different sections of society with differing social values and attitudes, or assess its impact on society as a whole
* the **scientific:** the writer might deal with the subject by examining in a detached and objective way the effect that depictions of sex and violence have upon the human mind and nervous system
* the **historical** . . .
    – and so on.

Most pieces of writing will approach their subject from some particular angle – unless of course the writer is trying to look at a topic from several different viewpoints in an attempt to be impartial.

Method of dealing with this

1 Run your mind over the letters of your essay-writing mnemonic: PHRASEEMS.
2 Read the piece carefully to see what approach to his subject the writer is taking.
3 Find the appropriate adjective from the mnemonic to describe the approach: political, historical, social, ethical/moral, and so on.

Activity

> The following is one of three extracts from weekly magazines about the famine in Ethiopia, television coverage of it and aid programmes. You will be given all three later as a comprehension exercise. Meanwhile, discuss the writer's approach to her subject in the passage below:
>
> 'What we've done is make starvation sexy' was how Keith Jendon, director of the Band Aid Trust, described Live Aid's contribution to the world of famine relief, as he and Bob Geldorf prepared to set out on their present two-week tour of Mali, Niger, and Chad, with 'attendant media', to publicize the wider Sahel drought. It wasn't an entirely fortunate way of putting it, but I knew exactly what he meant.

The pop-stars, the phone-ins, the young shaming their elders into giving more, the international camaraderie of the entertainment world, have indeed given the subject a glamour, a sexiness, it has never before quite possessed. Oxfam, speaking of those who give to them, says they are 'mid-everything' – middle-class, middle-aged, middle-of-the-road in their politics. There is nothing 'mid' about Band Aid's donors, whether the school-children sending in their tons of split-peas via Red Star to the old ILEA bus depot in Bloomsbury that is now the group's headquarters, or Hamdan al-Maktoum, racehorse owner, who gave them one million after the Live Aid concert last July.

More startling, anyway at the time, than the identity of disaster relief's new donors, was the scale of their response, first to the record at Christmas, later to the concerts. Band Aid themselves were surprised. It all seemed to happen so suddenly.

News of the famine first seriously impressed the western public in July 1984, after Michael Buerk visited southern Ethiopia and came back with appalling pictures for television of what seemed an entire nation with nothing to eat.

Caroline Moorehead, *New Society*

▓ *Task 4:* Discuss the writer's attitude to the subject

This asks you to assess how writers feel about their subjects. It also leads into an analysis of how they write, since feeling, or the absence of it, has a great effect upon style.

Method of dealing with this

For our purposes here the kinds of speech and writing we use to convey wishes, thoughts, and feelings can be put into three broad and over-lapping categories:

1 the instructional;
2 the informative;
3 the persuasive.

If we think of language as having an emotional scale ranging from hot at one extreme to cold at the other, you will see that the language used in these different categories registers different degrees of heat on that scale:

- **instructional** writing doesn't appeal to our emotions at all;
- **persuasive** writing does its best to stir them, while
- **informative** writing can move towards either extreme, depending on what it is trying to achieve.

The instructional category

Writing for instructional purposes has several fixed characteristics:

1 it proceeds step by step, usually in chronological order;
2 it uses an impersonal mode of address: either the imperative, as in, 'First connect the side supports to the back panel', or the third person singular or plural, passive mood, as in 'The side supports should first be connected

to the back panel'. (The first is preferable, being shorter, crisper, and more business-like);

3 it uses precise, objective language and technical jargon. Not, 'Turn the little black wheel on the side to near the top', but 'Set the thermostat to the required temperature'.

The informative category

The more closely a piece of writing is geared to instruction, the more impersonal and colourless its tone; the more factual its vocabulary, and the shorter and brisker its sentence structure. When the writer wants to make his or her readers understand the *reasons* for the instructions at the same time, the tone becomes warmer; the impersonal third person changes to the more intimate second person, *You*; the vocabulary becomes more emotive and the sentence structure more leisurely. Here, for example, is Sir Ernest Gowers instructing and educating civil servants in the art of writing letters to the general public in *Plain Words*:

> First, in letters written in the first person, be careful to avoid giving the impression that an all-powerful individual is signifying his pleasure. If the letter grants what is asked for, do not say that you are making a 'concession'. If it refuses a request never say 'I do not think you have made out a case'. Imply that your duty is not yourself to be your correspondent's judge, but merely to decide how the case before you fits into the instructions under which you work.
>
> Secondly, it is a mistake to mix these methods in one letter unless there is a good reason for it. If you choose an impersonal method, such as 'The Department', you may of course need to introduce the first person for personal purposes such as 'I am glad' or 'I am sorry' or 'I should like you to call here', or 'I am glad to say that the Department has . . . ' But do not mix the methods merely for variety, saying 'I' in the first paragraph, 'We' in the next, 'The Department' in the third and 'it is' in the fourth. Choose one and stick to it.
>
> Thirdly, do not use the impersonal passive, with its formal, unsympathetic phrases such as 'it is felt', 'it is regretted', 'it is appreciated'. Your correspondent wants to feel that he is dealing with human beings, not with robots. How feeble is the sentence, 'It is thought you will now have received the form of agreement' compared with 'I expect you will have received the form of agreement by now'. In brief, be short, be simple, be human.

The persuasive category

The language that belongs to this category is at the hottest end of the emotional scale and is used by people who want to sell us something – whether it is a religious ideal, a political ideology, or simply their own particular ideas about how we should think and act. (Advertising obviously belongs to this category but is dealt with separately in *The language of society*, page 176.) Writers in the persuasive category try to sell us their ideas by playing on our feelings. Journalists, for example, can slant the news in the direction they want by their use of words. Compare 'Mr X's firm rejection of this proposal' with 'Mr X's stubborn rejection of this proposal'. Which puts the speaker in a bad light simply by the choice of a 'loaded' word?

Activity

> **1** Write two short speeches, one supporting, the other attacking a politician or other public figure. Use some of the neutral and slanted words below in your writing.
>
> | | | | |
> |---|---|---|---|
> | prudent | timid | generous | extravagant |
> | enthusiastic | fanatical | consistent | dogmatic |
> | flexible | wavering | imaginative | far-fetched |
> | practical | expedient | thrifty | mean |
> | ambitious | greedy | courageous | reckless |
>
> **2** Good journalists do not over-use this technique, having a proper respect for the facts. Others have fewer scruples. Consider the article from the *Sun* on the facing page, then discuss the following issues:
>
> **a** Does the writer anywhere use value-laden language?
>
> **b** What impression do you think the headline might make on readers?
>
> **c** Does the writer distinguish clearly between fact and opinion in the first paragraph?
>
> **d** What is the function of the sub-headings?
>
> **e** Discuss the juxtaposition of facts in the paragraph:
> While little Peter was alone and slowly dying, his mother was out drinking at a NAAFI canteen where she had a barman friend. What effect does this have?
>
> **f** Is this good journalism? If so, in what ways is it good?
>
> **g** What criteria do you use to judge newspaper reporting? Discuss the presentation of this story on the basis of these criteria.

Journalists are restricted by their lack of time and column inches. Creative writers, politicians, and other public figures can spend more time, space, and energy on the task of moving our hearts and moulding our opinions. Whatever their motives, each uses basically the same techniques. They are listed below, in no particular order:

a Heightened language

Some of the vocabulary used may be archaic in flavour – so old-fashioned that we would be embarrassed to hear it in ordinary speech: words like *pledge, foe, brothers, split asunder, fatherland, motherland,* etc.

The effect of words like this is to remove us from the plane of ordinary life and lift us up into the realm of the ideal.

b Obsolete grammar

Heightened language is reinforced by the use of similarly old-fashioned grammar: inversions of the normal order of subject and verb, for example:

HORROR OF MOTHER ON A SPREE WHO LET HER BABY STARVE TO DEATH

By DOUG WATSON

Dorothy Taylor felt like having a good time with her friends.

But her two-year-old son Peter was a problem.

So she strapped him in his pram and left him alone at home . . . for a week.

Peter starved to death. He was eventually found, still strapped in.

His pram was littered with fragments of lining which he had ripped off in his terror and desperation.

Body

Under a table in the house at Hipswell, Catterick Camp, Yorks, police also found the body of an alsatian dog. It had been dead three weeks.

Yesterday, 36-year-old Mrs Taylor – parted from her husband and four other children – pleaded guilty to manslaughter.

Mr John Johnson, prosecuting, told Newcastle-upon-Tyne Crown Court that Mrs Taylor showed "utter disregard" for her baby.

While the child was dying, she was only a 10-minute walk away from him.

The pram, he said, had no mattress. Just the padded lining torn to shreds by the baby.

Drinking

"One shudders to think of that child, scrabbling with its little hands to do that kind of damage," Mr Johnson said.

While little Peter was alone and slowly dying, his mother was out drinking in a NAAFI canteen where she had a barman friend.

Mrs Taylor would have been away even longer than a week, the court heard – if friends had not said she could not stay with them any longer.

After the dead baby was found, Mrs Taylor told the police she had arranged for a girl to look after Peter.

But, the court heard, she could not name the girl.

Mrs Taylor was also alleged to have explained: "I thought the neighbours would hear him crying, and report it to someone who would come and take him away."

Before the baby's death Mrs Taylor was said to have turned down help offered by the welfare authorities.

Mr Nigel McCluskey, defending, said there was no evidence of mental instability.

A man had promised to marry Mrs Taylor. But he left her for another woman.

"The disappointment changed her from a caring mother to an irresponsible one," Mr McCluskey said.

He added: "What she has done, she has to live with for the rest of her life. That is part of her punishment."

Mrs Taylor was jailed for four years.

Suffer

Mr Justice MacKenna told her: "You went away to amuse yourself with friends and stayed away for a week.

"I am told that you hoped the child would be rescued by strangers. Perhaps you did.

"But you must have known that if he was not rescued he would suffer terribly. And that in the end, he would die."

'Ask not for whom the bell tolls', wrote John Donne in a seventeenth century Meditation; 'Ask not what your country will do for you', said J. F. Kennedy in the twentieth. The subjunctive, that out-of-date and neglected mood of the verb, may also be used: 'Let there be light,' God commanded in the Bible; 'Let the word go forth,' said Kennedy in his inaugural speech as President.

c Large and splendid images

These open up for us a wider world than that of every day. They are designed to excite readers or hearers, and give them a glimpse of something greater, nobler, and more splendid than ordinary life. The 'flame of freedom' for instance is more evocative than the plain word 'freedom' itself.

d Repetition

This is designed to drive home a point and emphasize it. Think of Mark Antony's repeated exclamation in his speech after Caesar's murder: 'Yet Brutus is an honourable man!'

e Sound-patterning

Speakers and writers may use alliteration to express their feelings and induce their listeners/readers to share in them. (Alliteration is the deliberate repetition of consonants at the beginning of words that are placed close together in a phrase or sentence: plosive *b*s express anger; plosive *p*s express contempt; softer sounds such as *s*, *w*, *m*, and *l* in contrast soothe and calm.) Reporters who write for tabloid newspapers like to use this technique emotively in captions like 'Brothers of Blood' (under a photograph of IRA terrorists).

f The use of antithesis

Key word

> *Antithesis:* the placing next to each other of words or phrases or clauses containing contrasting ideas, e.g.:
>
> My thoughts fly up, my words remain below.

Speakers and writers achieve two things by using antithesis:

1 a rhythmic, musical effect: the rising intonation of the first phrase (the *thesis*) is 'answered' by the falling intonation of the second (the *antithesis*), and we feel a harmonious, almost musical quality in the writing. (If you don't understand what I mean by one phrase or sentence 'answering' another, hum the first line of 'God save the Queen' then follow it immediately with the last line. You should be able to recognize how the last line completes or 'answers' the first.)

Antithesis can lend a wonderful impression of finality to a statement thanks to this rising and falling intonation. We listen, and we feel that the last word on the subject has been said. It is antithesis that makes the aphorisms of Oscar Wilde so devastating; for example:

Men marry because they are tired, women because they are curious; both are disappointed.

2 antithesis allows the writer to draw a sharper contrast between ideas than he or she could otherwise achieve. In the following example it is the similarity in structure of the two different clauses that brings out the contrast between their ideas. Look at the way in which the two statements below match grammatically, preposition with preposition, nouns with nouns, verb with verb:

In Ireland   men   are   oppressed by   the Church;

in England, the Church is   oppressed by   men.

Now look at the way in which their *ideas* contrast:

In Ireland   men   are   oppressed by   the Church;

in England, the Church is   oppressed by   men.

g Parallel phrasing

This technique uses matching phrases and clauses to express related rather than contrasting ideas. It is commonly used in speech-making, both to emphasize and strengthen a point, and to help a speaker or writer build up to a climax. Churchill used it to great effect in the following well known piece of wartime oratory (the parallel phrases are in italics):

> Even though large tracts of Europe and many old and famous States have fallen, or may fall into the grip of the Gestapo and all the odious apparatus of Nazi rule, we shall not flag nor fail. We shall go on to the end. *We shall fight in France, we shall fight on the seas and oceans, we shall fight with growing strength and growing confidence in the air. We shall fight on the beaches, we shall fight on the landing grounds, we shall fight in the fields and in the streets, we shall fight in the hills, we shall never surrender;* and even if, which I do not for a moment believe, this island or a large part of it were subjugated and starving, then our Empire beyond the seas, armed and guarded by the British Fleet, would carry on the struggle until in God's good time the New World, with all its power and might, steps forth to the rescue and liberation of the Old.

Talking point

> What other techniques mentioned above can you find Churchill using here?

An interesting variation of this parallel phrasing is the technique known as 'speaking in threes'. A speaker signals the climax of his speech by making three related assertions in rapid succession; for example:

We've shaken the West Wing, we've shaken the White House, and here in Georgia tonight we're shaking the world!

For some inexplicable reason this makes audiences burst into loud and and prolonged applause. Watch any Party Conference or Trades Union Congress and you will hear speakers use this technique to great effect.

Activity

Read the extracts below from two famous speeches, and complete the activities that follow.

Let the word go forth from this time and place, to friend and foe alike, that the torch has been passed to a new generation of Americans, born in this century, tempered by war, disciplined by a cold and bitter peace, proud of our ancient heritage, and unwilling to witness or permit the slow undoing of those human rights to which this nation has always been committed, and to which we are committed today . . .

Let every nation know, whether it wish us well or ill, that we shall pay any price, bear any burden, meet any hardship, support any friend, oppose any foe, in order to assure the survival and success of liberty. This much we pledge, and more . . .

Let us never negotiate out of fear. But let us never fear to negotiate . . .

And so, my fellow Americans: ask not what your country will do for you – ask what you can do for your country. My fellow-citizens of the world: ask not what America will do for you, but what together we can do for the freedom of man.

With a good conscience our only sure reward, with history the final judge of our deeds, let us go forth to lead the land we love, asking His blessing and His help, but knowing that here on earth God's work must be truly our own.

President J. F. Kennedy's inaugural speech, January 1961

This ceremony is held in the depth of winter. But, by the words we speak and the faces we show the world, we force the spring.

A spring reborn in the world's oldest democracy, that brings forth the vision and courage to reinvent America . . .

Americans deserve better. And in this city today, there are people who want to do better. So I say to all of you here, let us resolve to reform our politics, so that power and privilege no longer shout down the voice of the people. Let us put aside personal advantage so that we can feel the pain and see the promise of America.

While America rebuilds at home, we will not shrink from the challenges, nor fail to seize the opportunities of this new world . . .

Our greatest strength is the power of our ideas, which are still new in many lands. Across the world, we see them embraced – and we rejoice. Our hopes, our hearts, our hands, are with those on every continent who are building democracy and freedom. Their cause is America's cause.

The American people have summoned the change we celebrate today. You have raised your voices in an unmistakable chorus. You have cast your votes in historic numbers. And you have changed the face of Congress, the presidency, and the political process itself.

Yes, you, my fellow Americans, have forced the spring. Now, we must do the work the season demands.

We have heard the trumpets. We have changed the guard. And

now – each in our own way, and with God's help – we must answer the call.

President Bill Clinton's inaugural speech, January 1993

1 Discuss the techniques that Kennedy and Clinton use in these speeches to move the hearts of their hearers. Below is a list to prompt you:
  - heightened language
  - emotive language
  - large images
  - repetition of key words and/or phrases
  - alliteration
  - antithesis
  - parallel phrasing

2 Choose a subject on which you feel strongly and write a speech that attempts to persuade other people to feel like you. You might try the case for or against nuclear power, animal rights, or the return of capital punishment. If you don't feel strongly about anything, pretend you do.

Use as many of the techniques listed above as you can.

■ *Tasks 5, 6, and 7:* Discuss the audience targetted by the writer, his register, and style

Examiners frequently ask you to discuss the following points (numbers 5, 6, and 7 on our original list):
  the audience targeted by the writer;
  the register used in relation to this intended audience;
  the writer's style.

Consider these points carefully and you will see an overlap between the three: writers know the kind of readers for whom they are writing (5) and choose the register most appropriate for that audience (6). Combine this with the way they feel about their subject and the way they want their audience to feel, and the result is their style (7). (Style can also be influenced by the writer's bias, Task 8 on the original list.)

Register

Register refers to the kind of language writers use for particular audiences and particular contexts: their choice of words and phrases. Look, for instance, at the examples of the demotic (slang and/or colloquial expression, literally, 'of the common people'), common (from the common pool of language), and formal registers below:

Idea   Tabloid newspapers are not very good.
Register   The tabloids stink. (*demotic*)
    The tabloids are rubbishy papers. (*common*)
    Tabloid newspapers are unworthy of serious attention.
    (*formal*)

Activity

> Find at least four different ways of expressing the idea that books are not worth reading.

It would be pointless for a writer to use the formal register when addressing, say, *Sun* readers. Rational arguments expressed in long words and sentences are inappropriate to that audience. And the reverse is equally true. Blunt assertions would upset and alienate readers of papers like the *Times, Guardian,* or *Independent.* They prefer headlines such as *French intransigence irritates British Ministers* to *Hop off you Frogs; Britain resolute in face of Argentinian attack* to *Up yours, Galtieri; Belgrano sunk* to *Gotcha!.*

But register does not stand alone: it is a component of the larger entity we call *Style.*

Style

Key words

> *Content* is what a writer says, i.e. his or her ideas.
> *Style* is the way he says it, i.e. his or her expression.

A writer has to suit his or her style – that is, vocabulary, sentence structure, tone, imagery, and other techniques – to the targetted audience, or it will ignore the writer's message. Remember when assessing style that everything about it – diction, sentence structure, rhythm, imagery, irony – is broadly determined in the first place by:

- **a** how the writer feels about the subject, and
- **b** how he or she wants readers to feel – angry or pleased, admiring or critical. It is then modified to suit
- **c** the kind of readers he or she wants to reach: the audience.

Praise, for instance, has to be expressed in one way for tabloid readers ('Nice one, Gary!'), and in another for readers of the broadsheets ('Lineker headed in a brilliant goal with the fluency that is his trademark'). It may help therefore to ask yourself the following questions when evaluating a piece of writing:

Attitude

1 Does the writer write in a neutral, matter-of-fact way, giving us the evidence and leaving us free to make up our own minds? (What kind of audience might this imply?)
2 Is he or she amused by the subject and therefore good-humoured and relaxed in writing about it?
3 Is the writer earnestly trying to convince us of something?
4 Does the subject upset the writer in some way, causing anger or bitterness or resentment? Does the writer show contempt and dislike for what he or she is writing about?

Vocabulary

1 If 4 above is true, does the writer express emotion by using emotive language and insulting terms? Or does the writer keep his or her feelings under intellectual control and write in a coolly disapproving manner?

(What kind of audience might be indicated by the use of each of these methods?)

2 Is the vocabulary largely plain and Anglo-Saxon? Formal, with a number of Latinate words only where necessary? Or learned and esoteric, with mainly Latinate words? (What might the different kinds of vocabulary tell you about the audience targetted by the writer?)

Sentence structure

1 Are the sentences largely short and simple in construction, or lengthy and complex? Is there a variety of sentence lengths? (Again, what might this tell us about the kind of readers targetted?)

2 If the sentences are lengthy and complex, are the clauses within them so well-handled that they are easy to read, or do clauses cut across one another in a way that confuses the reader?

Imagery and other devices

1 Does the writer use imagery? If so, does it clarify his or her meaning or make it more vivid? If so, explain how. (You do this by explaining the similarities between the thing being described and the thing being used to describe it – as with Sir Osbert Sitwell's writings and tapestry in the passage below. For help with this, see the section on Metaphor and Metonymy, page 207.) (Can the kind of imagery and other techniques used tell us anything about the intended audience?)

2 Does the writer use irony? Antithesis? Repetition? Sound patterning? Parallel phrasing? If so, how does it help to express the ideas? Your job is to look for evidence of all these things and provide the examiner with proof of what you say.

Difficulties in assessing style

It is reasonably easy to recognize when writers are trying to play on our emotions – the persuasive techniques discussed above give them away. It is also fairly obvious when writers are angry about their subject: they use strong-sounding, often insulting words and they make forceful assertions, often in a sarcastic, angry, or contemptuous tone. Here for instance is William Cobbett expressing his contempt for public school and university men:

> . . . If I had been brought up a milksop, with a nursery-maid everlastingly at my heels, I should have been at this day as great a fool . . . as any of those frivolous idiots that are turned out from Winchester and Westminster School, or from any of those dens of dunces called Colleges and Universities.

Compare this with a neutral version of the same statement:

> If I had had a more sheltered upbringing I should be no wiser than men educated at public school and university.

Note the very physical noun, *milksop*; the humiliating image of the nursery-maid running after a child; the alliteration in *dens of dunces*, and the tone of contempt got through the use of the insulting adjective *frivolous* and the sarcastic phrase *as great a fool*.

Such writers never use modifying words and phrases like *almost*, *quite*, *perhaps*, or *on the whole*; neither do they use tentative verbs like *might*, or *could* – they would weaken the strength of their dogmatic assertions.

When a writer's mind rather than feelings are involved, however, it is much more difficult to assess his or her attitude towards the subject. At first sight the style may seem to lack any obvious distinguishing features, and you may be at a loss as to how to approach it. This kind of style, which for convenience's sake I shall call the 'academic', is discussed and illustrated below:

> Dame Edith Sitwell's posthumous short autobiography, brisk, digressive, written very much in a speaking style, might be considered as a kind of last rally against a certain type of critic she had long been at war with. There is nothing in the tone of this scrappy and lively and gossipy book, written though it was with a swollen hand and in conditions of physical pain, that suggests the slightly forced solemnities and the formal and not wholly sincere reconciliations of a death-bed. There is rather eldritch laughter, cackles of wild gaiety. There is no reconsideration of claims, recantation of attacks, or, indeed, failure of loyalties. There is a fine rashness and simplicity about the book; one thinks of some grand ship of the line going down in flames, but with its flags still flying, and its deck-guns firing to the last. Even the ranks of Scrutiny, perhaps, could scarce forbear to cheer. To use a distinction Miss Pamela Hansford Johnson has made about her, the paying off of old scores here is perhaps vicious (like a cat that scratches when its fur is stroked the wrong way) but not spiteful. Dame Edith could not hate people. Those who attacked her or bored her also made her laugh; and she conveys her helpless amusement, her sense of funniness, even where she cannot convey where exactly, for her, the joke lies.
>
> A writer in these columns, for instance, said about another very distinguished woman poet, one at the opposite pole from Dame Edith in that this other woman poet is noted not for her ornateness but for her transparency of diction: 'The frailty of these poems is their distinction. At their very best, they seem to be just on the verge of not being there at all.' One could perhaps think of happier ways of phrasing a sound critical perception. Dame Edith pins this unfortunate reviewer to her page and then relates how she remembers the poet in question (with a tactfulness towards her own sex she does not name her, but it was in fact Miss Kathleen Raine) saying to her: 'The mind is a vortex'. So, to be sure, the mind is. But Dame Edith then quotes a wonderful piece from Dickens:
>
>> 'Mind and matter,' said the lady with the wig, 'glide swift into the vortex of immensity. Howls the sublime and softly sleeps the calm idea in the whispering chambers of imagination. To hear it, sweet it is. But then, out laughs the stern philosopher, and saith to the Grotesque

''What ho! Arrest for me that agency. Go bring it here!'' And so the
vision fadeth.'

This is shockingly unfair but both Miss Raine and her reviewer would
have to admit that it is extremely funny.

Dame Edith was not good at abstract argument; but she was
wonderfully good at detecting possible false notes and at bringing out
the ludicrous side of persons or attitudes of which she disapproved. A
passage about Dr Leavis, similarly, is introduced with surprising
effectiveness by a quotation from Plato; and the passage ends with some
quotations from Dr Leavis's famous chapter on Milton, and with some
lines from *Paradise Lost* analysed by him. Dame Edith's comment is, 'It is
sad to see Milton's great lines bobbing up and down in the sandy desert
of Dr Leavis's mind with the grace of a fleet of weary camels.' Again, this
is strikingly unfair; but for visual aptness and grotesque humour, for a
quality which in poetry Dr Leavis himself calls 'enactment', it could
hardly be bettered . . .

The house of criticism has many mansions and, in heaven, Dame Edith
will perhaps share one with Swinburne and Landor. None of these three
is fair and balanced, each has a taste which is in some degree narrow
and eccentric. Each can praise memorably, and attack with humorous
fury. Each also is a performer, what Wyndham Lewis, one of Dame
Edith's other targets here, called a 'personal-appearance artist'.

Dame Edith combined two characteristics of the aristocrat, a frank
delight in personal display, and a certain fundamental reticence. She
does not go in detail in this book, for instance, into the unhappiness of
her childhood or into her conversion to full Christian belief. She says
little about her deep personal affection for her brothers. She disliked the
middle-class habit of what may, perhaps, most aptly be called
'unbosoming'. Thus having described the appearance and manners of
D. H. Lawrence vividly and with sympathy, she adds tartly:

Though courteous and amiable, he was determined to impress on us
that he was a son of toil (that was the great romance, apart from his
marriage with Mrs Lawrence, in his life) and he seemed to be trying
to make us uncomfortable by references to the contrast between our
childhood and his. But this was not our fault. Our childhood was hell,
and we refused to be discomfited.

Taken Care Of is not an elaborate, ornate, subtly composed tapestry like
Sir Osbert's autobiographies. It is abrupt, informal, tangential. Yet the
very slightness of structure and directness of attack means a lack of
disguise. Here is a very strange and rich personality, to be taken or left.
The humour, the sharpness, the good heart come out in this little
anecdote about Dylan Thomas: 'On another occasion he came to
luncheon with me, and as he arrived, said to me, ''I am sorry to smell so
awful, Edith. It's Margate.'' I said, ''Yes, of course, my dear boy, it's
Margate''.'

(from the *Times Literary Supplement*)

As this passage shows, writers with an academic, scholarly approach write in a cool, controlled, often urbane manner. They do not preach or harangue. They are relaxed enough to tell amusing little anecdotes or make scholarly in-jokes (like the deliberate misuse of 'Scrutiny' [a literary magazine known for the severity of its criticism] in place of 'Tuscany' in the quotation *Even the ranks of Tuscany could scarce forbear to cheer*). They sound knowledgeable, rational, and civilized.

How to evaluate the academic style

1 Make the fact that the style has no immediately obvious features into a feature in its own right.

> **Sample answer:** The writer's approach is the rational, scholarly approach of the academic critic writing in the *Times Literary Supplement*. It is based on rational thought rather than emotion, and this coolness of approach is reflected in an appropriately cool style. It contains no dogmatic, sweeping assertions, no strongly emotive language, no surging rhythms to persuade us of the truth of what he says.

2 Now go on to discuss the style in more detail:

a Diction

Assess whether the writer's diction is

1 drawn largely from the common pool;
2 erudite and full of Latinate expressions
3 colloquial.

> **Sample answer:** His diction is formal and educated but never pompous. It is made up of words drawn largely from the common pool*, such as *scrappy, lively, gossipy,* but is strengthened at times by more Latinate expressions found only in the register peculiar to academics: *digressive, recantations, solemnities, eldritch* in the first paragraph alone. This clearly shows that he is targetting an audience of his intellectual peers rather than addressing a wider readership in need of further education. Nowhere, as we might expect, does the writing descend into the register of colloquial language or slang.**
> [* see the section entitled *The Concept of Register*, page 36]
> [**see pages 36–39.]

b Mode of address

Assess whether the writer's mode of address is personal or impersonal.

Mode of address refers to the way in which writers address or 'speak' to their audience. They may use the intimate first person throughout, as if actually talking to their readers ('I have an almost feminine partiality for fine china'); they may address them as *you* ('You may judge for yourself whether this is likely to produce the desired effect'), or include them in a more intimate relationship by using *we* ('We who know better ought not to allow our feelings to sway our judgement in this affair').

Writers who write for readers whom they assume to be as well-educated, well-read, and interested in the subject as themselves often avoid the personal pronouns *I*/*we*/*you*/*us* used by those who wish to 'talk' to their readers in a friendly, conversational way, often to disguise the fact that they are trying to inform or educate them (after all, nobody likes being talked down to). They use instead the more remote third person impersonal pronouns, *it* or *one*, discussing their subject from a detached, scholarly viewpoint.

Talking point

> Consider the different degrees of detachment revealed in the statements below:
>
> I think the central idea is very badly expressed.
> The central idea is not particularly well expressed.
> One might have hoped for a happier phrasing of the central idea.

Sample answer: The writer treats his readers as his intellectual equals by using the impersonal pronouns *it* and *one*. 'One could perhaps think of happier ways of phrasing a sound critical perception', he remarks urbanely, crediting us with the same degree of knowledge, taste, and discrimination as himself. The use of *one* also allows the writer to make his point delicately, without subjective emotion. How much better than the writer does this critic know, we think on reading this, and how elegantly he has managed to put her in her place whilst still acknowledging the soundness of her perception.

Talking point

> 1 What difference do you find between the sentence quoted above and the following re-statements of the same idea?
>
> This is a foolish way to express a sound critical perception.
> In my opinion, this is an unfortunate way to express a sound critical perception.
>
> 2 What does the writer's use of *perhaps* tell us about his attitude towards his subject?

Note: in certain other contexts *one* may be used very differently:

a to up-grade a speaker's status by enhancing his importance, as in:

One has terrible trouble in finding people of the right quality to work for one today;

b to play down existing high status and make the speaker seem less self-assertive, more approachable. See such public pronouncements of the Prince of Wales as,

It crept up on one with a kind of ghastly inexorability that one would one day be King.

Talking point

> What do you deduce from the writer's use of
>
> a full titles for the women writers he mentions: *Miss Pamela Hansford Johnson* and *Miss Kathleen Raine*;
> b the term *woman poet* rather than *lady poet* or *poetess*?

c Syntax

Assess whether:

1   the writer uses a predominantly simple or complex sentence style;
2   phrases are used instead of clauses for economy and liveliness;
3   the arrangement of clauses is skilful enough to make his meaning clear and his writing easy to read. (See the section on the arrangement of clauses within sentences in *Clause analysis*, pages 92–93.)

> **Sample answer:** The grammatical structure of the writing is what we would expect of someone with a high degree of formal education. Most of the sentences are complex in structure and well over the twelve to twenty-five words limit recommended for clear expression. However, they are generally well-handled and perfectly clear: the first and second sentences, containing thirty-seven and forty-five words respectively, for instance, are easy to read, and the fifth, although technically thirty-six words in total, is actually made up of two shorter ones thanks to the use of a semi-colon.
>
> In paragraph 2, however, this tendency to write long sentences tends to cause confusion at times. In the opening sentence of this paragraph the writer gets as far as the object of the verb 'said' ('woman poet'):
>
> > 'A writer in these columns, for instance, said about another very distinguished woman poet . . . '
>
> then puts off telling us what was said for another twenty-six words. Before reaching the quotation we have to struggle through
>
> > **a** a phrase – 'one at the opposite pole from Dame Edith', and
> > **b** a lengthy dependent (noun) clause – 'in that this other woman poet is noted not for her ornateness but for her transparency of diction'.
>
> The result is that by the time we actually get to the end of the sentence, we are in danger of being thoroughly confused as to who is saying what about whom. Much the same criticism can be made of sentence 4 of the same paragraph, in which a lengthy interpolation in brackets cuts off the object ('the poet in question') from the verb ('saying to her'). However, the writer uses phrases well; see the first two sentences of the passage, where the phrases 'brisk, digressive, written very much in a speaking style' and 'written though it was with a swollen hand and in conditions of physical pain' add life and give a varied intonation to the writing.

d Rhythm

Look for rhythm created by:

1   the alternation of sentences of different lengths;
2   the use of antithesis and/or parallel phrasing or repetition within sentences.

> **Sample answer:** The writer shows a pleasing sense of rhythm and balance in his alternation of short, medium, and long sentences. This

can be seen to advantage in sentences 2, 3, and 4 of paragraph 1, and in the whole of paragraph 2 (excluding the quotation). Harmonious balance is also seen in the antithesis of, 'the paying off of old scores here is perhaps vicious . . . but not spiteful.' The writer makes no attempt to sway our emotions by the use of rhythm.

e Imagery

Writers use images

1 to clarify their meaning;
2 to add colour and life to their writing.

Assess how well each of the images used in this passage succeeds in these two aims.

> **Sample answer:** There are four major images here, each one just and appropriate without being strikingly original. The simile of the grand ship of the line dressed overall suits Dame Edith's flamboyant taste in clothes and her liking for personal display, just as that of the cat brings out her normally sleek and feline composure, disturbed from time to time by sudden flashes of spite. The 'house of criticism' metaphor is obviously a re-vamping of the biblical image, 'In my Father's house are many mansions'. It works because the idea of many separate houses conveys both the breadth of literary criticism – the fact that it has room for many very different theories – and the narrowness of the views of those critics who, like Dame Edith, shut the doors of their minds to the value of any kind of literature they do not like. Finally, the metaphor of the tapestry used to describe Sir Osbert's autobiographies contrasts his more detailed and meticulous and traditional craftsmanship and highly decorative style (all qualities of tapestry) with his sister's plainer, more loosely constructed and casually written final work.

f Bias

Examine the passage for signs that the writer favours Dame Edith to the extent that he plays down her faults to make the most of her good qualities.

> **Sample answer:** The writer makes it clear that he likes and respects both Dame Edith and her work, and though he is ready to point out her faults he does it in such a way that they are outweighed by her virtues. Thus, her failure to reconsider past claims and attacks is noted but not condemned – rather praised by implication in the statement, 'There is a fine rashness and simplicity about the book' and in the image of the ship that follows. In the same way, he admits that Dame Edith could be vicious, then tempers the admission by clearing her of the charge of spite – as if to suggest that viciousness is firstly more natural, secondly less unpleasant, and thirdly, more acceptable than spite; all dubious and highly debatable points.
>
> Further bias is shown in the way that he handles Dame Edith's

treatment of Miss Kathleen Raine. He agrees that it was 'shockingly unfair', then weakens the criticism immediately by insisting that both Miss Raine and the 'unfortunate' reviewer would have to admit that it is extremely funny. One wonders if they would.

Understatement is another technique the reviewer uses to present Dame Edith in a favourable light: thus, she was 'not good at abstract argument'. This is followed by praise that amounts almost to overstatement: she was 'wonderfully good at detecting possible false notes and at bringing out the ludicrous side of persons or attitudes of which she disapproved'. In the same way, he writes, 'None of these three [critics] is fair and balanced'; not, 'Each of these three critics is prejudiced and unbalanced', and if each has 'a taste which is . . . narrow and eccentric', it is narrow and eccentric only 'in some degree'. 'Here is a very strange and rich personality', the reviewer writes, 'to be taken or left'. But there is little doubt as to which he would have us do.

Activity

Read the following passages (A and B are extracts from newspaper articles, C is an extract from a textbook) and discuss them from the point of view of:

1 the writers' attitudes towards their subjects;
2 the relative position each would occupy on the linguistic heat scale (i.e. which extract contains the most, which the least amount of emotion);
3 the kind of reader targetted;
4 the appropriateness of the chosen register;
5 the quality of the writers' style (diction, syntax, mode of address, imagery, rhythm, etc.);
6 bias.

A Now we are colonized by journalistic muggers with cabbage ears and blocked noses who beat at their typewriters with leaden coshes. Under those indiscriminate blows the keys weld into mere slugs of metal within which there is no decipherable meaning other than hostility. The muggers do not forge words but blunt instruments with which to render those who read insensible, if not permanently brain-damaged. When you actually handle the newspapers for which they commit their acts of aggression, holding them away from you as you might an old sock, you realize that, indeed, time has a warp. Fresh from the presses each issue may be, but it already smells of its near future, the contents of dustbins and the wrapping of fish.

B Curiously, while standards have improved at one end of the market, on the popular front they are worse than I can remember. Quotations, even whole stories, routinely invented; intrusions into privacy commonplace; political 'angling' blatant. The *Star* is a shameless and shaming new phenomenon that makes even hardened popular journalists blench. The popular press lost its news role to television over thirty years ago and has since been in the entertainment business. And the drift to soft-porn – 'from gutter to sewer' as Joe Haines once famously put it – has been gradually coming for years, ever since the 60s revolution.

C There is criticism to be made, too, of the way in which the popular press, particularly, tends to trivialize and sensationalize news. Their readers are fed, day in and day out, on a diet of scandal, sex and over-simplification of serious issues. This is nothing new – their readers have always looked for entertainment rather than the serious information of the quality press. The 'tabloids' fill their readers with what they enjoy – bingo, competitions, and the activities of royalty and soap opera stars, in the reporting of which the boundaries between reality and fiction are increasingly blurred. Much of this is harmless escapism, but it is argued that a continuous diet of this can numb people's ability to get to grips with the real and important issues that face society.

Talking point

'Tone' is the term used to describe the emotional atmosphere that is created by a piece of writing: how the writer would sound if you were listening to him or her in person. The kind of words used to describe tone include:

angry	bitter	resentful	contemptuous	scathing
aggressive	cool	detached	aloof	calm
reassuring	conversational	intimate	soothing	humorous
light-hearted	sarcastic	ironical	pleading	pompous
patronizing	aggressive	confident	amused.	

In writing, where you cannot hear a writer's tone of voice, tone comes from the kind of language used, from the sentence structure, and from the mode of address. What differences of tone do you notice in the examples given above?

▦ *Task 8:* Examine the writer's style for signs of bias

All writers, even creative ones, are restricted by considerations of time and space. (If James Joyce had really recorded everything his hero thought and felt and did in the course of one day, how many volumes would *Ulysses* have run to?) Journalists with their limited number of column inches are obviously more restricted than most, but all writers have to select, and therefore all writers distort to some extent the material they present to their readers. All writers, in other words, have an inbuilt tendency towards bias.

Key word

Bias: an inclination or predisposition, often irrational, in favour of somebody or something(s).

We have seen bias at work in a small way in the comprehension passage on Dame Edith Sitwell, where the reviewer made light of his subject's faults and warmly praised what he saw as her virtues. In the following passage the writer uses a wider range of techniques to support his opinion that comprehensive schools are inferior to selective ones (grammar and secondary moderns combined).

Bias in graphic material

Key word

> *Graphic material:* drawings, photographs, graphs, statistical tables, etc. used in the illustration of books and articles.

Look at
- **a** the pictures at the head of the passage;
- **b** the headline (in larger, bolder print) between them;
- **c** the table of results below the main headline (reprinted in larger type on page 284);
- **d** the tabulated 'Outlines for an overhaul' at the bottom of the review (reprinted on page 287).

Sample answer: Bias is evident in the exaggerated drawings of the pupils from the two different kinds of school. They are stereotypes of unreal opposites, one representing all that is good, the other all that is bad. Thus the boy on the left is happy to learn: his smile, the unbelievable neatness of his uniform, the mannerliness of his posture (knees and feet tidily together), and the cared-for, orderly arrangement of his books all say so. The boy on the right in contrast is clearly unhappy: there is dissatisfaction in his scowl, defiance in his body language (chair tilted carelessly back, hands rudely shoved into pockets), and contempt for education shown in the disorderly treatment of his books. Thus, before any proper evidence has been given, readers are emotionally bounced into accepting the existence of two kinds of pupils in two different kinds of schools, one greatly superior to the other.

This visual impression is strongly supported by the bold headline, *Losers in a loaded struggle.* Clearly, we are expected to feel sympathy for the under-privileged, unhappy pupil on the right, who is losing a battle in which the odds have been heavily stacked against him by his school.

The statistical table below the headline [see also page 284] is again used to bounce readers into accepting the superiority of selective schools. At a quick glance it persuades us that selective schools beat comprehensives in every area except one – delinquency. A cool, hard look at it would show us that academically the gap between the two is not wide: 57.8 per cent A level passes for the comprehensives against 63.8 per cent for the selective system. Neither is the 3.0 per cent of grade A passes in the comprehensives bad when measured against the 6.4 per cent in the grammar schools, which cream off the brightest students in their areas. When results are set out like this, however,

THE INDEPENDENT Thursday 30 April 1987

EDUCATION

Peter Wilby on a new study that says some pupils are more equal than others in the state system

Losers in a loaded struggle

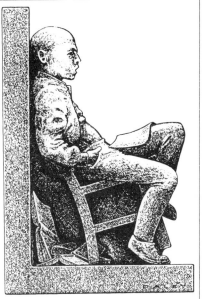

WHERE THE COMPREHENSIVES FAILED

	Selective system	Comprehensive system
Reading test	100.27	94.50
Attitude to school test 1	70.78	63.38
Attitude to school test 2	55.98	54.28
Delinquency	9.9%	18.9%
Attendance	78.8%	68.2%
Attempted A-levels	15.2%	14.0%
A-level passes	63.8%	57.8%
A grades at A-level	6.4%	3.0%

The first line shows the average scores of fourth year pupils on a reading test, where the national average for the age group would be 100.
The second and third lines show average scores for fourth year pupils on tests of pupils' perceptions of their school environment, teacher behaviour, fellow pupils' behaviour and the school organisation. The higher the score, the more positive the attitude to school.
The fourth line shows the percentage of pupils who had received a guilty court finding or an official caution.
The fifth line shows attendance rates for fourth year pupils.
The sixth line shows the percentage of pupils who went on to attempt A-levels. Note that all the selective schools went comprehensive after the pupils completed their fourth year.
The seventh and eighth lines show success rates at A-level among those who attempted them.

COMPREHENSIVE schools are failing because they are trying to imitate grammar schools. And the pupils they are failing most are those for whose benefit they were set up — the children of average and below-average ability.

This conclusion emerges from a detailed comparison of the selective and comprehensive systems, published today. It is based on what the researchers — David Reynolds of University College, Cardiff; Michael Sullivan, of University College, Swansea and Stephen Murgatroyd, formerly of the Open University — call "an experiment of nature" in a Welsh community. In the 1970s, one half of the area studied went comprehensive, the other half remained selective. On almost every available measure — social background, housing, maths and reading scores, intelligence — the type of pupils entering the two systems at the age of 11 were near enough identical.

This is the first British study allowing a direct comparison between two similar child populations. Previous research on the outcomes of different school systems has been plagued by comparing like with like.

By any reckoning, the results are bad for the comprehensives. On several criteria, and particularly those concerning social rather than academic outcomes, the results of the selective system (grammar and secondary modern schools combined) were superior.

The analysis is based on 328 pupils in their fourth year of secondary education. Children in the selective system did markedly better in a reading test and in one of two tests designed to measure their attitudes to school.

But the most startling results concern delinquency and attendance. The comprehensive pupils were twice as likely to get into trouble with the courts as their peers in the selective system. And the number of separate offences committed was more than seven times greater. Attendance rates, calculated from form registers for the whole fourth year, show that even the secondary modern schools comfortably outperformed the comprehensives. All these results are shown in the table above.

In the results of a further test, not shown in the table, the com-

Pupils thought life in comprehensives was ruled by fate

prehensive pupils did one-third better than those in the selective system. The test measured the extent to which children felt they had personal control over events that happened to them. Remarkably, it seems that one of the main outcomes of going to the two comprehensives in this study was a belief that life depended on luck, chance and fate.

Exam results for the sample of pupils are still awaiting publication. But analysis of overall A-level results for the areas served by the two systems suggest that the comprehensives were less likely to produce academically successful sixth-formers.

Which children did the comprehensives fail most? Many critics of comprehensives have assumed that they are worst for bright children. But the results of this research suggest the opposite. Bright children *did* do better in grammar schools, but only

slightly better. It was the children in the middle band of ability — those who would be in the top forms of secondary moderns — who lost out in comprehensives. In the secondary moderns, for example, their attendance averaged 91 per cent, in the comprehensives, only 66.4 per cent.

On some measures, such as attitude to school, the comprehensives did better with the least able children. But, on reading, the secondary moderns were superior. And, with these lower band children, the secondary moderns managed an attendance rate of 83.4 per cent. In the comprehensives, the rate was only 49.2 per cent.

So why did the comprehensives do so badly? The instability naturally created by a switch to a new system may have been one factor. Size was possibly another. Both comprehensives had well over 1,000 pupils, on split sites. This created management problems for the heads, who found it difficult to delegate. The greater areas that needed supervision increased the likelihood of truancy and vandalism. The large num-

Outlines for an overhaul

The authors suggest several proposals for making "pseudo-comprehensives" more effective:

■ **Publication of attendance and vandalism rates as well of exam results**
■ **Abolishing separate posts and management structures for pastoral care**
■ **More opportunities for lower-ability children to mix informally with teachers in social and sports events**
■ **Less movement between streams in order to maintain stable pupil friendships**
■ **More staff participation in school management**
■ **Parents to visit schools informally more often to talk over problems**
■ **Fewer school rules, particularly on uniform**

bers of staff led to inconsistency in enforcing rules. An average double lesson, the researchers estimate, was up to eight minutes shorter in the comprehensives because of the distances that staff and pupils had to travel.

Staff turnover was higher in the comprehensives: 12 per cent over two years, against four per cent in the selective system.

But the researchers balance these points against the comprehensives' clear advantages, such as their superior physical facilities and more favourable staffing ratios.

Their main conclusion is more far-reaching. The comprehensives' failure was inevitable, they argue, because they were not genuine comprehensives at all. They were pseudo-comprehensives, trying to offer a highly traditional grammar school education and ethos to the full ability range.

In general, the two comprehensives, in sharp contrast to the secondary moderns, emphasized academic at the expense of social and pastoral aims. And they still rated the achievements of the ablest children more highly

than those of the below-average. "The tendency was for all teachers, even those from the former secondary modern schools, to redefine their role as being merely an imparter of knowledge in the mould of the former grammar school teacher. Much informal interaction between teachers and pupils was therefore eliminated and many of the teachers progressively disassociated themselves from such things as playground and lunchtime supervision."

Middle band comprehensive children were set between 60 and 90 minutes homework each night,

Beating was twice as heavy as in the selective system

and many of them resented it; in the secondary moderns, no homework was set regularly though staff sometimes stayed after school to help children prepare for exams. In the comprehensives, academic promotion and demotion meant that at least a quarter of the children changed forms in the first three years at secondary school; in the secondary moderns, barely 10 per cent changed. Above all, the comprehensives tried to motivate children through grammar school-style competition: annual exams, termly reports, grading systems. In the secondary moderns, as one head observed, "we encourage each pupil to reach the best rather than pit one against the other".

As a comprehensive teacher put it: "The great mistake we made was in assuming that the academic horse would pull the social cart". In the academic race, the lower ability children were in-

evitably losers, and were more conscious of academic inferiority than they were in the secondary moderns. They thus became alienated from the school. In the comprehensives, few lower ability pupils took part in sports, societies and concerts. As the difficulties of controlling them grew, rules were enforced more strictly and punishments became more draconian. The researchers write: "Levels of corporal punishment began to rise until, in our estimate, the comprehensive system was beating twice as heavily as the selective system." Such developments further increased pupil alienation.

The writers conclude that if they are to succeed, comprehensives must change radically: "They must divert their attention away from the top third of the ability range towards the other sections and types of pupils."

They add: "The schools must learn that whether pupils actually attend, whether they are delinquent outside the school day, whether they have positive self-conceptions and whether they view themselves as in charge of their own lives are important educational goals, especially since there are a large number of lower ability pupils for whom these are the *only* educational goals that they are likely to attain ... in a world where there is a greater chance of a child attending psychiatric hospital than a university, such a reorientation of school goals towards social development seems only sensible."

The Comprehensive Experiment by David Reynolds and Michael Sullivan with Stephen Murgatroyd (Falmer Press, £14.95 hardback, £7.95 paperback).

without qualification or explanation, readers can hardly be blamed for forming a biased opinion. The caption above it, WHERE THE COMPREHENSIVES FAILED, also reinforces the bias by directing us to look for failure rather than success.

The tabulated 'Outlines for an overhaul' at the foot of the review [printed on page 287] are overshadowed by the graphical material at the head and by all that has been written in between. Readers can scarcely look at this box without being distracted by the subheadings above it to left and right in bolder and heavier print – these again stressing what is wrong with comprehensives rather than advocating reform.

The review itself (below) is followed by an examination of bias within the passage.

WHERE THE COMPREHENSIVES FAILED

	Selective system	Comprehensive system
Reading test	100.27	94.50
Attitude to school test 1	70.78	63.38
Attitude to school test 2	55.98	54.28
Delinquency	9.9%	18.9%
Attendance	78.8%	68.2%
Attempted A-levels	15.2%	14.0%
A-level passes	63.8%	57.8%
A grades at A-level	6.4%	3.0%

The first line shows the average scores of fourth year pupils on a reading test, where the national average for the age group would be 100.

The second and third lines show average scores for fourth year pupils on tests of pupils' perceptions of their school environment, teacher behaviour, fellow pupils' behaviour and the school organization. The higher the score, the more positive the attitude to school.

The fourth line shows the percentage of pupils who had received a guilty court finding or an official caution.

The fifth line shows attendance rates for fourth year pupils.

The sixth line shows the percentage of pupils who went on to attempt A-levels. Note that all the selective schools went comprehensive after the pupils completed their fourth year.

The seventh and eighth lines show success rates at A-level among those who attempted them.

COMPREHENSIVE schools are failing because they are trying to imitate grammar schools. And the pupils they are failing most are those for whose benefit they were set up – the children of average and below-average ability.

This conclusion emerges from a detailed comparison of the selective and comprehensive systems, published today. It is based on what the researchers – David Reynolds of University College, Cardiff; Michael Sullivan, of University College, Swansea; and Stephen Murgatroyd, formerly of the Open University – call 'an experiment of nature' in a Welsh community. In the 1970s, one half of the area studied went comprehensive, the other half remained selective. On almost every available measure – social background, housing, maths and reading scores, intelligence – the type of pupils entering the two systems at the age of eleven were near enough identical.

This is the first British study allowing a direct comparison between two similar child populations. Previous research on the outcomes of different school systems has been plagued by comparing like with like.

By any reckoning, the results are bad for the comprehensives. On several criteria, and particularly those concerning social rather than academic outcomes, the results of the selective system (grammar and secondary modern schools combined) were superior.

The analysis is based on 328 pupils in their fourth year of secondary education. Children in the selective system did markedly better in a reading test and in one of two tests designed to measure their attitudes to school.

But the most startling results concern delinquency and attendance. The comprehensive pupils were twice as likely to get into trouble with the courts as their peers in the selective system. And the number of separate offences committed was more than seven times greater. Attendance rates, calculated from form registers for the whole fourth year, show that even the secondary modern schools comfortably out-performed the comprehensives. All these results are shown in the table above.

Pupils thought life in comprehensives was ruled by fate

In the results of a further test, not shown in the table, the comprehensive pupils did one-third better than those in the selective system. The test measured the extent to which children felt they had personal control over events that happened to them. Remarkably, it seems that one of the main outcomes of going to the two comprehensives in this study was a belief that life depended on luck, chance and fate.

Exam results for the sample of pupils are still awaiting publication. But analysis of overall A level results for the areas served by the two systems suggest that the comprehensives were less likely to produce academically successful sixth-formers.

Which children did the comprehensives fail most? Many critics of comprehensives have assumed that they are worst for bright children. But the results of this research suggest the opposite. Bright children *did* do better in grammar schools, but only slightly better. It was the children in the middle band of ability – those who would be in the top forms of secondary moderns – who lost out in comprehensives. In the secondary moderns, for example, their attendance averaged 91 per cent, in the comprehensives, only 66.4 per cent.

On some measures, such as attitude to school, the comprehensives did better with the least able children. But, on reading, the secondary moderns were superior. And, with these lower band children, the secondary moderns managed an attendance rate of 83.4 per cent. In comprehensives, the rate was only 49.2 per cent.

So why did the comprehensives do so badly? The instability naturally created by a switch to a new system may have been one factor. Size was possibly another. Both comprehensives had well over 1,000 pupils, on split sites. This created management problems for the heads, who found it difficult to delegate. The greater areas that needed supervision increased the likelihood of truancy and vandalism. The large numbers of staff led to inconsistency in enforcing rules. An average double lesson, the researchers estimate, was up to eight minutes shorter in the comprehensives because of the distances that staff and pupils had to travel.

Staff turnover was higher in the comprehensives: 12 per cent over two years, against four per cent in the selective system.

But the researchers balance these points against the comprehensives' clear advantages, such as their superior physical facilities and more favourable staffing ratios.

Their main conclusion is more far-reaching. The comprehensives' failure was inevitable, they argue, because they were not genuine comprehensives at all. They were pseudo-comprehensives, trying to offer a highly traditional grammar school education and ethos to the full ability range.

In general, the two comprehensives, in sharp contrast to the secondary moderns, emphasized academic at the expense of social and pastoral aims. And they still rated the achievements of the ablest children more highly than those of the below-average. 'The tendency was for all teachers, even those from the former secondary modern schools, to re-define their role as being merely an imparter of knowledge in the mould of the former grammar school teacher. Much informal interaction between teachers and pupils was therefore eliminated and many of the teachers progressively disassociated themselves from such things as playground and lunchtime supervision.'

Beating was twice as heavy in the selective system

Middle band comprehensive children were set between 60 and 90 minutes homework each night, and many of them resented it; in the secondary moderns, no homework was set regularly though staff sometimes stayed after school to help children prepare for exams. In the comprehensives, academic promotion and demotion meant that at least a quarter of the children changed forms in the first three years at secondary school; in the secondary moderns, barely 10 per cent changed. Above all, the comprehensives tried to motivate children through grammar school-style competition: annual exams, termly reports, grading systems. In the secondary moderns, as one head observed, 'we encourage each pupil to reach the best rather than pit one against the other'.

As a comprehensive teacher put it: 'The great mistake we made was in assuming that the academic horse would pull the social cart'. In the academic race, the lower ability children were inevitably losers, and were more conscious of academic inferiority than they were in the secondary moderns. They thus became alienated from the school. In the comprehensives, few lower ability pupils took part in sports, societies, and concerts. As the difficulties of controlling them grew, rules were enforced more strictly and punishments became more draconian. The researchers write: 'Levels of corporal punishment began to rise until, in our estimate, the comprehensive system was beating twice as heavily as the selective system.' Such developments further increased pupil alienation.

The writers conclude that if they are to succeed, comprehensives must change radically: 'They must divert their attention away from the top third of the ability range towards the other sections and types of pupils.'

They add: 'The schools must learn that whether pupils actually attend, whether they are delinquent outside the school day, whether they have positive self-conceptions and whether they view themselves as in charge of their own lives are important educational goals, especially since there are a large number of lower ability pupils for whom these are the *only* educational goals that they are likely to attain . . . in a world where there is a greater chance of a child attending psychiatric hospital than a university, such a reorientation of school goals towards social development seems only sensible.'

Outlines for an overhaul

The authors suggest several proposals for making 'pseudo-comprehensives' more effective:

* Publication of attendance and vandalism rates as well as of exam results
* Abolishing separate posts and management structures for pastoral care
* More opportunities for lower-ability children to mix informally with teachers in social and sports events
* Less movement between streams in order to maintain stable pupil friendships
* More staff participation in school management
* Parents to visit schools informally more often to talk over problems
* Fewer school rules, particularly on uniform

Bias in written material

Sample answer: Wilby does his best to make us pre-judge the case. In his opening lines, he reveals his bias in several ways.

Firstly, he places the statement *Comprehensive schools are failing* ... at the very beginning of the review, before telling us, *This conclusion emerges from a detailed comparison of the selective and comprehensive systems.* This positioning gives the statement the ring of established truth; readers are persuaded to accept it as proved before they have had chance to weigh the evidence.

Wilby proceeds to identify himself completely with the researchers by the definitive quality of the verbs he uses: comprehensives *are failing*; this fact *emerges*. Such verbs leave no possibility of doubt. Had he wanted to discuss the case impartially he would have put things rather more tentatively, leaving room for doubt: he would have used such verb forms as *Comprehensive schools **may** be failing*, and *This **seems** to emerge* ... or ***seems** to be suggested by* ...

Furthermore, Wilby uses the verb *failing* in a blanket way: he doesn't qualify it by adding *in certain ways* or *in the social and pastoral aspects of their education* (facts which emerge only much later), and so readers are early led to believe that nothing at all is right with comprehensive schools ...

You might then cover some or all of the following points:

1 In paragraph 4, the use of the intensifying phrase *by any reckoning*; this cuts off any possibility of finding good in the results, before they are actually given.

2 Also in paragraph 4, the selection and emphasis of those particular results which suit the reviewer's case:
On several criteria, and particularly those concerning social rather than academic outcomes, the results of the selective system ... were superior.

3 In paragraphs 5 and 6, the use of intensifying adverbs and adjectives that have an emotive effect on readers:
Children in the selective system did *markedly* better;
But the most *startling* results ... ;

4 In paragraph 8, the treatment of unproved hypothesis as evidence:
... analysis of overall A level results ... suggest that the comprehensives were *less likely* to produce academically successful sixth-formers.

5 In paragraph 9, the technique of begging the question: that is, taking for granted a statement that hasn't yet been proved:
Which children did the comprehensives fail most?
There is a clear implication here that comprehensives failed *all* children in their care – an implication not born out by evidence elsewhere in the review.

6 In paragraph 10, the discounting of the opposite point of view by cancelling out points in its favour with points against:
On some measures, such as attitude to school, the comprehensives did better with the least able children. *But, on reading, the secondary moderns were superior. And, with these lower band children, the secondary moderns managed an attendance rate of 83.4 per cent* ...

7 In paragraphs 11, 12 and 13, the mention of disadvantages that help to explain why comprehensives did less well than selective schools (paragraphs 11 and 12) is cancelled out by the listing of advantages (paragraph 13) which outweigh them. Again, the careful placing of the fact Wilby wants to emphasize helps to make his case: as we saw in the unit on essay writing it is always best to put the case for your opponents first and then demolish it.

The rest of the review is less subjective, and cooler in tone: it sticks to statements of fact, gives direct quotations from the study, and the writer distances himself from its authors by the use of such phrases as *The writers conclude*. Paragraphs 1 to 13 have set the tone, however, and the review can hardly be called balanced and fair.

Talking point

> Which opinion do you think most readers of this review would be left with: that comprehensives schools are potentially good and need only re-shaping on the lines suggested to become really successful; or that the comprehensive system is a failure and should be abolished?

Activity

> Now that you know what is expected of you, try your hand at the comprehension passages below.
>
> The following are three extracts from weekly magazines published late in 1985 about the famine in Ethiopia, television coverage of it and aid programmes.
>
> Read them carefully and answer the questions which follow.
>
> **A** 'What we've done is make starvation sexy' was how Keith Jendon, director of the Band Aid Trust, described Live Aid's contribution to the world of famine relief, as he and Bob Geldorf prepared to set out on their present two-week tour of Mali, Niger, and Chad, with 'attendant media', to publicize the wider Sahel drought. It wasn't an entirely fortunate way of putting it, but I knew exactly what he meant.
>
>   The pop-stars, the phone-ins, the young shaming their elders into giving more, the international camaraderie of the entertainment world, have indeed given the subject a glamour, a sexiness, it has never before quite possessed. Oxfam, speaking of those who give to them, says they are 'mid-everything' – middle-class, middle-aged, middle-of-the-road in their politics. There is nothing 'mid' about Band Aid's donors, whether the school-children sending in their tons of split-peas via Red Star to the old ILEA bus depot in Bloomsbury that is now the group's headquarters, or Hamdan al-Maktoum, racehorse owner, who gave them one million after the Live Aid concert last July.
>
>   More startling, anyway at the time, than the identity of disaster relief's new donors, was the scale of their response, first to the

record at Christmas, later to the concerts. Band Aid themselves were surprised. It all seemed to happen so suddenly.

News of the famine first seriously impressed the western public in July 1984, after Michael Buerk visited southern Ethiopia and came back with appalling pictures for television of what seemed an entire nation with nothing to eat.

Caroline Moorehead, *New Society*

B Resettlement or genocide?

To report a disaster on the Ethiopian scale successfully would be difficult under any circumstances. To do so when there is no background framework of understanding, when access for journalists is severely restricted, and where political, professional, and humanitarian motives come into conflict is near to impossible. In absolute terms, reporting of the Ethiopian famine has failed.

In relative terms, of course, journalists need not feel so disheartened. Their work, after all, has been responsible for the largest mobilization of popular concern and assistance the West has ever seen. There is also a chance that some comprehension of more fundamental issues – notably the relationship of rich to poor countries – will outlast the current tragedy. But principally success has come through simplicity – the argument that people 'out there' are dying for lack of food. You have money. Give some of it to stop them dying.

What has been obscured by that simplicity is the complex set of factors which led to the famine, which maintained the tragedy and which, even now, may underlie the most terrifying genocide programme since Pol Pot's Kampuchea. Please note the qualification: this is a plea for investigation, not in itself an accusation.

Diverse Reports' film, *Hand to Mouth* (Wednesday C4 8.30–9 pm) takes Germaine Greer to Ethiopia to report on the resettlement programme, the project by which the Ethiopian government is seeking to move populations from the war-torn, famine zones of the north to areas of development in the south-west. It is a central thesis of the film that the refusal of Western governments and aid organizations to assist in this programme, for political reasons, will render useless the emergency aid supplied so far and will probably lead to the failure of the project itself. The result, it is argued, will be a repetition of the famine disaster, with blame to be laid at the door of the West for its denial that resettlement is the only long-term solution.

The film's view of the resettlement programme is positive – there are interviews with a government representative and with Kurt Jansen, the United Nations co-ordinator in Addis Ababa. We see examples of camps in the resettlement zones and hear from some of those who have moved there. There is commentary to the effect that termites are a major problem and that these could be dealt with by a chemical manufactured by Shell, if only the hard currency were available. There is mention of Malaria and how better methods of prevention than drugs could be used with more aid. In short, the overall view is that which the Ethiopian government would like to project – that those in the resettlement camps are volunteers, pioneers opening up virgin territory where conditions are hard but where, with work and government assistance, a new future can be made, far from the hopeless deserts of Tigre, Eritrea, and Wollo.

There is, however, a different view of resettlement. That it is not completely voluntary. That people die in the Russian Antonov planes which carry them because there is no oxygen or pressure in the cargo bays. That large areas of the new zones are malarial swamps. That families are broken up, deliberately, in order to destroy any vestige of opposition to the central government. That resettlement is not so much a long-term solution as a final solution. None of these fears is mentioned in Greer's report, not even so that they can then be disproved.

The film ignores one of the most crucial aspects of the Ethiopian disaster – that a civil war is raging, based in the famine areas of Tigre and Eritrea. It also ignores the fact that a resettlement programme to give people new and productive land coincides with a possible desire to depopulate, by movement or death, the very areas where opposition to the ruling Derg is strongest.

John Marshall, *New Society*

C I blame the BBC for much of the violence in our cities. Politicians may refer to 'inner city deprivation', moralists to the 'irresponsibility of parents' – ignoring the fact that most people don't have parents nowadays. What the BBC does is to create nightly an unhealthy craving for excitement by showing news bulletins which consist almost entirely of violent scenes and disasters, the camera zooming in whenever possible on disturbing detail – a black man being clubbed by police in South Africa, flies buzzing round a corpse in Lebanon. Certain clips of film are repeated whenever possible – like the Bradford Football stadium holocaust.

The apologists for showing this type of material dictate that we have to see the nasty nature of the modern world if we are to change it. But this is pure humbug. Even the moving film of the starving in Ethiopia had little effect compared to Band Aid. It was the sight and sound of noisy pop groups that got the cash flowing in. As it is, we have reached a stage now when parents of young children will have to think hard about whether they ought to have a television set in the house.

Richard Ingrams, *The Listener*

1 'Sexy' is an unusual adjective to use with 'starvation'. What do you think Kevin Jendon meant by it?

2 The 'simplicity' of the film he was reviewing obscured certain important facts, in John Marshall's opinion. What were these?

3 a From what particular angle does each of the three writers approach the famine in Ethiopia?
 b What attitude does each writer take towards it?

4 What does the language used in each piece show about:
 a the personal bias of each writer;
 b the readers for whom it was intended?
 Give evidence from the passages for your views.

5 Which piece contains the 'best writing' in your opinion? Make sure that you explain the criteria by which you judge good writing.

Answers to short questions

• •

page 14   liaison   rendezvous   parole   moustache   brunette
restaurant   fiancé(e)   prestige

page 27
2 abjure, conjure, jury, perjury
3 liberal, liberate, libertine
4 manage, manicure, manipulate, manual, manufacture, manuscript
5 inter alia, intermediary, international, intercommunicating, interrupt, intercontinental, intersperse, interdependence, interval, interject, intervene
6 conjugal, conjunction, junction, juncture, subjugate

page 62

helping	pancakes	cream	cheddar	thought	dieting
mind	remorse	good	chase	idea	focus
publisher's	party	year	secretary	understanding	
block	tackle	days	cup	tea	luncheon
egg	salt	roll	fluff	plastic	apple
regime	banquets	abuse	plate	mints	mouth
man					

page 63

affectionate	physical	all	tactile	kinaesthetic	other
friendly	35	warm	sensual	unpossessive	
loving	mutual	telephone			

page 65

cried	fitted	stubbing	hurried	stepping	shot
prodding	detached	turned	burned	tossed	let
trickle					

page 66   sleepily   obliquely   westward softly   thickly   slowly
faintly

page 67   with   by   of   in   at   to   on   out

page 79   **Noun clauses:**
a object   **b** object   **c** object   **d** object   **e** object
f subject   **g** subject   **h** apposition   **i** complement

pages 81–82   **Adjectival clauses:**
that were used for the meal
that was made from the recipe
that featured a cream sauce
that dried on the plates
that went into the washer
that has a powerful triple spray
that gets things [so] sparkling clean
that go into the exceptionally quiet machine

that has five fully automatic programmes
that include two for economy
that makes running costs [so] low
that is a feature of the dishwashers
that come with a Free Five Year Parts Guarantee and . . .
that give [such] peace of mind

The following are **adverbial clauses**:
so . . . that it doesn't matter
how dirty the pots and pans are
so . . . that it's no more expensive than washing by hand
such . . . that it's no wonder people say . . .

page 87 **a** noun clause **b** adjectival clause **c** adverbial clause of result

page 100 **1** The convention that conjunctions **join** sentences, rather than begin them.
2 They have no independent main clause at their head. It is in the previous sentence, cut off by a full stop.
3 Paragraphs 2, 7, 8, and 9.
4 'Again and again.'
5 The cult of 'machismo' – male pride in potency and strength.
6 Efficiency of function.
7 There is a sexual innuendo here, related to male potency and sexual performance. There is also the promise of appeal to the opposite sex.
8 It suggests that this is a genuine potency, as opposed to the simulation of it.

page 120 pen•cil   big•   big•ger   bi•ology   bio•logical

page 121 **1** John could only see his wife from the door.

2 John could only see his wife from the door.

3 John could only see his wife from the door.

pages 155–156 wenevə wılı wɒs ın trʌbəl hız θɔts tɜnd tuwɔdz plæntıŋ sidz ın hız bæk jad. hi rızented hız bɒs, wɒz fed ʌp wıð hız wɜk, ænd sæd ðæt bıf, hıs sʌn, wɒz dʒʌst bʌmıŋ aloŋ, ınsted of plænıŋ əhed. fɔ wılı, tru sʌkses ment ɜnıŋ hʌndrədz of dɒləz ænd wınıŋ rıspekt frɒm əðə men.

lındə dıd nɒt nəʊ wɒt tu seı tu hɜ hʌsbənd. ʃi saıd ænd tʊk ʌp hɜ dɑnıŋ. ıf əʊnlı bıf wʊd stɒp hız bʌmıŋ əraʊnd ænd setəl daʊn. wılı wʊd bi səʊ hæpı ðen, ıt wʊd gıv hım sʌmθıŋ tu tʃıə əbaʊt. hi kɜəd səʊ mʌtʃ fɔ bıf, ænd ʃi kʊd nɒt beə tu wɒtʃ hız sləʊ drıft tuwɔdz deθ. ıt wɒz pjʊə tɔment tu hɜ.

page 218 **1** Features that make form suitable for subject:
  * short, to suit small size of germ
  * four-stress line creates jaunty rhythm that makes poem pleasant and easy to read, and makes us feel light-hearted
  * stresses fall on words in such a way that they bring out the amusing mismatch of scale in *mighty/smaller, germ/pachyderm*.

2 **a** Ancient, traditional yet simple nature of 4 × 4 form makes it appropriate for expression of general truths about nature of sexual love.

   b Effect of unrealized beats:

   line 6: creates feeling of waiting in suspense for lover's reaction;

   line 8: different readers will find different things here: silent pause instead of realized beat could indicate shock, dismay, inability to speak in response to what is happening, etc.

   line 12: again, individual responses may differ: silent recognition and acceptance of the inevitable, perhaps? A sinking into crushed silence?

page 219 2 |I wan|dered lone|ly as | a cloud|

   |That floats | on high | o'er vales | and hills,

   |And all | at once | I saw | a crowd,|

   |A host | of gol|den daff|odils.|

page 221 **a** Iambic foot

   b Two consecutive off-beats in line one: on the (sight)

   Two equal stresses perhaps on Save where in line 3

   c Iambic pentameter

page 225 1 **a**

line 117:	These	always	pinched	end
line 118:	excuse	don't	pinched	end
line 119:	What	bones	Epsom	Heath
line 120:	seen	that	papers	
line 121:	You	papers		
line 122:	don't	all	pinched	end
line 123:	woman	runs	terrible	risk
line 124:	Let	Sweeney	continue	story

   b *lines 120* and *121* have an unrealized beat.

   c *line 117:* stresses create effect of Swarts making an assertion.

   line 118: stresses create effect of indignant denial.

   line 119: stresses fall naturally where they would in real life when asking a rhetorical question.

   line 120: stresses give impression of finality, of offering incontrovertible evidence.

   line 121: stresses show Snow going on the attack, demanding agreement from Swarts.

   line 122: stresses create impression of angry, totally dogmatic statement.

   line 123: even stresses give impression that Doris is repeating a bit of well-worn wisdom she's heard often before; no excitement.

   line 124: even stresses give impression of polite command; neutral attitude.

   d *lines 15–20* in particular: 'Yes, I'll eat you . . . crocodile isle.'

Index

Acknowledgements

• •

The author and publisher are grateful for permission to reprint the following copyright material:

Kingsley Amis: from *One Fat Englishman* (Harcourt Brace Jovanovich), by permission of the Peters, Frazer & Dunlop Group Ltd.; **W.E.K. Anderson:** from *The Written Word* (1963), by permission of Oxford University Press; **Baugh & Cable:** from *A History of the English Language*, 4th edition, © 1993, by permission of Prentice Hall, Englewood Cliffs, New Jersey, U.S.A.; **Steve Bell:** 'If . . .' cartoon from *The Guardian* (1985), by permission of the artist; **F. Bodmer:** from *The Loom of Language* (George Allen & Unwin, an imprint of HarperCollins Publishers Ltd., 1987) by permission of the publishers; **Mary Byrne:** from *Eureka* (1987), by permission of David & Charles, publishers; **David Crystal:** from *The Cambridge Encyclopedia of Language* (1987) and from *English Today* (1987/88) by permission of Cambridge University Press, from *Listen to Your Child* (Penguin Books, 1986) copyright © David Crystal 1986, by permission of Penguin Books Ltd.; **Viv Edwards:** from *The West Indian Language Issue in British Schools* (Routledge & Kegan Paul, 1979) by permission of International Thomson Publishing Services Ltd., and from *Language in a Black Community* (1986) by permission of Multilingual Matters Ltd., Frankfurt Lodge, Clevedon Hall, Victoria Road, Clevedon, Avon BS21 7SJ; **Ian Fleming:** from *Dr No* (Cape, 1958) © Glidrose Publications Ltd., 1958, used by permission; **Alastair Forbes:** from a review in *The Spectator*, by permission of the author; **E.M. Forster:** from *A Passage to India* (Edward Arnold, 1924) by permission of King's College, Cambridge and The Society of Authors as the literary representative of the E.M. Forster Estate; **Dennis Freeborn:** figures from *Varieties of English* (1986, 2nd edition 1993), by permission of Macmillan Press Ltd.; **Stella Gibbons:** from *Cold Comfort Farm* (1932), by permission of Curtis Brown, London, on behalf of the author's Estate; **Sir Ernest Gowers:** from *Plain Words* (HMSO, 1973) Crown ©, by permission of the Controller of Her Majesty's Stationery Office; **Martyn Harris:** from 'The Story of English' in *New Society*, by permission of *New Statesman & Society*; **Russell Hoban:** from *Riddley Walker* (Cape), by permission of David Higham Associates; **Simon Hoggart:** from an article in *The Guardian*, by permission of the author; **Philip Howard:** from *The State of the Language: English Observed* (Hamish Hamilton, 1984), copyright © Philip Howard 1984, by permission of Penguin Books Ltd.; **Ted Hughes:** from *The Hawk in the Rain*, and *Wodwo*, by permission of Faber & Faber Ltd.; **Richard Ingrams:** from an article in *The Listener*, by permission of the author; **Rory Johnson:** from an article first published in 1991 in *The Guardian* ©, by permission; **Anthony Jones & Jeremy Mulford:** from *Children Using Language* (1971), by permission of Oxford University Press; **T.W. Knight:** from *A Comprehensive English Course* (University of

London Press, 1962) by permission of Hodder & Stoughton Ltd./New English Library Ltd.; **Roger Lass:** from *The Shape of English* (Dent, 1987) by permission of J.M. Dent; **D.H. Lawrence:** from the works of D.H. Lawrence by permission of Laurence Pollinger Ltd. and the Estate of Frieda Lawrence Ravagli; **Tom Leonard:** from *Intimate Voices* (Galloping Dog Press) by permission of Cathie Thomson on behalf of the author; **Bernard Levin:** from a review in *The Times*, by permission of the author; **David Lodge:** from *Nice Work* (Martin Secker & Warburg Ltd., 1988) © David Lodge 1988, by permission of Reed Consumer Books Ltd.; **John Marshall:** from 'Resettlement or Genocide' in *New Society* (1985), by permission of *New Statesman & Society*; **W. Somerset Maugham:** from 'Sheppey' in *Selected Plays* (Wm. Heinemann Ltd.) by permission of Reed Book Services; **Caroline Moorhead:** from an article first published in *New Society* (1985), © Caroline Moorhead 1985, by permission of Shiel Land Associates Ltd.; **George Orwell:** from 'Down the Mine' in *Inside the Whale and Other Essays* (1957), and from *1984* (1949) by permission of A.M. Heath on behalf of the late Sonia Brownell Orwell and Martin Secker & Warburg Ltd.; **John Price:** article from *The Times Educational Supplement* (1985) by permission of the author; **Randolph Quirk:** from *The Use of English* (1962), by permission of Longman Group UK, and from *The English Language and Images of Matter* (1972) by permission of Oxford University Press; **Anthony Sampson:** from 'London Hotels' in *The Observer*, by permission of the Peters, Frazer & Dunlop Group Ltd.; **Fritz Spiegl:** from an article in *The Listener*, by permission of the author; **Jill Tweedie:** from an article in *The Guardian*, by permission of Rogers, Coleridge & White Ltd.; **Doug Watson:** article in *The Sun*, by permission of Newsgroup Newspapers; **David C. Webb:** from a letter to *The Guardian*, by permission of the author; **Peter Wilby:** article in *The Independent* (1987), by permission of Newspaper Publishing Plc.; **Sir Peregrine Worsthorne:** from an article in *The Spectator*, by permission of the author; and **Richard C. Wydick:** from 'Plain English for Lawyers', first published in *The California Law Review*, © 1978 California Law Review Inc.

Also for: extracts from *The Authorized Version of The Bible* (*The King James Bible*), the rights in which are vested in the Crown, by permission of the Crown's Patentee, Cambridge University Press; 'Sound Bites', first published 31.8.88 in the *Weekend Guardian* ©, and a leader from *The Guardian* ©, first published 16.9.80, both by permission of *The Guardian*; advertisement by permission of Hotpoint Ltd.; British Rail 'Letraset' advertisement by permission of InterCity, British Railways; extract from 'Rediscovering Poverty' in *New Society* (1986) by permission of *New Statesman & Society*; extracts from the *New English Bible* © 1970, by permission of the Oxford and Cambridge University Presses; extracts from a leader in the *Times Education Supplement*, 15.12.61, © Times Newspapers Ltd. 1961, and from a review of 'Taken Care Of' by G.S. Fraser in the *Times Literary Supplement*, 8.4.65, © Times Newspapers Ltd. 1965, by permission of Times Newspapers; Volkswagen advertisement by permission of V.A.G. (UK) Ltd.; and Whitbread Trophy Bitter advertisement by permission of Whitbread and Collett, Dickinson, Pearce Advertising Agency.

Although every effort has been made to trace and contact copyright holders before publication, we have not been successful in a few cases. If notified, the publishers will be pleased to rectify any omissions at the earliest opportunity.